THE TEACHING AND PRACTICE OF PROFESSIONAL ETHICS

THE TEACHING AND PRACTICE OF PROFESSIONAL ETHICS

edited by

John Strain and Simon Robinson

Copyright © 2005 John Strain & Simon Robinson

The moral right of the author has been asserted.

Apart from any fair dealing for the purposes of research or private study, or criticism or review, as permitted under the Copyright, Designs and Patents Act 1988, this publication may only be reproduced, stored or transmitted, in any form or by any means, with the prior permission in writing of the publishers, or in the case of reprographic reproduction in accordance with the terms of licences issued by the Copyright Licensing Agency. Enquiries concerning reproduction outside those terms should be sent to the publishers.

Troubador Publishing Ltd
9 De Montfort Mews
Leicester LE1 7FW, UK
Tel: (+44) 116 255 9311 / 9312
Email: books@troubador.co.uk
Web: www.troubador.co.uk

ISBN 1 905237 33 2

Typeset in 11pt Stempel Garamond by Troubador Publishing Ltd, Leicester, UK

Contents

Foreword   vii
Bernadette Porter

Introduction   ix

Acknowledgements   xi

Author Biographies   xiii

PART ONE: ISSUES IN PROFESSIONAL ETHICS

1. Professional Ethics and Higher Education   3
   John Strain

2. The Marketisation of the University: Professional, Commercial and Ethical Dilemmas of Academic Life   18
   Helen Johnson

3. Humanising Professional Ethics   40
   Peter Lucas

4. Learning and Earning in the Knowledge Society: Some Ethical Considerations   51
   Peter Jarvis

5. "Academics at the Coal Face": Ethical Dilemmas in the Real World – Lessons from Research into Social Exclusion   65
   Nic Walters

6. Is there Space for 'Moral Development' in Education?   74
   Anna Abram

7. Ethics and the Teaching Profession   91
   Ron Best and David Rose

8. Responsibility for Nature: A Challenge to Reflect Critically on Cultural Values   105
   Jens Christensen

PART TWO: TEACHING PROFESSIONAL ETHICS

9   Beyond Unilateralism in Ethics: A South African
Multilateral Ethics Expertiment 1997–2003   117
Martin Prozesky

10   Applied and Professional Ethics: A Comparison   127
Susan A. lllingworth

11   "Wisdom Cries Aloud in the Street": Using Service-Learning
to Teach Ethics Across the Curriculum   147
Elizabeth Ozarak

12   The Challenge of Raising Ethical Awareness:
A Case-based Aiding System for Use by Computing
and ICT Students   155
Don Sherratt, Simon Rogerson and N. Ben Fairweather

13   An Approach to Developing Ethical Sensitivity
in Student Nurses   175
Patricia Perry and Janis Moody

14   Teaching Ethics in Higher Education   187
Thomas Borchman and Poul Bonde Jensen

15   Enabling Professions   199
Simon Robinson

Foreword

Dr Bernadette Porter
Formerly Vice Chancellor, Roehampton University

In the comprehensive review of higher education in the UK that Lord Dearing undertook in 1977, two purposes of higher education were set alongside each other: inspiring and enabling people to develop their intellectual abilities to the highest potential levels throughout their lives; and equipping people for work in ways that help shape a democratic, civilised and inclusive society. Much debate about higher education is inevitably about quality, funding, organisational relationships and information technology, all of them vitally important. But it is too easy to lose sight of the essential ethical character of what Dearing and many others have identified in the purposes of higher education. Equity in whom we admit to universities, no less than how we prepare people to be not just capable engineers, accountants and doctors but good engineers, accountants and doctors, with all the nuances of quite what we mean by good, are above all ethical questions.

This book began its life in a conference held in 2003 at what is now Roehampton University. This conference, the Real World, Real People conference was, we believe, the first international conference in teaching applied and professional ethics in higher education. It had three themes. The first was to explore the ethical challenges that arise in the broad range of professional life. Secondly, the conference explored the implications of these challenges on how we prepare our students in higher education for the world of work. But ethics, like politics, is intrinsically contested. It requires a climate of discourse in which claim and counter claim can be scrutinised with respect as well as rigour, remembering always that ethical claims arise not just as cognitive propositions but as claims about people's lives, sometimes as claims about other people's lives that are deeply treasurable to them. And so the third theme of the conference was to examine the relationship between people's faith, spirituality or personal philosophy and the ethical claims we make on each other.

It was my view at the time that the exploration of these themes in relation to higher education would persist far beyond the confines of a single conference. I am delighted that John Strain and Simon Robinson have put together this valuable volume which draws on so many of the contributions to the 2003 conference. I am delighted too that the conference continues to grow building on a range of academic and professional networks. This is an enterprise with an important future.

Introduction

This book attempts to portray some of the interdisciplinary richness inherent in learning and teaching in professional ethics. Its contributors include sociologists, psychologists, philosophers, theologians, educationalists, nurses, engineers and scientists. Part one of the book explores ethics as it arises in professional practice, particularly in relation to the university as a locus of professional practice in teaching and research. Part two explores learning and teaching in professional ethics.

The first chapter sets a context for reflection on both professionalism and ethics as well as some implications for how professional ethics is taught. Teaching in higher education is itself a professional activity and one which has been traumatically challenged by the changing political context of higher education in which a public service ethos is challenged by demands upon universities to satisfy educational markets. This marketisation of the university has provoked not only a series of ethical dilemmas for academics but has removed some of the sense of freedom within which these dilemmas and their solutions can be fully owned by academics. The richness of Johnson's thesis lies in her poignant and honest account of her own experience of coping with this transition as well as in her call for organisational development to point towards solutions.

The role of philosophy in teaching professional ethics is an important component in Lucas' paper. He reminds us that for Aristotle, the virtuous life in practice requires not just moral virtues but also intellectual virtues. Lucas offers a powerful warning note to those who would exclude philosophy from the teaching of professional ethics. More specifically, Lucas makes a powerful case for the significance of Aristotelian virtue ethics as making a far better bridge between the theory-practice gap than either consequentialist theories such as utilitarianism or the principled rationality of Kantian ethics. There is much in Lucas' paper which bears on the teaching of ethics but the paper is included with those focusing on the practice of ethics because the story that he has to tell is as much about the practice of healthcare ethics and environmental ethics as with the teaching of ethics.

Jarvis takes up the theme of the shifting ground of universities that Johnson outlined and amplifies it relation to the emerging knowledge economies in which universities no longer have any monopoly on knowledge production. Research has become a far larger networked activity than any single university could manage. But there are ethical implications that Jarvis explains.

Abram takes up the theme of virtue ethics from Aristotle beginning with his insistence that ethics is not just about knowing what is good. It is about becoming good. There is therefore an essentially developmental aspect of ethics just as there is with education. So the relationship between education and ethics is persistent as well as symbiotic. Abram contextualises the virtues in a framework of personal development that would surely have appealed to Aristotle himself.

Best and Rose take us away from the university as the locus of professional ethics and focus instead on teaching in schooling. But the story they have to tell includes some powerful reminders that all is not well. Their concern is with the political context within which state schools function and with the implications of this context for the way in which teachers exercise moral judgement. They ask some awkward but challenging and helpful questions. They feel that teaching of professional ethics to aspirant teachers has a hollow ring to it at a time when schools are being marketed in a framework in which caring parents working in partnership with teachers are transformed into sovereign consumers of commodified knowledge.

In part two, the focus of the book shifts to the teaching of professional ethics. There can be few testimonies more powerful to the importance of creating conditions of dialogue in the teaching of ethics than the deeply moving story Prozesky tells of the creation of the Unilever Ethics Centre at the University of Kwa Zulu Natal in South Africa. He observes that "while the creation and violent maintaining of apartheid was largely the work of a culture steeped in a single Christian ethos, its defeat was the shared project of morally committed people from many belief and value systems, secular as well as religious." He describes an approach to teaching ethics that combines, inter alia, a sensitivity to traditional, ethnic moralities such as those of Africa and Australia with the ethics of the western philosophical tradition. It is an approach that is deeply committed to inclusivity. It raises the question of how commitments to inclusivity can provide an adequate framework for mutual comprehensibility without the philosophical treatment that provides that framework becoming in some sense primary.

Illingworth reflects on the distinction between professional and applied ethics. She examines how professional ethics has developed and its impact in Higher Education. She then looks at the differences between professional and applied ethics in learning and teaching objectives, learning and teaching methodologies, and in relation to the different stakeholders. Interestingly, she finds that professional ethics moves more into the area of virtue ethics, and thus to the development of virtues. The connection of this to broader issues such as citizenship is brought out. Finally, the effect of all this on the perceptions of disciplines, not least on the idea of supradisciplinarity is discussed.

If ethics is about how people act rather than the apprehension of propositions about what might be right or wrong, then learning through experience has a particular salience. Ozarak provides an account of service learning in which the provision of services in the community that meet identified needs is made into an integral part of the curriculum in a way which allows mutual illumination of service and learning. She provides weighty evidence that this form of experiential learning is capable of supporting long term retention of knowledge together with the capability to apply it, more effectively than many variants of classroom learning. But service learning has an importance beyond pedagogic effectiveness in that it is itself an intrinsically ethical endeavour, closely related to the ethics of care.

Sherrat *et al.* point towards the growth of new professions as new technologies such as information and communication technologies (ICTs) emerge. They are concerned with developing new courseware and pedagogies to help students recognise the ethical issues that arise in the use of ICTs.

They recognise the importance of learning ethics through scenarios and case studies but understand the limitations of these when real life cases are simplified to reveal particular learning points and hence lose realism and credibility. They describe the development of a teaching tool that draws on the techniques of artificial intelligence to present students with rich materials for ethical analysis. For any given ethical dilemma and scenario that a student might present, the tool presents a comparable scenario from a library of ethically analysed cases which reflect the conflicts and dilemmas that might arise in the use of ICTs in practice.

The question to what extent computers, however allegedly intelligent, resemble human beings is itself of course a matter of enormous ethical debate, one which Herbert Dreyfus has engaged in passionatelyfor over thirty years and argued ferociously against treating computers as ethical intentional agents in any significant way like human beings.

Perry and Moody remind us that the nursing curriculum has always included an ethics component. The increasing potential of innovative medical treatments, a more litigious society, developments in the nurse role and the scarcity of specific resources all combine to create an increasing emphasis on ethical decision making in the pre-registration nursing curriculum, a requirement formalised in the re-organisation of nurse education in the Project 2000 and in Fitness for Practice initiatives at the turn of the millenium. They provide an interesting case study of how different approaches to ethics including principalism, virtue ethics and the ethics of care can be seen as complementary components in an authentically ethical nursing curriculum.

Part of this authenticity comprises an acquisition and development of what Borchmann and Jensen call critical agency. They are referring to an aspect of self understanding in which aspiring professionals become aware of themselves as committed and engaged ethical agents, a process which might be important for all professionals not just nurses. This process of acquisition is one they explain in terms of Perry's (1970) four stage progression: from a dualism in which right is contrasted starkly with wrong; through a complex dualism in which different contenders for right and wrong are appraised; through a relativism in which the contradictory claims of different ethical demands are recognised to, finally, what is called a commitment in relativism in which aspirant professionals make their own ethical commitments as engaged participants in the world of work.

Some might cavil at the use of the word relativism to describe circumstances in which people hold different views as to what is ethically appropriate in similar circumstances. Aristotle, for example, was no relativist. He believed that what would count as virtuous conduct is what someone of practical wisdom would do when acting rationally, or in accord, as he put it, with right reason. But Aristotle was no less clear that people would see things from different perspectives and see differences in detail. But Borchmann and Jensen make a powerful case for a pedagogy for an ethics of personal commitment in organisational behaviour and management, a domain in which instrumentalist thinking and virtue ethics has dominated.

In the final chapter Robinson suggests one plausible view of the professions, as enabling the client and other stakeholders. This argues against the view of the professions as disabling (Illich), and invites us to consider what enabling might mean in relation to autonomy. A relational view of autonomy is argued for and illustrated in four professional areas. If this view of the professional has any plausibility then it follows that there are critical attributes analogous to those embodied in a Rogerian view of counselling and teaching that need to be developed appropriately in the pre-professional curriculum and professional development. A framework for such teaching is developed.

REFERENCES

Dreyfuss, H. L. (1972) *What Computers Can't Do*. New York: Harper & Row.
Gilligan, C. (1982) *In a Different Vooice*. Cambridge, MA: Harvard University Press.
Perry, W. (1970) *Forms of Ethical Intellectual Development in the College Years: A Scheme*. New York: Holt, Rinehart and Winston.

Acknowledgements

This book was John Strain's idea but it would never have come to fruition without the unstinting generosity and careful efficiency of Simon Robinson whose editorial skills have been pearls beyond price. The book has been extraordinarily long in its gestation. Both of us are indebted to all the contributors for their forbearance with us and for the generosity with which they supported the project, and to Jeremy Thompson and the team at Troubador Publishing Ltd for his abundant and understated skills.

There are three particular people that John Strain would like to thank. First, Professor Patrick Dowling, former Vice Chancellor of the University of Surrey whose support for the Centre for Applied and Professional Ethics at Surrey and Roehampton Universities was persistent, unwavering and deeply sympathetic; secondly, Professor Richard Harper, former Director of the Digital World Research Centre, University of Surrey. This is not the book that Richard wanted him to write but John remains deeply grateful for Richard's scholarly encouragement. And thirdly, Margaret, whom I met in discussion over Catullus, and for whom *Quid datur a divis felici optatius hora.*

Author Biographies

JOHN STRAIN
John Strain is a Chartered Psychologist and a priest in the Church of England. After studying History and Philosophy at the University of Keele, UK, his career began as an officer in the Royal Navy. He was given a mid-career opportunity to train as an Occupational Psychologist at London University. After many years conducting research and consultancy in organisational change within the Ministry of Defence, John worked as a management consultant before training for the priesthood. John holds degrees in history, philosophy, theology and psychology. He is the Director of the Centre for Applied and Professional Ethics at the University of Surrey. He has a particular interest in spirituality and professional ethics in mental healthcare. He has a wide portfolio of academic publications in systems and management, philosophy, psychology, ethics and in the ethnography of digital technologies in domestic settings.

SIMON ROBINSON
Simon Robinson is Professor of Applied and Professional Ethics, Leeds Metropolitan University, Associate Director, Ethics Centre of Excellence, and Visiting Fellow in Theology, University of Leeds. Educated at Oxford and Edinburgh Universities, Simon entered psychiatric social work before being ordained into the Church of England priesthood in 1978. Simon entered university chaplaincy at Heriot-Watt University, and the University of Leeds, developing research and teaching in areas of applied ethics and practical theology. His research interests include: religious ethics and care; professional ethics; ethics in higher education; spirituality and professional practice; corporate social responsibility; and ethics in a global perspective. His books include: *The Social Responsibility of Business*; *Ethics in Engineering*; *Agape, Moral Meaning and Pastoral Counselling*; *Case Studies in Business Ethics* (ed. with Chris Megone); *Living Wills*; *Spirituality and Healthcare*; *Ministry Amongst Students*; *Values in Higher Education* (ed. with Clement Katulushi).

HELEN JOHNSON
Helen Johnson is the Director of the Professional Education Research Centre at Roehampton University. She is Principal Lecturer in Education

Management and Accreditation Adviser in the School of Education Studies. Her other research interests are voluntary sector schooling; citizenship education; teaching and learning in higher education; and education marketing in higher education. She researches from an organisational studies perspective, and is particularly focused on values, culture, roles, identity and managerial processes and their impact on organisational, staff and children's development. She has published widely in these fields in the academic press.

PETER LUCAS
Peter Lucas, is Senior Lecturer in Philosophy, and Course Leader for the MA in Bioethics and Medical Law, at the University of Central Lancashire, Preston, UK. He received his doctorate from Lancaster University in 1998, and has since taught philosophy and ethics at the universities of Bolton, Lancaster, and Central Lancashire. His current research interest lie in post-phenomenological continental philosophy, virtue ethics, and the philosophy and ethics of science and technology. He has contributed articles to *Philosophy of the Social Sciences, Environmental Ethics* and *Environmental Values*, and is in the process of completing a book on ethics and self-knowledge.

PETER JARVIS
Peter Jarvis is a former head of the Department of Educational Studies at the University of Surrey and Adjunct Professor, Department of Adult Education, University of Georgia, USA. He has received many academic honours including the Cyril O Houle World Award for Adult Education Literature from the American Association of Adult and Continuing Education. He was the first non-North American to be elected to the International Hall of Fame of Adult and Continuing Education in USA. He was Noted Scholar at the University of British Columbia, and has been a Visiting Professor at the universities of Ljubljana, Pedagogical University of Tallinn, Tennessee, Alaska at Anchorage and Maryland. Peter has written and edited about 30 books and 200 papers on adult education and learning, continuing professional education, nurse education, primary school education, distance education and third age education.

NICHOLAS WALTERS
Nicholas Walters is Senior Staff Tutor in Political, International and Policy Studies at the University of Surrey. His academic interests focus on unemployment and social exclusion. He is responsible for the University's interests in community education for socially disadvantaged adults, and has developed a portfolio of international research, and research and development projects. He has special interests in refugees, migrants and

asylum seekers, together with former substance mis-users. He was the project manager for an European Union initiative assisting former active addicts into employment and was responsible for the UK research in the European Union's "Workalo" project. Nick has published work in the UK, the United States and in Europe. Nicholas is also an Anglican priest with a particular interest in ethics and values.

Florina Zoltan and Linda Townsend were Research Officers on the Workalo project.

ANNA ABRAM
Anna Abram works at Heythrop College, University of London; at the Missionary Institute London; and at the Catholic University at Leuven. Born in Poland and educated in both Poland (Cardinal Wyszynski University, Warsaw) and in the UK (Heythrop College), Anna is a specialist in Christian Ethics and moral development. Her other interests lie in 'Christian-Jewish dialogue'. Her publications include: 'Virtue Ethics As a Tool for Tackling Global Economic Issue', in A.O'Mahony and M.Kirwan (eds), *World Christianity: Politics, Theology, Dialogues*, London: Melisende, 2003; 'Chmielowski Adam (Brother Albert)', in *Dictionary of Christian Biographies*, London: Continuum, 2001;'Christian Feminist Ethics – What is it?', *Collectanea Theologica (1998)*

RON BEST
Ron Best is Professor of Education and chair of the Ethics Board at Roehampton University. He took his doctorate at the University of East Anglia where his thesis concerned the organization of 'remedial education' in comprehensive schools He has researched and written widely on aspects of pastoral care, affective education and spirituality. He is President of the National Association for Pastoral Education and a founder-member of the European Affective Education Network. He is currently researching deliberate self-harm amongst adolescents where ethical issues concerning confidentiality, referral and the rights of parents are raised in teachers' professional work. His books include *Education for Spiritual, Moral, Social and Cultural Development* (Continuum, 2000) and *Tomorrow's Schools – Towards Integrity* (with Chris Watkins and Caroline Lodge, RoutledgeFalmer, 2000).

DAVID ROSE
David Rose is Principal Lecturer in Education and Director of Masters' Provision within the School of Education at Roehampton University. He is also Director of the Centre for Research in Religious Education and

Development. His areas of work include religious education, curriculum policy and research methods in education. He taught in secondary schools for 16 years and has served as Advisory Teacher for Religious Education. For the past 19 years he has been at Roehampton working on undergraduate and post-graduate programmes in education. Many of his publications have been related to religious education in schools, especially in relation to visual imagery and the teaching of multi-faith RE. He has also written concerning religious education policy. His research interests involve cultural restorationism and how it finds expression in curriculum policy and its implementation.

JENS CHRISTENSEN
Jens Christensen is Associate Professor, Department of Development and Planning, Aalborg University, Denmark. His research area is the theory of knowledge in relation to technological and social practice and interaction with nature, including cultural and historical perspectives; and in integrating ethics in knowledge and practice. He has published extensively in Danish about fundamentals of practical knowledge and man's relation to nature. His publications in English include: *Reflections on Problem-based Learning* in: Anette Kolmos et al. (eds). *The Aalborg PBL model. Progress, Diversity and Challenges.* Aalborg University Press, 2004; and forthcoming *Practical Knowledge – Challenges of the Heritage from Francis Bacon: Between Truth, Utility and Goodness"* in an anthology on Engineering Knowledge and Skills.

MARTIN PROZESKY
Martin Prozesky holds the Unilever Chair of Comparative and Applied Ethics and is Director of the Unilever Ethics Centre at the Pietermaritzburg Campus of the University of KwaZulu-Natal, South Africa, positions he has held since 1998. Prior to that he was Dean of Humanities and a Professor of Religious Studies at the former University of Natal. Martin is author and editor or co-editor of a number of books in the philosophy and history of religions published in the UK, the USA and South Africa, as well as of many journal articles. His current work deals with the quest for a genuinely inclusive global ethic.

SUSAN ILLINGWORTH
Susan Illingworth is Research Administrator for the School of Geography at the University of Leeds. After gaining first class honours in the History of Ideas from the Open University and in Philosophy from London University she went on to full time post-graduate research into theories of human rights at Bristol University, gaining her PhD in 1995. Susan was recently the Co-

ordinator for an ethics project for the UK Learning and Teaching Support Network. This project focused on interdisciplinary collaboration in ethics and investigated the needs of ethics learning and teaching for those whose primary subject area lies outside philosophy and religious studies. Differences were identified between the concerns of applied ethics, with its emphasis on objectivity, detachment and reasoned argument, and those of professional ethics, which introduces new issues and concerns by seeking to guide professional conduct and improve accountability.

ELIZABETH OZORAK
Elizabeth Weiss Ozorak is Professor of Psychology at Allegheny College in Meadville, Pennsylvania, USA. She received her first degree from Wesleyan University and further degrees from Harvard University. In 1999, she created the Values, Ethics & Social Action programme at Allegheny College, an interdisciplinary program that teaches students about social problems and pathways of change through community-based learning embedded in a sequence of academic courses. She continues to coordinate and teach in the programme and has mentored colleagues in developing community-based pedagogy. She is also a trained facilitator for nonviolence workshops. Her research is mainly in the area of psychology and religion, and she has published a number of scholarly articles and book chapters in this area as well as two recent articles on service-learning.

SIMON ROGERSON
Simon joined De Montfort University in 1983, following a successful industrial career which culminated in being the Computer Services Manager for Thorn EMI. He now combines lecturing, research and consultancy in the management and ethical aspects of computing. He has published and presented papers in many countries about these issues. In 1995 he became the Director of the newly formed Centre for Computing and Social Responsibility. He conceived and co-directs the ETHICOMP conference series on the ethical impacts of IT. He is a member of the Parliamentary IT Committee in the UK, a Fellow of the Institute for the Management of Information Systems and a Fellow of the Royal Society for the encouragement of Arts, Manufactures and Commerce.

BEN FAIRWEATHER
Ben Fairweather is Research Fellow at the Centre for Computing and Social Responsibility at De Montfort, University, Leicester. He is editor of the journal *Information Communication Ethics and Society* and Associate Editor, Telematics and Informatics. His has wide interests in the broad area of computing ethics including Codes of Ethics, Surveillance, Privacy,

Encryption and Electronic Voting, Health Issues in Computing, Teleworking and the ethics of Robotics and Artifical Intelligence.

DON SHERRATT
Don Sherratt is a doctoral student at the Centre for Computing and Social Responsibility at De Montfort, University, Leicester.

JANIS MOODY
Janis Moody is a nurse lecturer in the School of Acute and Continuing Nursing at Napier University, Scotland. Her main area of expertise relates to professional, ethical and legal issues in nursing and healthcare. She holds an MSc in Nursing and Health Studies from the University of Edinburgh and an MA in Medical Ethics and Law from Keele University. Her research focuses on accountability in nursing and what it means to practising nurses. She is particularly interested in facilitating the link between theoretical content and practice in teaching, helping students to apply and make sense of ethics in their day-to-day professional practice. She has published several articles on dementia care and on euthanasia.

PATRICIA PERRY
Patricia Perry is currently a nurse lecturer in the School of Acute and Continuing Care Nursing at Napier University, Scotland. Her main area of expertise is nursing theory and practice and more particularly in professional, ethical and legal issues in nursing. She is module leader for modules addressing moral and ethical issues in health care for nurses, veterinary nurses, health science students and complementary therapists. She has a particular interest in ethical decision-making, consent, patients' rights, confidentiality, privacy, organ transplantation and ethics and genetics. She is also interested in developing approaches to learning, teaching and assessment which link ethical theory and clinical practice and promote the development of skills useful to the undergraduate student nurse and the postgraduate registered nurse.

THOMAS BORCHMANN
Thomas Borchmann is associate professor at the Department of Communication at the University of Aalborg, Denmark. His subject of specialisation is communication within organisations. Thomas holds a Masters degree from the Department of Philosophy at the University of Aarhus and a PhD from the Department of Organisation and Management at the Aarhus School of Business. His research is centred on critical and value-oriented analysis of discourses concerning work, organisation, management, technology and learning as these are articulated in local

contexts, theory-building, media and curricula. Thomas has published several contributions to including a chapter in Kolmos, Fink & Krogh "*The Aalborg PBL Model*, Alborg University Press.

POUL BONDE JENSEN
Poul Bonde Jensen is the Organisation and Human Resource Manager at Jyske Bank (Northern Region) in Denmark. After completing his Master of Political Science degree at Aarhus University, specializing in regulatory politics, Paul studied for this PhD at Aarhus Business School with a dissertation on value-based management and leadership. His particular interests include business ethics with a focus on how to enlighten practical matters with philosophical or theoretical considerations. Among the numerous approaches employed in this respect, game theoretical experiments and studies in practical settings have proved especially fruitful – and sometimes entertaining as well.

PART ONE

ISSUES IN PROFESSIONAL ETHICS

1
Professional ethics and higher education

John Strain

INTRODUCTION

Professionalism and ethics are both deeply contested concepts. What people mean by being a 'professional' and by being 'ethical' varies considerably and the ambiguities associated with their meaning reflect different and deeply personal investments and commitments about both. In this chapter I shall explore some of the ambiguities surrounding both professionalism and ethics and describe a rationale for teaching professional ethics in higher education that addresses these ambiguities.

AMBIGUITIES IN PROFESSIONALISM

The medieval inheritance of professionalism

The emergence of professions as distinct occupational groups claiming authoritative competence over a particular field of knowledge and practice is, in part, an outcome of modernity, a product of task specialization and the division of labour that accompanied post-medieval industrialisation. But the relationship between professional practice and higher education has much older roots, lying in the somewhat chaotic fashion by which universities emerged in medieval Europe. Critics of contemporary universities who are uneasy with the emphasis attached to the employability of graduates, looking back perhaps to a purer ideal of liberal education in the medieval universities (Maskell and Robinson, 2002) might be inclined to forget just how strong was the link between the curricula of the thirteenth century *studia* at Bologna or Paris and the demands of the three specialist and cerebral occupations of lawyer, doctor and priest. Law, medicine and theology constituted, as Dunbabin (1999) explains, the higher faculties of what came to be called, by the fifteenth century a *universitas*. Those who are uneasy at the combination of the academic and the vocational in higher education do well to remember the reason for the emergence of higher education. In Bologna, the University emerged from an alliance between city governors, who exacted oaths from lecturers that they would serve the interests of the city first; and Pope Gregory IX who wanted a canon law school to assist his efforts at ecclesiastical reform. This is not to claim that higher education has its origins solely in what became the *grandes ecoles* or polytechnics. But it offers a pointer towards the delicate balance in the dynamics of supply and demand for higher education, in mediaeval universities as much as contemporary ones. This is a balance which has on one side the demand for vocational and professional education. On the other side lies the recognition that the professions require people who are embarked on journeys of learning to think and converse well for life, understanding themselves, their relationships with others and the manner in which peoples interests are best served.

The three original learned professions of lawyer, doctor and priest, what Elliot (1972) called the 'status professions', gradually gave way to a broader occupational structure of 'occupational professions' associated with the specializations of industrialization. Freidson (1994) distinguished between two categories of profession: those with specific and shared ideological traits and values producing distinct occupational identities with legally protected licences to practice; and less prestigious, more labile occupations with greater reliance on protection by professional bodies. In the first category there was an emphasis on the importance of professionals using their own discretionary judgements. In the second there is an emphasis on practising in accordance with declared and publicly available standards.

Brown and McCartney (2000) show how these occupational professions emerged differently in the UK and USA from continental Europe. In the former, the state (and it might be added the universities) had minimal role in providing training and licensing of these new occupations with the consequence that each occupational profession hosted its own movement and, in time, institution, for establishing qualifications, maintaining loyalty and protecting its members. In continental Europe, the status and protection of the new professionals was maintained by state controlled elite institutions of advanced education which ensured the privileges of its graduates who went to work either in the expanding civil services or in technical-managerial positions in industry. One consequence of this difference between what might be called an open market professionalism and state (and university) sponsored professionalism was that open market professionalism needed some way of demonstrating a shared common feature of what was meant by professionalism. The development of shared objective standards and benchmarks of practice (and perhaps, more recently, so called quality standards), has been part of an attempt by occupational professions to define their relationships to each other as professionals. What defines them has been a commitment to doing the job properly, as defined in standards, on the grounds that it would be 'unprofessional' to do otherwise. There are two observations worth making here. First, this 'standards oriented' professionalism has an ethically appealing inclusivity about it. We can all be professionals by doing our job properly, no matter what our status or occupation. Secondly, it is a concept of professionalism which is at odds with the emphasis attached by members of status professions to using discretion, wisdom and judgement in their work. Some of the frequently reported distrust between doctors and health service managers may be underpinned by a difference between doctors, as status professionals, who see the emphasis on publicly available procedures and processes as a threat to their professional judgement; whereas health service managers as occupational professionals see the development of such standards as what constitutes being a professional; and furthermore, as part of the contribution to be made by professionals to the call for greater accountability, with all its ethical resonance.

Ambiguities within professionalism

These historical considerations help illuminate some of the contemporary ambiguities about what it means to be a professional. The inheritance of this ambiguity within professionalism helps illuminate the concern expressed by Helen Johnson in the next chapter, that increasingly complex quality standards expected of the school teaching profession constitute an assault on the professional discretion of teachers rather than a reflection of the accountability associated with occupational professions.

The historical inheritance also illuminates the ambiguity over expectations about coherence between behaviour at work and out of work. A barrister, priest or military officer might be considered guilty of conduct unbecoming his calling if caught cheating or misbehaving outside work whereas a plumber's behaviour outside of work might be deemed irrelevant to his capacity to be a good plumber. There are borderline cases which suggest that the distinction between status profession and occupational profession is more permeable than sometimes suggested. Nurses might be considered a case in between the two, less a status profession than doctor but something more than an occupational profession. The nursing profession with its strong emphasis on caring for people raises a further ambiguity within the concept of professionalism: the extent to which the choice of a particular profession reflects a calling or vocation where the choice of work is linked strongly with a person's identity and deeply held values rather than the contractual rewards of work. Tradition might have it that this applies particularly to the nurse or priest. But one might also be an artist, a writer or a racing horse jockey, primarily because of the intrinsic rewards of the work that make sense only in respect of deeply held values.

These ambiguities suggest a further distinction between what I shall call discretionary or vocational professionalism and behavioural or competence professionalism. In discretionary professionalism, the freedom to act with discretion together with a personal commitment to occupational values figures strongly. In competence professionalism, the surety that what is done accords with declared standards figures strongly together with a commitment to accountability in respect of these standards. Vocational professionalism relates strongly to an individual's first person choices. They relate to 'my discretion' and 'my vocation'. Competence professionalism relates strongly to the demands upon the professional from outside agencies, demands about how the professional behaves at work and outside work.

There is a further aspect of the meaning of professionalism which contrasts amateur with professional, a difference about doing things for remuneration or not; a difference closely linked to the difference between a vocation followed regardless of remuneration and a professional competence which is the basis for remuneration.

In this brief and somewhat inconclusive survey of the ambiguities surrounding the concept of a professional, some of the tensions in the way the word is used are apparent. The tensions are perhaps most apparent in the UK National Health Service where vocation, occupation, competence, professional boundary and status all jostle for space in a complex kaleidoscope of different professional histories and changing requirements. It is a competition for space, perhaps partly for dominance and perhaps partly to resist the dominance of others. But it is also a forum on which deeply held values are involved, values which connect with what we mean by ethics. But before we explore the vagaries of the concept of ethics, it is time to take stock.

What I wish to suggest is that if students are properly to understand the complexity of professional ethics including the conflicts between the different meanings of what it is to be a professional, conflicts between professional autonomy and professional conformance and accountability, between vocations and competences, between life choices and remunerations all of which populate the canvas of professional ethics, then the interdisciplinary nature of the subject needs to be appreciated. Teaching and learning in professional ethics are deeply interdisciplinary and necessarily ethical. It is a subject in which the history, sociology and psychology are as much part of the canvas as philosophy and management science.

Ambiguities in ethics

The conflict between autonomous professionals and authorities who seek professional conformance leaves out a third group of key stakeholders in professional ethics, the beneficiaries of professional services, the clients themselves. How each professional relates to their clients forms the primary canvas of professional ethics.

Bernard Crick once wrote a famous book about politics, *In defence of politics* (Crick, 1962). The title might have indicated that politics was on the back foot or in need of some encouragement. Not so; the late 1950s and 1960s were a period of intense political engagement in which ideology, pragmatism, democracy, socialism, pacifism and capitalism all competed for space in an intense debate in the aftermath of the Second World war. Crick's mission was less about encouraging debate than about bringing a degree of order to it. His was a quest to defend political activity as Aristotle once understood it, as the pursuit of the management of differences between free people living together in a community in which all individuals would flourish. And so Crick defended politics from too close an association with democracy, with ideology and with idealism of various hues.

Ethics at the beginning of the 21st century might need its own defence in a similar vein to that which Crick once provided for politics. Like politics, ethics is an intrinsically contested subject. And just as there was once passionate debate about politicising the curriculum of higher education; so today there is intense debate over the whether and how ethics should be included in the curriculum of higher education. Rather than make a attempt to define what is meant by ethics, it might be no less illuminating to identify what ethics is not, by identifying what ethics might need defending against. In particular, I shall defend professional ethics against the philosophers and against the righteous proponents of conformance.

A defence against philosophers

It might seem strange to consider defending ethics against philosophy. Generations of undergraduates have encountered ethics as a sub-discipline of philosophy. Alongside epistemology and ontology, ethics has figured as one of the core elements of the philosophical curriculum and students have read Plato and Aristotle, Kant and Hume, Mill and Austin for theories surrounding such concepts as right, good, virtue, benefit and duty. There have, of course, been far more people academically interested in ethics than just philosophers. Doctors, engineers and management theorists, to name but a few, have been deeply interested in what it is for a doctor, an engineer or a manager to act ethically. But so powerful has been the regard for philosophy within ethics that the relationship between philosophy and the applied ethics of doctors, engineers and managers has been seen as that of principalism. In medical ethics, perhaps the branch of professional ethics with the strongest claim to longevity, there is a strong tradition of doctors studying medical ethics as a branch of applied philosophy. Beauchamp and Childress *Principles of Biomedical Ethics* (2001) is perhaps a paradigm treatment of principalism in which the concepts of autonomy, non-malevolence, beneficence and justice constitute four overarching principles. Three variants of principalism can be identified. The first, what might be called weak principalism, is the argument that the mapping of generic concepts such as virtue, obligation, benefit, nature and goodness to the phenomena we confront in professional life form a helpful conceptual vocabulary with which to articulate ethical dilemmas and avenues out of them. And furthermore, the tradition of philosophical writing from Plato to Heidegger illuminates this mapping.

There is also a stronger version of principalism that might be characterised as the thesis that certain principles of ethics are capable of being derived independently of any application in a particular profession and then 'applied' in the sense that particular classes of conduct are assessed in respect of conformance to principles. O'Neill (2002, 50) provides a helpful schema of different accounts of the principalist thesis of practical reason. Within this schema, she distinguishes between principles of practical reason that arise in realist accounts of metaphysical moral truths, in the manner that Plato once enjoined, and in 'particularist' conceptions of reasoned action in which reasoned action is shaped by norms and particular commitments to people or causes rather than by more general principles. The quest for principles and rules is one which, in the particularist's view, entails an abandonment of that degree of sensitivity to the nuances of every particular person or situation without which the pursuit of ethical conduct would be pointless. For the particularist, the very concept of applied ethics is suspect. The distinction between ethics and its application reflects a misunderstanding of how ethics works in the practice of our lives. Much encouragement of this view derives from Wittgenstein's critique of rule-following in general and his conception of philosophy, not as the provision of substantive knowledge nor as answers to general questions, but rather as clarification or even, therapy. For Wittgenstein, as Thornton (1998) puts it, explanation has no place in philosophy and should be replaced by description.

> 'Philosophy may in no way interfere with the actual use of language; it can in the end only describe it.' (Wittgenstein, 1953, section 124).

McDowell (1981) adopted this Wittgensteinian perspective to suggest that the incapacity of rules to determine action entails that this under-determination of conduct is in fact, a non-determination of it. But this is not the opposition to principalism that I wish to commend here. Indeeed, there is some minimal sense of principalism that would be required for any sense to be made of learning in ethics. And the fact that principles underspecify conduct is not necessarily to remove the value of principles. Principles, in mathematics as much as in ethics, frequently underspecify the appropriate actions that are consistent with a principle. O'Neill (2002, 124) uses the analogy of solving a design problem under multiple constraints. None of the different constraints that limit the range of solutions are capable of generating the solution of themselves. Imagination and practical judgement are required to generate candidate solutions which might then be assessed in terms of conformance to principles.

Because principles can only be articulated within a particular culture or a particular tradition, it does not necessarily follow that the principles so articulated are not reliable guides. Macintyre (1989) insists that there is no Archimedean or neutral standpoint from which traditions, cultures and practices may be approached. On the contrary, he suggests, to be initiated into a tradition is a precondition for meeting and understanding other traditions. To be formed within a particular tradition of ethical practice, for living and for working, requires more than knowledge acquisition. As Verstraeten (2002) reminds us, how we act in different situations needs to be integrated into a narrative harmony of our lives. In the conditions of our knowledge oriented society, we are drawn inexorably into the possibilities of ever increasing perplexity and fragmentation. Paul Ricoeur (1990) encouraged the integration of one's personal *idem* identity that maintains itself through time, and the persistently challenged *ipse* identity that emerges through the encounter with 'the other'. This 'other' might be a person, a community or a text; all of them avenues by which a person is able to imaginatively reconfigure what is important in the account one gives of the continuity of oneself in the encounter with others.

What is important in developing this process is the opening before oneself of the array of experiences and meanings which people in relationships, including those between professionals and clients, in hosts of different practices, have made sense of each other. It is the study of literary texts, novels, poems, stories and religious testimonies that open up the arena of otherness in which the moral imagination can develop and flourish.

This brings us to the third variant of principalism that professional ethics needs to be defended against. This version of principalism is a pedagogical claim that only the study of philosophy can provide a satisfactory basis for the principles of conduct that require application across the various disciplines. It is not even clear that Aristotle, Hume, Wittgenstein or Heidegger would have themselves subscribed to such a version of principalism. In practice, some of the most eloquent illuminations of the relationship between our inclinations and the articulation of the circumstances within we must act, have come not so much from academic philosophy but from novels and plays. F R Leavis' taught generations of students of English Literature by means of an analysis of the 'great tradition' of moral sensibility in English literature. His teaching was a certainly an ethical endeavour in what it sought to inculcate. But it was never an endeavour that was dependent on academic philosophy. To the extent that professional ethics needs to be defended from this pedagogical version of principalism, ethics needs defending against philosophy.

As well as understanding principles, to be educated ethically requires sufficient capability to place oneself empathetically in the shoes of others and it requires sufficient emotional intelligence to be able to articulate how actions might be understood by the other. Martha Nussbaum (1997) presents a powerful case for the development of narrative imagination which will allow professionals to learn to place themselves as spectators in the circumstances of people they might serve in their professional life.

A defence against righteous conformance

Ethics can be a tough task master. What is not permissible is logically condemnable; whenever you fall, you are necessarily in the wrong. Different words are available to remove the sting of wickedness without destroying the bases for condemnation. Deeds may be 'inappropriate' or 'misguided' rather than plain wrong but the condemnatory force survives. Such condemnation was once associated with old fashioned religion and in some places and some times still is. But there are countless secular versions of righteous indignation at wrong-doing. And if religion has been responsible for its share of inculcating guilt through the centuries, the insistence on God's preparedness to forgive with persistence and in love, has at least ameliorated the onslaught of the righteous.

Secular versions of righteousness do not always have the same insistence on forgiveness. Those who have offended against animal rights have seen their property and persons attacked. Offences against the environment offend against common and deeply held values and the pursuit of accountability and openness can be a source of bitter recrimination against those who fall short. This passion for the righteousness of new causes appears at the same time as the rejection of those standards of truthfulness and objectivity that modernity provided. Paradoxically, the post-modern rejection of grand narratives, whatever fears it might have inculcated of an 'anything goes' relativism, has in fact heralded a passionate variant of righteousness. The point perhaps is that there is now a plurality of different hues of righteousness. Systematic syntheses of political theory, handmaidens all of them of modernity, once encouraged us to see political life as the stage for ethical conduct on a grand stage. Locke, Rousseau, Marx, Mill and Dewey gave us ethics writ large whether of liberty, nature, socialism or liberty. Ethics was almost subsumed within politics. But such grand commitments, together with the political associations that implemented them have yielded ground to careful expositions of how we should treat one another in particular contexts and over particular issues. Ethics has replaced politics as the arena of discourse about what we treasure most in our life in the community whether it is respect for the environment, resistance to globalisation or the avoidance of child labour in supply chains.

However worthy such causes are, passionate enthusiasm for 'people causes' risks encouraging us to forget that human beings are frail things, vulnerable, all of us, to the charge of hypocrisy if by that strange word we simply mean failing to act consistently with what we preach. But it may be that we don't use the word hypocrisy very sensibly. Government ministers applauding family values are liable to ridicule when they are caught behaving *in flagrante*. But a more telling charge against them might be that they erred not so much by failing to act in accordance with what they believe, but rather, they failed to tell us truthfully what in fact they believe. The wickedness of hypocrisy lies not so much in the vulnerability to sin we all share but in the commitment to lying about what we deeply believe about ourselves.

Friedman *et al.* (2002) analysed fifty professional codes of conduct between 1999 and 2000 and demonstrated how three types of obligation are generally found in these codes. The first is a very broad injunction that professionals should obey existing laws of the state or of superior authorities such as bodies constituted by governments to regulate the professions. The second type of obligation is to practise with competence and provide a quality service. The third type of obligation is to reflect certain values on one's behaviour, such as courtesy, care, loyalty and dignity. Now it may be that some of what these authors describe as obligations are in fact not obligations in the sense that Kant would have understand an obligation, but are in fact injunctions to act virtuously as Aristotle would have enjoined. But what is interesting is the weight of evidence these authors bring that codes of professional ethics are sets of rules to be obeyed. Professional ethics needs to be defended against the righteous who fail to remember that, as Orwell once remarked, 'people wish to be good.... but not too good...and not all of the time.'

Perhaps one of the most important aspects of righteousness in professional ethics is the too close identification of ethics with conformance to rules. One of the very frequently encountered discourses in professional ethics concerns the conformance of some particular conduct with the rules of the professional body or ethical code. Attendance at frequent meetings of ethics committees associated with research within the National Health Service provides copious examples of rules, codes and procedures by which proposals for research or medical conduct are to be assessed. The situation is not very different in other professions. Psychologists, psychotherapists, computing scientists, engineers and architects all work to professional codes of conduct. Indeed, it may be that the shift towards ethics that has been observed since the 1980s (Seedhouse, 1988, 1) is in reality a shift towards conformance with publicly available codes. For professionals to have such rules, for them to keep to these rules and for these rules to be publicly available are all ethically worthwhile features of professional life. But the plethora of rules and the plethora of different codes for so many different categories of profession raise two questions. First there is the danger that we equate ethics with conformance with rules rather than with the criteria by which such rules are themselves judged as good rules or not. Secondly, the complexity of these rules rather suggest that rules can be provided for every circumstance in which an ethical dilemma arises. As Aristotle remarked it is inevitable that we cannot expect to be exact in matters of ethics but be content with general guidance. The danger of reliance on the rulebook approach to ethics is the risk of encouraging the principle that what is not forbidden is thereby virtuous. Ethics is to defended against conformance with rules.

It would be misleading to suggest that the intemperate demand for righteousness in ethics arises only from commitments to secular causes. People of religious faith have not been lacking in commitments to righteousness.

The impact of modernity on religious faith has been ambiguous. On the one hand, it has sought to marginalize religion to the sphere of the private and to 'reduce' religion to culture by seeking to explain away religious beliefs in terms of concepts and artefacts used to explain culture more generally. Religions are best understood, in this view in 'terms applicable to culture: texts, language, stories, rhetoric, societies, politics and self-understanding' as Hardy (1996) complained, with little account given of their transcendental content. On the other hand the outcome of the Enlightenment's concern with 'rights' and reciprocal duties has resulted in a degree of protection for a person's religion and religious practice that has recently been enshrined in Human Right legislation such as Article 9 of the European convention on Human Rights.

Taken together, the cultural reductionism of religion and minimal protection of it under the law form the basis for the minimalist treatment of religious faith in the management of organisations: tolerated, respected even, if it helps being work well for the organisation, but otherwise to be treated as a personal matter. Maclagan's (1998) treatment of the conditions under which an organisation might become an ethical community makes no reference to the members of the organisation having any religious faith. But the liberal enlightenment project under which reductionism and minimal protection have flowered have both come into conflict with a new respect for particular traditions and a determination to honour locale and particularity amidst the forces of globalisation. It has found a voice in Macintyre's (1988) onslaught on the Enlightenment project and the recovery of the validity of traditions in ethics as part of his account of the tradition-bound character of rationality. Macintyre's project sees ethical practices embedded in and not dissociable from people's histories and traditions. The evaluation concepts, maxims, arguments and judgements that comprise a morality are nowhere to be found except as embodied in the lives of a particular people. "Morality which is no particular society's morality is to be found nowhere" (Macintyre, 1981, 266). Central to the project is Aristotle's treatment of virtue, the habitual dispositions that both facilitate and contribute to human goodness.

The re-awakening of a concern with 'virtue ethic' has coincided with recognition of the need for toleration of different traditions in which dialogue and mutual respect have a primacy, understanding each other without subjugation to them. For Hans Georg Gadamer (1989) such an endeavour treats as futile any attempt to find a common reference point to which all interpretations of behaviour can be assessed in an unbiased way. Instead, he suggests a 'fusion of horizons' is possible between the author of an action and an observer, a fusion in which sense can be made of interpersonal activities. Rejecting the Enlightenment's hostility to prejudice and tradition, Gadamer recognised that listeners of texts or commentators on human events 'give meaning' to a text or event, as necessarily prior to both perceptions of a text (or event) and their understanding. But, critically, Gadamer saw this preliminary understanding of an event not as an entirely serendipitous or whimsical initiative by a sovereign interpreting subject, but as something which connects with the interpreting subject's past or story. A reader seeing or "interpreting" the events in Huckleberry Finn as racial stereotyping is not something whimsically invented, but rather, as something connected to the circumstances and perspective of the interpreter's situation or perspective. But these situations or perspectives are locatable in history. They are not our own, but parts of traditions. Understanding an action is, for Gadamer, a dialogical pursuit of an understanding with others of different positions. By exposing our prejudices, by learning of other points of view and approaches to life we can learn to enrich our own point of view.

Macintyre (1988) shows how the holders of a particular moral tradition may experience irresolvable conflicts within their own traditions. In circumstances of crisis, alternative constructions of what is crucial within the tradition will arise. Consistent with his rejection of modernism, Macintyre rules out any quest for a 'tradition independent' yardstick by which to assess these rival constructions. This might open him to a charge of relativism – with no way of judging between them. But Macintyre argues that rival constructions of traditions (or of traditions themselves) are indirectly commensurable in virtue of, as Fergusson (1988) explains, 'one tradition's ability to use language to accommodate the insights of another while also resolving new problems which are incapable of resolution in the rival account.' Interestingly, Macintyre explains this is in quasi-Gadamerian terms concening language. Although traditions are, *sub specie aeternitatis*, incommensurable, translation is possible from the discourse of one to another. Not only can we come to learn a second language, we can sometimes find that certain things can be said in the second language that cannot be said in the first. For language, substitute moral discourse, and there is possibility of changing a moral tradition by means of the insight provide by another.

This debate about toleration, respect and post-modernity is a rich one and there are other voices which defend the separateness of particular communities and their ethics in a manner which is no less respectful of difference but is less concerned with dialogue between them. Hauerwas (1995, 218) rejects the epithet 'postmodern' but his approach has similarities with Macintyre's. He shares Macintyre's rejection of 'modernist' liberalism and rationalist ethics, insisting that people become members of a particular community, formed by religious convictions which define their ethical position. The celebration of toleration, pluralism, and personal autonomy which is inherent in liberalism is at odds with the religious person's celebration of being bound to a particular God, a particular way of life, and to one another, according to Hauerwas. Trust, patience hope, gratitude, hospitality and forgiveness are the hallmarks of what a religious person might celebrate because these are the virtues which can be shown in their story. Stories, for Hauerwas, provide more moral guidance than principles can. They help us imagine what sort of person each of us thinks we ought to be. Such imaginings may be at the level of unrealized fantasy. Or they can point us to the practice of virtue and character, formed not in isolated moral quandaries but in the practices of good lives, helping shape the lives of others.

The difficulty with Hauerwas' account is that it has a propensity to re-introduce the very problem which the hermeneutically oriented postmodernism of Gadamer was intended to solve: how to provide a basis for communication across radical differences. Nor, as Hauerwas (1981, 94) recognizes, does his account of an ethical community altogether solve the problem of what he calls "vicious relativism". His account provides no treatment of morality that could offer the basis for co-operation between different people in order to secure generally desirable outcomes such as justice. Narratives in religious traditions provide powerful accounts of how a morality is constituted. But Hauerwas' refusal (Hauerwas, 1981, 97) to recognize 'a story of stories', a grand narrative to provide a basis of truth across different traditions might seem prone to encourage hostility across different communities.

Professions will be practised in a world of increasing diversity in which toleration, respect and mutual understanding will be critical in a world of plural religious faiths and value systems. Professional ethics will therefore need to be taught in ways which respect these faiths. Faith is understood here very broadly. It includes all religious faiths and also traditions of spirituality, ordered approaches to conduct in life and sets of values that people might not describe as religious.

A RATIONALE FOR TEACHING PROFESSIONAL ETHICS

Ethics, like politics, is an intrinsically contested activity. Its teaching will need to be defended against pedagogic colonization by the philosophers and defended against the righteous. It will need to be intrinsically inter-disciplinary in that history, sociology, literature and psychology are as much part of the canvas as philosophy. The teaching of professional ethics needs to be defended against the righteous in three senses. It needs to be defended against those who understand ethics merely as conformance to rules rather than the analysis of the criteria by which we judge whether rules are good rules or not. Secondly, it will need to be defended against those whose enthusiasm for justice excludes all scope for forgiveness. And thirdly it needs to be defended against those who would exclude all reference to religion and instead recognise that in a diverse post-modern world, it will be essential to include a commitment to dialogue between people of different faiths as a major factor in professional ethics. A careful balance will need to be struck between the claims of those who see ethics as so prescripted and unchallengeable that no analysis is needed; and between those who would exclude all reference to the dependencies that have been claimed between people's beliefs, religious or otherwise, and people's conduct.

REFERENCES

Barnett, Ronald (1984) *The Limits of Competence*, Buckingham, Society for Research in Higher Education and Open University Press

Barnett, Ronald (2000) *Realizing the University in an age of Supercomplexity*, Buckingham, Society for Research in Higher Education and Open University Press

Beauchamp, T L & Childress, J F (2001) *Principles of Biomedical Ethics*, Oxford, Oxford University Press

Benner, Patricia and Wrubel, Judith (1989) *The Primacy of Caring: Stress and Coping in Health and Illness*, Boston, Addison Wesley

Blake, Nigel, Smith, Richard and Standish, Paul (1988) *The Universities we need: Higher Education after Dearing*, London, Kogan Page

Brown, R B & McCartney, S, (2000) Professionalism definitions in 'managing' health services, in Malin, N (ed), *Professionalism Boundaries and the Workplace*, London, Routledge

Crick, B (1962) *In Defence of Politics*, London, Weidenfeld & Nicolson

Dearing, Ronald (1997) *National Committee of Inquiry into Higher Education (The Dearing Report)*, London, HMSO

Delanty, Gerard (1988) Rethinking the University: the autonomy, contestation and reflexivity of knowledge, *Social Epistemology*, 12 (1) pp 103-13

Dunbabin, J (1999) Universities c 1150- c 1350 in Smith D and Langslow A K (eds) the Idea of a University, London, Jessica Kingsley

Elliot, P (1972) *The Sociology of the Professions*. London, Macmillan

Freidson, E (1994) *Professionalism Reborn: Theory, Prophecy and Policy*, Cambridge Polity Press

Friedman, A, Phillips, M & Timlett, R (2002) *The Ethical Codes of UK Professional Associations*, Bristol, PARN

Habermas, Jurgen (1984) *Theory of Communicative Action*, Vol 1, Cambridge, Polity Press

Handy, Charles (1996) *Beyond Certainty, Beyond Certainty: the Changing Worlds of Organizations*, Harvard, Harvard Business School Publishing

Hauerwas, Stanley (1981) *A Community of Character: Toward a Constructive Christian Social Ethic*. Notre Dame, Ind.: University of Notre Dame Press.

Hewitt, J (2002) A critical review of the arguments debating the role of the nurse advocate, *Journal of Advanced Nursing*, 37 (5) pp 439-445

Johnstone, Megan-Jane (1998) *Bioethics: a nursing perspective*, Philadephia, W B Saunders

Macintryre, A (1989) *Whose Justice ? Whose Rationality?* London Duckworth

MacIntyre, A (1981) *After Virtue*, London, Duckworth

Maskell, D & Robinson I (2002) *The New Idea of a University*, Exeter, Imprint Academic

McDowell, J (1981) Non-Cognitivism and Rule Following, in Holtzman, S and Leach, C (eds), *Wittgenstein: To Follow a Rule*, London, Routledge Keagan Paul

Newman, John Henry (1986) *The Idea of a University*, Illinois, University of Notre Dame Press

Noddings, Nell (1984) *Caring, a feminine approach to ethics and moral education*, Berkeley, University of California Press

Nussbaum, M C (1997) *Cultivating Humanity*, Cambridge MA, Harvard University Press

O'Neill, O (1996) *Towards Justice and Virtue*. Cambridge, Cambridge University Press

Rice, David (2001) Ethics and the Multinational Corporation, *The Moral Universe*, London, Demos

Ricoeur, P (1992) *Oneself as Another*, translated by Kathleen Blamey, Chicago, University of Chicago Press

Rogers, Carl (1961) *On Becoming a Person*. Carl London, Constable

Rogerson, Simon (2004) Launching the Great Curriculum Debate, *Ethical Space: The International Journal of Communication Ethics*, Vol 1, No 3 pp 7-8

Scott, Peter (1997) The Postmodern University? in Smith, Anthony and Webster, Frank (eds), *The Postmodern University: Contested visions of Higher Education in Society*, Buckingham, Society for Research in Higher Education and Open University Press

Seedhouse, D (1988) *Ethics The Heart of Health Care*, Chichester, Wiley

Strain, John (2004) What is distinctive about ethics in particular professional disciplines and what is transferable across them? in *Approaches to ethics in Higher Education, Ethics across the curriculum*, Leeds, HEFCE Learning and Teaching Support Network

Thornton, T (1998) *Wittgenstein on Language and Thought*, Edinburgh, Edinburgh University Press

Verstraeten, J (2002) *Healthy Thoughts, European Perspectives on Health Care Ethics*, European Ethics Network, Core Materials for the Development of Courses in Professional Ethics, Leuven, Peeters

Wittgenstein, L (1953) *Philosophical Investigations*, Oxford, Blackwell

2
The marketisation of the university
Professional, commercial and ethical dilemmas of academic life

Helen Johnson

INTRODUCTION

Professional roles, based on autonomous and disinterested decision-making, could perhaps be expected to develop and evolve incrementally in response to environmental factors. But what happens if those factors change radically, experiencing a profound paradigm shift? As with the rest of the public services, higher education has been subject to restructuring and profound alterations to funding. Once virtually guaranteed public funding, institutions are required to generate income in order to survive and thrive. The professionally disinterested service to society is now much less emphasised, in the face of the need to perform in a business-like, commodified, market-orientated way. With the market has come the increasing use of marketing techniques to attract customers to the suppliers of competitive public services.

With these changing structures, cultures and functions have come concomitant changes in organisational and group cultures, and with them, individual roles. In this, academics within universities are experiencing changes in expectations about their participation in enhanced marketing activity and the solution of accompanying professional, commercial and ethical dilemmas. With reference, in particular, to the work of John Gray (1996) and Erich Fromm (1990), this chapter explores certain structural determinants or influences on choices about professional behaviour that are derived from a number of areas. In part one I will examine:

- the underlying philosophical differences within the paradigm shift within the public services;
- the importance of 'managed' organisational structures and cultures;
- the new 'marketised' role of academics in higher education institutions.

In part two I will detail an autobiographical case study of an ethical dilemma based on the possible clash between commercial advocacy and professional disinterestedness. In part three I will draw some tentative conclusions.

THE PARADIGM SHIFT IN THE PUBLIC SERVICES AND IN HIGHER EDUCATION

Over the last twenty-five years or so, under prime ministers Thatcher, Major and Blair, many types of change have been implemented in different parts of the British public services. However, they all express the same policy rationale, namely: the retreat from direct involvement by government in areas of social policy that up to the mid or late 1970s was seen as essential (Le Grand and Bartlett, 1993; Pollitt, 1993). The withdrawal in the 1980s took place as an expression of a political and philosophical view about the limited role of government, and also as a means of reducing government expenditure (Pollitt, 1993). Significantly, such a withdrawal was accepted and has been continued by the Labour governments of Tony Blair, first elected in 1997 (Marquand, 2004) and now re-elected for a third term in 2005.

The rationale that drove and drives the reforms links election success with changes, or at least no perceived increases, in personal income tax. With reduced governmental expenditure comes reduced taxation; and vice versa. This is significant, as taxation can be regarded as an expression of the relationship between individual citizens, the role of the state and the nature of community. The essential ethical question that is present in any discussion of taxation in these terms is both profound and ancient: What obligation do I have towards my fellow citizens?

The philosophical and ethical underpinnings: communitarianism or individualism?

Underpinning any discussion about the role of government and the provision of public services such as higher education, are ideas about the size and purpose of the public domain. As discussions started in the 1970s – after the consensus of the post-war period – two philosophical viewpoints were very influential. Both were American and were diametrically contrasting.

Rawls' (1971) integrated theory of justice places freedom, equality and fraternity in some kind of a balance. In a social contract of justice, individual citizens are able to participate and take responsibility for government. In this agreement, justice is regarded as being fairness, in which there is a basic equality in the distribution of rights and duties in society. Inequality is tolerated if it can be shown that all citizens derive some benefit from it. The interdependence of autonomy, state intervention to help the socially disadvantaged, and co-operation, can form the moral and social ties that help to integrate a society and make a community.

On the other hand, another influential philosopher of this period, Robert Nozick (1974) places narrow limits on the arena of the public domain and stresses the freedom of individual choice and allocation through free competition in the market place. It is the views of Nozick (and others) about the moral and ethical superiority of the market that are clearly recognisable in the public sector restructuring of the last two decades.

Of course, there is a duality of purpose in the public domain in which citizens are able to express a collective choice, in which elected politicians operate in the general interest and where citizens as individuals make choices as customers. How are these to be balanced? Ethical judgments about the appropriateness of decision-making, whether organisational or individual, have to effect such a balance. What is regarded as appropriate and fair will be considered in the light of values and attitudes derived from the social environment in which organisation and individuals are placed. These values, which enable choices between alternatives to be made, will become the 'taken-for-granted' ways of behaving in organisations, and will be expressed in professional codes of appropriate attitudes and conduct.

The overall paradigm shift in the public services has had an accompanying move to individual autonomy and decision-making, away from the professionals' view of the collective interest. Thus, ethical problems around, say, disinterested advice or conflict of interest, are increasingly an individual matter to be decided upon, for instance, on the basis of furthering the interests of the majority, or out of a sense of duty or through reasoned judgment (Kitson and Campbell, 1996).

The consequences of the market as a structural innovation

Government reforms introduced in the early Thatcher period stressed delegated decision-making, and many did introduce competition in some form into previously nearly monopolistic public services. If the 'market' is an ideal type, the market form that was introduced into the British public services in the 1980s can be seen to be more pragmatic (Le Grand and Bartlett, 1993). The aim was to replace bureaucratic and monopolistic state providers by competitive, independent providers, who because of the transformed nature of public funding arrangements, would respond to customer demands. Implicit in this, is the view that the paternalism of the public sector bureaucracies (however well intentioned) and the control of the definition of needs by professional elites should be replaced by the market mechanism. This mechanism is to be driven by actual customer wants, and behaviour. The relationship between the supplier or provider of the service and its recipient or customer is now supposedly 'equal', being contractual or quasi contractual in form. In this 'contractual' relationship, that in most instances is more rhetorical than legal, the 'generalised public' is replaced by a specific individual and the actual relationship 'narrowed' to become two or more specified parties. It is clear that a concern about equity and social justice is, if not totally absent, not the focus of such a mechanism.

Arguments for markets

Other commentators dispute this type of attack on markets and argue for them in terms of having positive and progressive social consequences. John Gray, in particular, makes some interesting comments about the social consequences of marketisation. For Gray (1996), the use of the markets has placed the worlds of producer-capturing and self-interested elites under attack. He supports the argument that emerged in the 1990s both in the U.K. and the U.S.A., for communitarian liberalism, that affirms the need for a sense of community within a market economy (Etzioni 1996; 2000). According to Gray (1996,10), what has happened is nothing less than 'the sweeping away of old class deferences and hierarchies' and that 'individual autonomy presupposes a strong public culture in which choice and responsibility go together'. He does, however, recognise limitations. Market exchange, for example, makes no inherent contribution to the autonomy (and empowerment) of the individual. Therefore, he argues that market competition must be limited in particular contexts, such as broadcasting and urban development (Gray, 1996, 10), where its impact on such autonomy may be disabling rather than enhancing. Arguing for the central insight of communitarian liberalism and drawing from Etzioni (1996; 2000), he asserts further:

> 'that the conceptions of autonomy and fairness are not embodiments of universal principles, but local understandings, grounded in particular forms of life.' (Gray, 1996, 10)

He emphasises the specific context and culture, in which this discussion around 'autonomy and fairness' takes place, and notes that:

> 'Conceptions of autonomy and of fairness are local notions, both in the sense that they express the ethical life of specific cultures, and because their content varies greatly, depending on the domain of the social activity in which they arise in any particular culture. In this morality, equality is demanded as a safeguard against exclusion... The justice with which communitarianism is concerned is not universal. It is the local justice which matches goods to social understandings, as they arise in particular cultures...'(Gray, 1996,10)

So, with autonomy and fairness as components of social justice, it must be noted that for some commentators, they too are relative, originating and belonging to their specific cultures. The best, Gray (1996) asserts, that can be realised is a 'local justice'.

An important part of Gray's argument, in support of some form of modified, social markets, is that to many observers (and recipients) the political accountability offered by the public services before their reform was at best unspecific and vague, and at worst, bogus and unresponsive. Arguably, such accountability, unless it has real, practical efficacy, leaves the recipient as much at the mercy of the lazy, uncaring or distant politician, as the market leaves the customer subject to the whims of an arbitrary market and a self-interested provider.

The market's impact on higher education's structures

Until the early 1980s, it was possible 'to view the whole structure of [higher education] in Britain... as reasonably autonomous'(Becher and Kogan, 1992, vii). In this freedom, the university could be seen as the organised anarchy of the 'garbage can' (Cohen and March, 1974) or as a political struggle between competing groups (Baldridge, 1978). As the university became a business, there was a need for rational, planned activity and an increasing need, acceptance and implementation of goals (Williams 2003). 'Unplanned' or 'anarchic' organisational-types were seen as increasingly inappropriate and ineffective when confronted with an environment, both within the institution and outside, that is subject to management discipline. In short, the university, once in Weick's (1976) terms a loosely-coupled system:

> 'is becoming more recognisably a formal work organisation, a social

unit ... that has been explicitly established for specific goals.' (Thomas and Taylor, 1974)

However, even less than twenty years ago, it was still possible to say the purpose of most universities was 'habitually avoided' (Allen, 1988). Subsequently, in the brave new world of the reformed public services, there have been innovations that resonate of business and the private sector: for example, the Higher Education Funding Council, England (HEFCE) now require university strategic plans to be constructed and published. As early as the beginning of the 1990s, Williams (1992,18) explored the behavioural consequences of structural and funding changes, asserting that: '... financial success is the main way in which institutional heads are being judged'. He went on to say that a major factor in the appointment of future vice-chancellors will be their 'likely success in promoting the institution externally and in attracting funds'. Eleven years later, Williams (2003) was discussing whether or not the 'enterprising university is becoming nothing more than as seller of services in the knowledge industry'. Once things started to move, they moved on very quickly.

Thus, formal strategic management has been deemed necessary and required by government and the HEFCE. In this way, each university must determine its own market segment; type and spread of activities; and establishment and management of institutional image in an increasingly varied and competitive post-compulsory education sector. Organisationally defined terms such as 'mission', 'objectives' and 'goals' give the university direction and 'discipline' through an increasingly turbulent and competitive environment (Johnson, 2003).

Universities in the market

Given these environmental and organisational changes brought about by government, it would seem that universities are now to see themselves as education businesses. The structures, the funding that follows the student, the forms of service delivery are changing – as is reflected in the new prevailing managerial discourse (Exworthy and Halford, 1999). All of these changes can be described as effecting the marketisation of higher education (Niklasson, 1996). Barnett (2000) has encapsulated one perception of the changes wrought on the higher education sector by saying that the contemporary university is now 'part supermarket, part cathedral'. In this, custodians of the western liberal intellectual tradition are now also competing in the market for 'bums on seats'.

Marketing is a specialised and professional discourse and is concerned with the matching of the university's resources and the demands of its customers. Anecdotal evidence would suggest that sometimes academics equate (with a shudder at its vulgarity) marketing with selling. Such shuddering is perhaps occurring less as realities take hold. However, on the most practical level, a marketing approach could be seen as appropriate for any institution that has services to offer and that wishes to identify and respond to the demands and interests of those who may use these services (and so keep the university open). Peters and Waterman (1982) influentially called this awareness, 'the need to be close to the customer'. It can also be seen as part of the new relationship encouraged by the policies of successive British governments, specifically through Citizens' Charters in the Major era (Harrow and Talbot, 1993; Pollitt, 1994) and other similar initiatives that enforced quality standards. In this way, through the need to market and promote its services, the university is made conscious of its customers' behaviour – and very importantly, its own.

Marketing as a function

Amongst many definitions, the British Chartered Institute of Marketing (quoted in Morgan, 1991, 5) defines marketing as: '…the management process responsible for identifying, anticipating and satisfying consumer requirements profitably'. In this definition, market and profit are accepted as though they were politically neutral or, at least, as though political comment was unnecessary. However, other practitioner literature does recognise that such a definition may be inappropriate to the wide range of public services, including higher education, that are likely to have objectives other than profits. Kotler, a leading figure in the practitioner literature, recognises this. Using the fundamental concept of the transaction, that is the 'exchange of values between two parties', he says that that: 'Marketing is specifically concerned with how transactions are created, stimulated, facilitated and valued' (Kotler, 2003, 4). It is the transaction - the exchange relationship – that underpins marketing. In such a relationship, a quid is exchanged for a quo, thus establishing mutual dependencies through negotiation. The term 'negotiation' carries with it, if not a total equality between the parties, some sense that discussion is possible until a mutually satisfying agreement is reached.

Engaging with the customer

It is a marketing truism that the focal point of all the activities of any organisation should be the wants and needs of its customers (Leavitt, 1960). This outward looking orientation reflects an interactive view of the organisation (or university) and its environment. The university cannot function effectively if it exists as a closed, inward-looking system (Trist and Bamforth, 1951). There is an expectation that the university must enter into connections, transactions and exchanges with the 'world out there', specifically with its market. For this to happen effectively, it would be necessary for there to be within the university itself an organisational culture that recognises, encourages and supports such transactions. But what is being exchanged in these transactions? From the overall organisational perspective, *what* and perhaps *who* is being marketed?

The immediate response is to identify certain services, such as undergraduate and postgraduate programmes. However, an established trend is for *relationship* marketing (Buttle, 1996). In this context, what is to be marketed is more than the academic award. It is the university itself as a functioning organisation, with its own particular culture as expressed through the behaviour and attitudes of its employees. Of the latter, it is those who interact with students, and other customers and stakeholders are particularly important.

Influencing through promotion

Promotion itself is the sum of the various activities an organisation undertakes to communicate the merits of its products or services (Kotler and Fox, 1995). The desired outcome of this activity is that targeted customers are persuaded to buy, or enrol, through exposure to information that is both incomplete and subjective. So this function is clearly not the same as that of a 'Which' magazine report, in which the advantages and disadvantages of a product or service are listed, direct comparisons made with similar goods or services, and rationally considered 'best buys' recommended. Examples of promotional media are videos, flyers, web sites, entries in compendia, advertising, public relations, the still influential university prospectus (Whitby, 1992) the increasingly important website (Albrighton and Thomas, 2001), and presentations by academics to groups of prospective students.

The issue of professional culture

Moving the discussion from generalities about marketing and changing organisational cultures and practices, it is possible now to focus more directly on the cultural issues raised by shifting occupational roles. As discussed elsewhere (Johnson, 2003), Halsey (1992) has described the 'decline of donnish dominion'. Moreover, the academic's 'crisis of professional identity' has also been much examined (Nixon, 1996). The discussion in this chapter will focus on the arguments that have revolved around the definition of the term 'professional', in an attempt to distinguish it from the term 'managerial' (and 'commercial').

Conventionally, Barber (1963) stressed two essential elements within a profession: firstly, that its members should have undergone a lengthy period of training in a body of abstract knowledge, and secondly, that its members should have a strong service tradition. This service tradition can be seen in terms of disinterest, objectivity and some sort of fiduciary relationship, in which there is a duty of care. More critically, Friedson (1970) has argued that a profession is engaged in the struggle for control over a designated area of work that professional status (with its implicit autonomy) has legitimised. Here, professionalism can clearly be seen as a project or control or capture, in which producers of special services seek to constitute and dominate a market for their expertise. The depth of 'professional culture' and its societal position is significant and its discussion can be placed in a wide context. In his comprehensive overview of the English professional classes, Perkin (1989, 2) states that:

> '...since 1800, British history can be seen in terms of the rise to pre-eminence of 'professionals', who rule by virtue of human capital created by education and enhanced by...the exclusion of the unqualified.'

He further (1989,17) contends that 'certified expertise' has been:

> '...the organising principle of post-war society...in which the expert has displaced once-dominant groups (working class organisations, capitalist entrepreneurs and the landed aristocracy) and their outdated ideals (of co-operation and solidarity, of property and the market, and of the paternal gentleman) with the professional's ethos of service, certification and efficiency.'

Over twenty six years ago, Gouldner (1979,153) identified a new class of employee 'composed of intellectuals and technical intelligentsia', that according to Webster (1995):

> '...while in part self-seeking and often subordinate to powerful groups, can also contest the control of established business leaders....'

To Gouldner, the 'new class' is an occupational group that has a political role that can provide vocabularies with which to discuss and debate the direction of social change; while to Perkin, these professionals 'create new ideals for organising social affairs'. As a contrast to these views, a Marxist perspective must be added. This stance, close to Friedson (1970), sees professional elites of all kinds engaged in projects of self-interested 'occupational enclosure', whatever the rhetoric of the groups to the contrary. As a matter of fact rather than as a political intention, there is an inherent inequality in the relationship between the professional and the professional's client. Lawton (1998, 21) identifies the issue of information and notes that, characteristically, professional relations have inequalities in information. Issues arise when one side uses the power that can emerge out of unequal dependencies. This is where trust comes in: we have to trust professionals because we do not have the expertise to judge the rightness or wrongness of their judgements.

Whatever the lasting outcomes of the changes brought about by the market reforms, some of which directly address this 'unequal relationship' and 'trust' within the education service as a whole, and certainly within universities, there is a culture that in some form is recognisably 'professional'. This can be described as the basic norms or values, which direct behaviour, attitudes, symbols and self-perceptions of those who call themselves academics. However, there can be, '...a tendency to overlook major discrepancies between the symbols of a professional and everyday realities' (Olesen and Whittaker, 1970).

Nixon (1996, 7) sees these as perhaps reinforcing those uncertainties and tensions:

> '...the changing conditions of academic work have placed a premium on the professional identity of the university teacher as researcher, capable of attracting external funds within an increasingly competitive research culture.'

Even within that professional identity, the activity with the arguably lower status, namely teaching, is under pressure. In a context where the kind of students has or is changing - and demanding pedagogical and curriculum response - the academic's professional identity is now 'as a *teacher* (Nixon's italics), capable of developing and *marketing innovative programmes*' (my italics) (Nixon, 1996, 7).

Contextual changes are responsible not only for a newly formulated sector, containing organisations referred to generally as universities, but they have also impacted in varying ways on the activities of the academics working within them. Funds have to be raised for research, sometimes in fierce competition with many others. In terms of lecture hall and tutorial group interaction, teaching and learning strategies also have to respond to perhaps the increasing size of student groups, student 'preparedness' for higher education and expectations.

Through surveys in the sector, Becher (2001) has shown that in many cases 'the academic tribes' acquire their culturisation from their experiences as undergraduates. Additionally, there can be a simplistic understanding of higher education that is 'rooted in a view of culture as primarily "enacted" rather than "constructed"' (Trowler, 1998). Thus, any questions asked about what comprises ethical academic behaviour must be aware of the complexity of the university and its academics (Hamilton, 2002). What are the consequences in terms of professional role and its underpinning ethical position when professional behaviour crosses over into an area of values and activities that can be more accurately described as managerial, commercial and business-like?

AUTOBIOGRAPHICAL CASE STUDY

> 'For there is far greater peril in buying knowledge than in buying meat and drink...'(Plato, 'Protagoras' quoted by Eric Fromm, 1990, 3)

The ethical problem

The 'problem' to be explored has been derived from my own professional experience. In the course of previous employment in an educational institution, I was required to recruit a specified number of students for a MBA programme. Income targets had been set and it was financially imperative that they should be met. It was clear that I was to meet these targets or my job was on the line. Thus, in Lyotard's term, as used by Ball (1994), I was under pressure from 'performativity', as my overall performance would be judged in terms of these targets.

I noticed that prospective students were asking me for advice about what they should do. Should they enrol for this MBA or should they do another course? Their asking for advice in such terms made me realise that their expectation was that they would receive disinterested, essentially professional, advice from me.

I was also aware that in my presentation about the MBA in question, which had been given to me to deliver (complete with expensively and attractively produced overhead projector slides), certain phrases and a certain language had been used in ways to promote the merits or 'sell' the degree. The information given was not disinterested or neutral and was structured in terms of the 'benefits to the customer' and followed the steps outlined in standard texts about selling (for example, Allen, 1993). My targets for enrolments had been set (and without their achievement the course would not run); and so, like it or not, I was engaged in a commercial activity. I was curious about how the prospective students interpreted my behaviour and how they themselves responded to it. Did they see themselves as prospective students or as possible customers? Did they recognise that I was engaged in a 'double', and perhaps, contradictory activity and role? They might have had certain expectations about my behaviour, but these were not necessarily consistent with the way that things really were, what I *really* had to do.

So, various expectations were in play. My employers had clear expectations of me as defined by my recruitment targets. Prospective students asked for advice and in so doing, asked me to put their interests above those of my employers; and, of course, I had my own expectations about how I should or should not behave in a certain situation. So, I experienced exchanges with a number of people who, though different in themselves and in what they wanted to receive or obtain, had found themselves in the same situation. My role had made me become the focal person within this set of interacting people. The interaction within my role set was on a variety of terms and for a number of purposes; some conflicting, some not. But it was these conflicting demands that resulted in an ethical dilemma that in organisational terms could be described as cognitive dissonance. The latter, as conceptualised by Festinger (1956), states that when an individual finds himself in a situation when the cues he receives from reality do not accord with his prevailing image of what that reality should be, he will experience dissonance.

Experiencing dissonance

Why did I experience this dissonance? Up to this point in my career, I had worked in public sector organisations that had had a strong 'public service ethos', and I had been socialised in that disinterested ethic (Ouchi, 1980). I was now in an organisation that was totally orientated to the market and had an operating stance where only the bottom line - the financial outturn - mattered.

Not unexpectedly, such dissonance, experienced through role ambiguity, incompatibility and conflict, can lead to work stress. Of course, some types of stress can be regarded as beneficial as the individual is prompted to a performance that is perhaps beyond the level previously achieved. However, other kinds of stress can be harmful and move the individual into role strain. This can be manifested as tension, low morale and the withdrawal from communication. In my case, it presented itself as situational and anticipatory stress (Cartwright and Cooper, 1997) – an ethical crisis. My marketing and professional roles seemed in complete conflict and, I had:

> 'to tolerate the dissonance, reduce it by altering either (my) image of reality or the reality, or find a way of explaining or rationalising, the discrepancy.' (Handy 1999, 383)

Digging deeper than the surface appearance or playing out of the role, the dilemma or conflict can be can be seen as more than about the 'boundaries' and substance of a role. More profoundly, they can be seen as part of an individual's self-concept. While not exploring this idea in detail, it is enough to note it is a self-concept that gives coherence, stability, predictability and security to our own understanding of who we are in terms of our identity and personality. It is not a new idea that the self-concept is itself formed through a process of interaction. Charles Horton Cooley (1922) talked of the 'looking glass self' in which the mirror that we use to see ourselves is the interaction with other people. Our personality is thus the result of this 'reflecting back'. In this way, most people learn, accept and use most of the attitudes, values, beliefs and expectations of the society in which we grow up. Mead (1934) talked of the two components of the self: 'I' and 'me'. The former, the personal self, is unique to the individual and comprises conscious and compulsive aspects. 'Me' is the social self in which the individual has internalised the norms and values of society (and those of the organisations with which s/he is involved).

In my own particular case, what had caused this 'dis-ease' that seemed to be coming from the depth of my personality? Just after the Second World War, Erich Fromm (1990, 67) accurately predicted what was to happen in the second half of the twentieth century. He did so by identifying the 'marketing orientation 'as developing as 'a dominant one only in the modern era', in which emphasis is placed on exchange value rather use value. I was perhaps able to accept the marketing orientation as 'freeing up' society from deference (in John Gray's terms) – or at least, its seeming inevitability – at a societal and organisational level. But, and this was a profound 'but', I certainly experienced severe difficulties when playing out a marketing role in organisational and individual terms. In short, I felt that not only was I experiencing the special practice of education as a commodity, but that I myself had become commodified, placed in a situation where:

> 'Success depends largely on how well a person sells himself (sic) on the market, how well he gets his personality across, how nice a 'package' he is; whether he is 'cheerful,' 'sound,' 'aggressive,' 'reliable', 'ambitious'...'(Fromm, 1990, 69-70)

I had become 'not concerned with 'life and happiness, but with becoming saleable' (Fromm 1990, 70). At best, the communication between myself and my potential students had become inauthentic (Taylor, 1991) insincere, and by definition, *unprofessional*. Fromm (1990, 70) puts it, thus:

> 'This feeling might be compared to that of a commodity, of handbags on a counter, for instance, could they feel and think. Each handbag would try to make itself as 'attractive' as possible in order to attract customers and to look as expensive as possible in order to obtain a higher price than its rivals.'

Going deep into the self-concept, such a commodification of the personality has direct psychological consequences, and once again, Fromm says (1990, 72):

> 'Since modern man experiences himself as both the seller and the commodity to be sold on the market, his self-esteem depends on conditions beyond his control. If he is 'successful', he is valuable; if he is not, he is worthless. The degree of insecurity which results from this orientation can hardly be overestimated.'

Thus, insecurity and dis-ease comes not only from the clash of cultures and roles but from the very nature of commodification and exchange, in which the possibility of authenticity is denied or compromised. Such a denial is important as authenticity is something 'we have to attain to be full and true human beings' (Taylor, 1991, 26) – or, at least, to attain mental health.

A political and ethical interpretation of personal experience

Gramsci (1971), Burawoy (1979) and Willmott (1993), amongst others, have examined how actors or workers within organisations go about understanding their own work experiences. Such experiences can be interpreted by individuals in terms of structural and political determinants and influences - and oppression. They can also be regarded as personal issues of internalisation, arising from individuals' own career history, and moral and ethical positions.

If such internalisation of distress and dissonance is attempted, conscious or not, certain strategies can be used. Three common ones are repression, rationalisation and withdrawal. There was also a fourth option: to leave the organisation. This was the option I chose. The consequences of taking such a course for the organisation are obvious. The status quo in that workplace was left unthreatened and victorious. In Gramscian terms, its hegemony was undisturbed. (And I had walked away from a dilemma that I was going to find in any public services organisation!) Eden and Huxham (1999, 297) note that:

> 'The way social order is maintained in organisations has been characterised as a feat of social construction. Actors interpret their situations and seek to 'make sense' through negotiating meanings, some temporary some less so, with their fellow workers.'

Expressed in this way, such negotiation is a cognitive process, 'conducted by thinking, meaning-seeking souls who invent and invoke social rules' (Eden and Huxham, 1999, 297), to help them exist and operate within an organisational context. Weick (1993) focuses on the 'commitments' that develop between organisational actors as they share interpretations about the organisation and what is expected of them. But as Eden and Huxham (1999, 297) comment, Weick does 'not reveal what makes a commitment', and pace my own circumstances, 'where the different strengths of commitment come from or feel like – such as being driven by fear, or by loyalty, pride or affection'. Clearly, there is more present here than purely a cognitive process, as 'different commitments reflect different emotional contracts' with the organisation and with other organisational actors – and most importantly, with the individual's own sense of self (Pfeffer, 1982). Arguably, it is from such emotional contracts – that express themselves in the self-regulatory feelings of shame, embarrassment and guilt or satisfaction and pleasure – that organisational order and control are derived.

Reflections and concerns about changes in role

Reflecting on this experience led me to my first concern about the changes that have occurred in the role of the professional in higher education (Nicholls, 2001). My question at this time was: are professionals (essentially, academics) being required, or finding it necessary to take, on new managerial and business activities? As time has passed, it is clear that in many instances they are. The question then becomes: does participation in such activities require new skills and attitudes? This is no simple matter as the ethical and professional, commercial and ethical become intertwined. After all, much of the language, much of the vocabulary, used in the literatures that describe professional and business behaviour, can be regarded as antithetical to each other. For example, the type of business orientation explored above urges its customers to *caveat emptor*, whereas the relationship between the professional and client is predicated on trust.

On the other hand, as has been recognised by Kotler (2003, 2003a), much is the same or similar, underpinned by what can be regarded as the common desire for effective personal interaction and communication (for example, the marketer's customer-centredness and the educator's student-centredness). Given these commonalties of process, if not of purpose and outcome, a third issue arises. In this changing and performance-orientated environment, is it possible to be sure that certain types of behaviour can be compartmentalised confidently into professional or commercial categories and kept convincingly apart? A tangential issue is about identifying where responsibility for behaviour and attitudes lies. Given the difficulties in recognising the real, perhaps complex and contradictory nature of behaviour, might it be that the only true awareness and responsibility for such behaviour can reside only with individuals themselves?

The final concern is perhaps the one that is the most important. Why does all this anxiety matter? Is such anxiety just over-sensitivity? Is it 'just academic'? Are we choosing to cripple ourselves with angst, taking away from institutions their responsibilities for how they require their staff to behave? As individuals, should we care at all about our behaviour and its consequences for others? After all, in a recently modernised and refurbished capitalist system, should not caveat emptor prevail? Are individuals to adopt an-ends-justify-the-means philosophy? Or are we to conform to standards of behaviour based on, say, some Kantian sense of a higher duty? Should we aspire to authentic behaviour, to a totally truthful communication, whatever that may be…? And, even if such an authenticity can be satisfactorily defined, can it ever be satisfactorily attained?

TENTATIVE CONCLUSIONS

This chapter has attempted to explore at societal, organisational and individual levels, the structural determinants or influences that academics face when making choices to do *this* rather than *that*. Whether we approach the difficulties we have defined as ethical as utilitarians or with a Kantian sense of duty or with confidence that we can reason our way out of this (Kitson and Campbell, 1996), we would seem to be left with very little space to make the dilemma and its solution truly ours.

Today, some academics within universities may be continuing to conceptualise their occupational role in terms that reflect the nature of the higher education sector before its marketisation. This in itself is important; it becomes even more significant if this remains the model of the academic that is passed down and used by subsequent generations. Such a continuance can be seen as an expression of vested interests. However, this may be a generational issue that will 'solve itself' in the retirement of those socialised in their occupational and professional values before the public sector reforms of the 1980s.

It could be that there are groups of academics, who despite governmental pressure, are determined to retain their own 'moral and conceptual frameworks' (Becher and Kogan, 1993, 3). Such a stand-off between two value systems could have direct and detrimental organisational consequences. There could be an organisational battle between competing groups, in terms that Baldridge *et al.* (1978) would expect. Such warfare could be disruptive and costly. More likely, as would seem to be happening, is that the academic profession is splitting into two discernible pathways. One pathway does not become deeply involved in the management of the university and withdraws to 'get on' with its research and, perhaps, teaching. The other pathway, either immediately on entry (or, perhaps more likely, later in their careers), focuses on management and administration. Each pathway has its own objectives, ambitions, discourse – and values. It is open for debate which group is marginalizing the other.

However, there is another way forward through an organisational development (OD) intervention that allows what is relevant from the past to be retained while the realities of today and tomorrow are fully explored – and perhaps, even enjoyed. It would also enable the two pathways to keep in touch. A form of synthesis could be attempted and in this way, a new professional culture for academics developed (Trowler, 1998). In this learning process (Brew, 1995; Easterby-Smith, Araujo and Burgoyne, 1999), staff members are given a sense of the university, in terms of its values, needs and priorities.

The need for organisational development

Nicholls (2001, 80) has noted that as 'a consequence of changing conditions', a new professionalism in academia is emerging. She goes on to say (Nicholls 2001, 80) that Nixon and Ranson (1997, 94):

> '... characterize this 'emergent' professionalism in terms of new forms of agreement-making that seek to reinforce the primacy of

the relation between professionals and their publics and the need to ground that relation in an ongoing dialogue regarding the ends and purposes of learning.'

Importantly, she follows the point through by noting such a dialogue will produce 'learning professions', occupational groups 'whose sense of professional identity is derived from their capacity to listen to, learn from and move forward with the communities they serve (Nicholls, 2001, 80-81).

Thus, the student-centred and environmental and market watchfulness become entwined once more. But nevertheless, however more 'acceptable' or 'palatable' to some academics at least, it is to present market-awareness as interaction with the university's served communities, certain realities remain. These realities are currently commercial and business–orientated. Decisions about the activities and direction of the university will have to be made – and not simply on academic terms. So while, Nicholls writes of a new professionalism that revolves around the researching and teaching duality (as exemplified in Eraut, 1994; Ramsden, 1992; Biggs, 2003), it is necessary for academics of the future to have at least some form of market-awareness and market orientation and to have participated in discussions about the ensuing educational, professional and ethical dilemmas. In this way, the structural determinants or influences on behaviour can be 'pushed back' and space made for autonomous decision-making. 'Keeping one's head down' or walking away from such dilemmas can be regarded as short-sighted and ultimately short-term coping strategies.

The living and growing – and learning organisation

Arie de Geus (1997), in his award-winning book about how companies live, addresses the issues of growth, learning and longevity in business. Though based on his career experience at Royal Dutch/Shell, his argument about the need for individual and organisational growth would seem to have equal applicability in other organisations, such as universities. He states:

> 'The company is clearly a unit, with a single identity; but the people and substructures within that unit show a rich variety. They are composed differently from each other; they have different characteristics and different potential. But they are all part of a cohesive whole.' (De Geus, 1997, 128).

Thus, in a successful organisation, certainly in one that survives, there is a set of common values (say, an acceptance of a western, liberal view of education). The organisational actors, whatever their occupational identity, according to De Geus (1997, 131) believe that 'the goals of the company will help them to achieve their own individual goals', be it that they wish to rise through the management hierarchy or to write a leading book in their field. He concludes his point by quoting some words attributed to William Stern:

> 'It is important that the individual goals of the substructures are harmonious with and best served by the goals of the higher level system. In crude terms, this means that the overarching structure should make it clear and prove to its components down to the individual human beings, that their survival and their self actualization are best served by working together towards the survival and the development of the whole.'

Thus, no argument is being made for a diminution of the essential educational and ethical core of what academics do. However, a case is made for that role to broaden, to have an awareness of the market, an understanding of the marketing orientation (that could include a knowledge of marketing practice and the various political possibilities that its three sub-discourses offer) and for an organisational role set that includes marketers. As seen earlier, Barnett (2000) perceptively saw the contemporary university as 'part cathedral' and 'part supermarket'. Such a balancing of tasks with political and moral perspectives surely must be addressed in the induction and subsequent training offered by universities to academics. Such training and development would allow them to deal with and flourish in an increasingly complex world – and in increasingly 'business-like' organisations. If they do not have such awareness and knowledge, they are unlikely to contribute influentially to the strategic decision-making processes in the restructured higher education sector. How will the university survive and thrive, and on whose terms, if such managerial and marketing realities and possibilities are not fully understood and addressed by academics themselves?

REFERENCES

Albrighton, F. and Thomas, J. eds. (2001) *Managing External Relations.* Buckingham: Open University Press
Allen, M. (1988) *The Goals of the University.* Milton Keynes: SRHE/Open University Press
Allen, P. (1993) *Selling: Management and Practice.* London: Pitman
Ball, S. J. (1994) *Education Reform.* Buckingham: Open University Press

Barber, B. (1963) *Some Problems in the Sociology of the Professions.* London: Daedalus
Barnett, R. (1992) *Learning to Effect.* Buckingham: SRHE/Open University Press
Barnett, R. (2000) *Realising the University in an Age of Supercomplexity.* Buckingham: SRHE/Open University Press
Becher, T. (2001) *Academic Tribes and Territories.* Buckingham: SRHE/ Open University Press
Becher, T. and Kogan, M. (1992) *Process and Structure in Higher Education.* London: Routledge
Biggs, J. (2003) *Teaching for Quality Learning in Higher Education.* Buckingham: Open University Press
Brew, A. (1995) Research and Teaching: Changing Relationships in a Changing Context. *Studies in Higher Education,* 23(3): 291-301
Burawoy, M. (1979) *Manufacturing Consent.* Chicago, Ill., USA: University of Chicago
Buttle, F. (ed.) (1996) *Relationship Marketing: Theory and Practice.* London: Paul Chapman Publishing
Cartwright, S. and Cooper, C. L. (1997) *Managing Workplace Stress.* London: Sage
Cohen, M. and March, J. (1974) Leadership and Ambiguity: The American College. *Administrative Science Quarterly,* 17(1):1-25
De Geus, A. (1997) The Living Company. *Boston, Mass.: Harvard Business School Press*
Easterby-Smith, M., Araujo, L. and Burgoyne, J. (1999) *Organizational Learning and the Learning Organization.* London: Sage
Eden, C. and Huxham, C. (1999) Action Research for the Study of Organizations. In S.R. Clegg and C. Hardy (eds.), *Studying Organization: Theory and Method,* London: Sage
Eraut, M. (1994) Developing Professional Knowledge and Competence. *London: The Falmer Press*
Etzioni, A. (1996) The Responsive Community: A Communitarian Perspective, *American Sociological Review* (61): 1-11
Etzioni, A. (2000) *The Third Way to a Good Society.* London: Demos
Exworthy, M. and Halford, M. eds. (1999) *Professionals and the New Managerialism in the Public Sector.* Buckingham: Open University Press
Festinger, L (1957) *A Theory of Cognitive Dissonance.* Stanford, CA: Stanford University
Friedson, E. (1970) *Professional Dominance.* New York, NY: Altherton Press
Fromm, E. (1990 ed.) *Man for Himself.* London: Routledge
Gouldner, A. (1957) Cosmopolitans and Locals: Towards an Analysis of Latent Social Roles – 1, *Administrative Science Quarterly* 2(3): 281-306
Gouldner, A. (1979) *The Future of Intellectuals and the Rise of the New Class.* London: Methuen
Gramsci, A. (1971 ed.) translated by Hoare, Q. and Smith, G. N., *Selections from the Prison Notebooks.* New York, NY: International
Gray, J. (1996) *After Social Democracy.* London: Demos

Halsey, A.H. (1992) *The Decline of Donnish Dominion.* Oxford: Oxford University Press
Halsey, A.H. (1995) *Change in British Society.* Oxford: Oxford University Press
Hamilton, N.W. (2002) *Academic Ethics: Problems and Materials on Professional Conduct and Shared Governance.* Westport, USA: ACE/Praeger
Handy, C. (1999) *Understanding Organisations.* London: Penguin
Ind, N. (2001) *Living the Brand.* London: Kogan Page
Johnson, H. (2003) The Marketing Orientation in Higher Education: the Perspectives of Academics about its Impact on their Role. In Williams, G., ed. *The Enterprising University*, Buckingham: SRHE/Open University
Kitson, A.and Campbell, R. (1996) *The Ethical: Ethical Theory and Corporate Behaviour.* Basingstoke: Macmillan
Kotler, P. (2003) *Marketing Management: Analysis, Planning, Implementation and Control.* Upper Saddle River, NJ: Prentice Hall
Kotler, P. &. Andreasen (2003a) *Strategic Marketing for Non-Profit Organisations.* Englewood Cliffs, New Jersey, USA: Prentice Hall
Kotler, P. and Fox, K (1995) *Strategic Marketing for Educational Institutions.* Englewood Cliffs, New Jersey: Prentice Hall
Lawton, A. (1998) *Ethical Management for the Public Services.* Buckingham: Open University Press
Leavitt, T. (1960) 'Marketing Myopia', *Harvard Business Review,* July-August, 45-56
LeGrand, J. and Bartlett, W. (eds.) (1993) *Quasi-Markets and Social Policy.* London: Macmillan
Marquand, D. (2004) *Decline of the Public: the hollowing out of citizenship.* Cambridge: Polity
Mead, G. (1934) *Mind, Self and Society.* Chicago, Ill.: University of Chicago Press
Morgan, N (1991) *Professional Services Marketing.* London: Butterworth Heinemann
Nicholls, G. (2001) *Professional Development in Higher Education.* London: Kogan Page
Niklasson, L. (1996). Quasi Markets in Higher Education – a comparative analysis, *Journal of Higher Education Policy and Management,* 18 (1): 7-22
Nixon, J. (1996) 'Professional Identity and Restructuring of Higher Education', *Studies in Higher Education,* 21 (1); 5-16
Nixon, J. and Ranson, S. (1997) Theorising Agreement: the Bases of the New Professional Ethic, *Discourse: Studies in the Cultural Politics of Education,* 18(2), 197-214
Nozick, R. (1974) *Anarchy, State and UtopiA.* New York: Basic Books
Olesen, V. and Whittaker, E. (1970) *The Silent Dialogue: a Study in the Social Psychology of Professional Socialization.* San Francisco: Jossey Bass
Ouchi, W.G. (1980) Markets, Bureaucracies and Clans, *Administrative Science Quarterly,* 25: 129-41
Perkin, H. (1989) *The Rise of the Professional Society: England since 1880.* London: Routledge

Peters, T. and Waterman, R. (1982) *In Search Of Excellence*. New York, NY: Harper and Row
Pfeffer, J. (1982) *Organizations and Organization Theory*. Marshfield, Mass.: Pitman
Pollitt, C. (2nd ed. 1993) *Managerialism and the Public Services: Cuts or Cultural Change in the 1990s*. Oxford: Blackwell
Pollitt, C. (1994) The Citizen's Charter: a Preliminary Analysis, *Public Money and Management*, 14, April-June: 9-14
Ramsden, P. (1992) *Learning to Teach in Higher Education*. London: Routledge
Rawls, J. (1971) *A Theory of Justice*. Cambridge, Mass: Harvard University Press
Taylor, C. (1991) *The Ethics of Authenticity*. Cambridge, Mass, USA: Harvard University Press
Trist, E. and Bamforth, K.W. (1951) Some Social and Psychological Consequences of the Longwall Method of Coal Getting, *Human Relations*, 4: 3-38
Trowler, P. (1998) *Academics Responding to Change*. Buckingham: SRHE/Open University Press
Webster, F. (1995) *Theories of the Information Society*. London: Routledge
Weick, K.E. (1976) Education Organizations as Loosely Coupled Systems? *Administrative Science Quarterly*, 21(1): 1-19
Whitby, Z. (1992) *Promotional Publications: A Guide for Editors*. Leeds: HEIST Publications
Williams, G. (1992) *Changing Patterns of Finance in Higher Education*. Buckingham: SRHE/Open University Press
Williams, G. (ed.) (2003) *The Enterprising University*. Buckingham: SRHE/Open University
Willmott, H. (1993) 'Strength is Ignorance: Slavery is Freedom: Managing Culture in Modern Organizations', *Journal of Management Studies*, 30(4): 515-52

3
Humanising professional ethics

Peter Lucas

My title is the humanisation of professional ethics. I shall argue that one of the unsung virtues of an Aristotelian approach to professional ethics is that it has the potential to bring about a humanisation of professional ethics. However, the idea that professional ethics stands in need of humanisation might well be news to many people. I shall therefore begin by talking about dehumanising tendencies within professional ethics, before moving onto what it might be reasonable to do about them.

I have heard it said that professional ethics is not a branch of philosophical ethics.[1] The suggestion being that students can be taught professional ethics without at the same time being required to get to grips with moral theory. If professional ethics were primarily about persuading students to respect established professional codes of conduct, with no requirement that they understand what might underpin such codes, then that suggestion might be a reasonable one. But it is far from clear that that is what professional ethics is primarily about. In any case if we are to properly consider whether students should be made aware of the theoretical background to professional ethical codes, we need at the same time to consider the variety of ways in which theory is thought to have a role in ethics.

Perhaps the most intuitively appealing of these putative roles of moral theory is a primarily instrumental role: theory is a tool that helps us perform moral actions more efficiently or effectively, should we choose to make such use of it. An alternative and more 'philosophical' view thinks of moral knowledge/understanding as essentially connected with moral practice. That is to say: knowing/understanding what moral goodness is itself belongs to what it is to be morally good. This latter view comes in at least two forms:

either virtue simply is knowledge (as Socrates claimed,[2] many would say implausibly), or moral knowledge/understanding is an indispensable component of virtue (rather than just a means to virtue).

Three possible alternative views are implied here then:

1. Moral knowledge/understanding is only contingently connected with moral goodness, and thus is neither necessary nor sufficient for moral goodness.
2. Moral knowledge/understanding is both necessary and sufficient for moral goodness.
3. Moral knowledge/understanding is necessary but not sufficient for moral goodness[3].

I have suggested that (1) is perhaps the most intuitively appealing view on this list. My reason for doing so is that such a view seems to be the default setting for many of the students I encounter. And the reason for this is not hard to find. It is a commonplace that consequentialism, and in particular utilitarian forms of consequentialism, represent what is in effect an ethical default for the majority of our society. Utilitarian thinking has infiltrated all levels of public decision making, through the widespread use of economic methods such as cost-benefit analysis. For many students then, utilitarianism seems almost indistinguishable from ethical common sense, and one often has to work quite hard to persuade them that there could be other ways of thinking about ethics.[4] It seems likely, however, that the pervasiveness of utilitarian thinking has shaped not only the substantive content of 'common sense' ethical thought, but also its more formal aspects. Again I only have anecdotal evidence for this, but alongside what often seems to be a knee-jerk acceptance of utilitarianism, many students seem to accede to a consequentialist conception of the theory/practice relation with minimal reflection. For consequentialists theoretical knowledge/understanding is only contingently connected with moral goodness. It is the job of theory to point the way to the correct moral decision. But since it would always have been possible to arrive at the correct decision by a variety of routes, including pure chance, theory is always in principle dispensable. No special merit is held to attach to being guided by the principle of utility, for example. Acting as if one were guided by the principle will do quite as well, so long as the consequences of doing so remain the same.

Such then seems to be the likely explanation for the tendency of students to find view (1) most appealing. And perhaps the same factors explain the somewhat dismissive attitude of some teachers of professional ethics toward moral philosophy: given a consequentialist conception of the theory/practice relation, philosophical accounts of what makes an act morally admirable will appear to be primarily of academic interest. None of which means that we have good reason to think that the consequentialist view of the theory/practice relation is a correct one. Combining that view with what Bernard Williams (1973, 130) refers to as the 'total assessment' position implicit in act utilitarianism (that is, the idea that in assessing the morality of an act we should take the widest view of its consequences that is practically possible), yields the result that, for utilitarians, 'the utility of anything is open to question, including... that of utilitarianism as a personal and social phenomenon.' It is perfectly possible that people would be more likely to act in a generally beneficent manner where they were entirely ignorant of utilitarianism as a theory. For example, it is possible that the maximisation of the general happiness would be best achieved by ensuring that people acted spontaneously, rather than by calculating the detailed consequences of their actions. It follows, however, that if utilitarianism were true we might have a moral responsibility to ensure that people remained ignorant of the theory. And with this the whole enterprise of teaching moral theory to students of professional ethics would be called into question. A consistent utilitarian might respond that what would be most important would be that we taught students whatever would be most likely to turn them into rational maximisers of the general happiness. However, we would also need to consider the students' own perspective in this. If the consequentialist view that theory is only contingently related to practice is implicit in what they are taught, they are likely to exit from ethics courses wondering what the point of ethical theory is: if what matters is that we do the right thing, why should it matter whether we understand why it is right? If students are to be taught theory at all then, we owe it to them to tackle the question of the theory/practice relation explicitly, for how else can they be expected to understand why they are being taught theory at all? On the other hand, if they are not to be taught moral theory (perhaps because utilitarianism has turned out to be true, and teaching utilitarian theory has turned out not to be the most efficient way of turning students of professional ethics into rational utility maximisers) it is hard to say why we would want to teach ethics at all, rather than say using some form of behavioural conditioning to procure conformity to utilitarian principles.

This idea that if utilitarianism were true we might be better off not teaching moral theory at all, and using some form of behavioural conditioning, suggests a further worry. In addition to potentially making the teaching of theory look pointless, the view that the theory/practice relation is a contingent one encourages the demoralisation of students, and the dehumanisation of practice. It is extremely hard for consequentialists to explain why it is actions and not events that are the preferred units of moral assessments – since both have what utilitarians consider to be morally relevant consequences. In some contexts (e.g. environmental ethics) it might even be cited as a virtue of consequentialist theories that they can make moral assessments of both actions and events. But where there appears to be no need to affirm an intrinsic link between human or quasi-human agency and moral significance, it is hard to say why any human quality should have a non-accidental relation to moral goodness (it may be that the cultivation of certain qualities will be an effective means to maximum happiness, but we shouldn't count on it). This being so, if it should turn out that in certain spheres of professional activity replacing humans with machines will maximise beneficial outcomes, then that will, at the same time, look like a morally preferable state of affairs.

In case this sounds too far-fetched, consider the increasing use that is made of robots in surgery. One surely wants to say that a skilled and conscientious surgeon not only acts in a technically admirable manner when s/he does all s/he can to bring about a beneficial outcome in a particular case, but that s/he also acts in a morally admirable manner (assuming that s/he isn't simply in it for the money, or the prestige). Now we know that robots already perform certain surgical operations better than humans, and will soon be performing very much better. From a policy standpoint then, we may reasonably feel that we have a moral duty to ensure that surgery is automated where doing so will maximise beneficial outcomes. Nevertheless, it is hard to see how the replacement of human surgeons by robots could lead to a state of affairs that was morally preferable in and of itself. The point may be clearer if we elaborate the example a little: suppose that the automation of surgery came about not through any deliberate human policy, but through the play of impersonal market forces – robots came to replace human surgeons, but no-one could legitimately take credit for this. Perhaps this situation would be preferable in many respects to the present situation. But could anyone really say with hand on heart that it was a morally preferable situation? The fact that the more efficient delivery of care could not be credited to any individual, or group of individuals, would mean that we could not speak of a moral improvement here, notwithstanding the various reasons we might have for preferring such a situation.

The above example concerns only an imagined possibility. Nevertheless it has important implications precisely because it is an example we can imagine. If surgeons, nurses, or other health care workers go into employment knowing that they are potentially replaceable by a machine not only in the technical aspects of their labour but in its ethical aspects too, this is surely demoralising. The consequentialist severing of moral goodness from any distinctively human qualities of the agent - consequentialism's dehumanisation of morality – leads quite straightforwardly to the demoralisation of humanity – in this case to the demoralisation of healthcare professionals. I do not mean to suggest here that the automation of healthcare would be morally wrong, or a mistake (though I don't think that it is a development we can afford to be complacent about). My point is simply that professional ethics has an interest only where human or quasi-human agency has a presence, and if a given ethical theory is insensitive to this, then this can legitimately be taken as a reductio of the theory in question. If the consequentialist conception of the theory/practice relation implies the dehumanisation of the professions, and the demoralisation of professionals, then so much the worse for consequentialism.

Let us assume these points are taken. Where might we turn for a more adequate view of the theory/practice relation? It would be natural to turn from consequentialism to a Kantian view. For Kant there is nothing morally significant about the maximisation of human happiness in and of itself. Only insofar as a rational agent wills in obedience to the moral law, does s/he do what is morally admirable (see Kant 1996a). Kant is somewhat ambiguous on the question of the extent to which such good willing involves theoretical understanding. In the essay 'On the common saying: That may be correct in theory but it is of no use in practice' he suggests that an adequate theoretical understanding of morality is a necessary condition for our actions to be morally good:

'[T]he worth of practice rests entirely on its conformity with the theory underlying it, and all is lost if the empirical and hence contingent conditions of carrying out the law are made conditions of the law itself.'(Kant 1996b, 280)

Kant's *Groundwork of the Metaphysics of Morals* presents a somewhat qualified view. Here he tells us that what his own account of morality makes theoretically explicit is already implicit in the common sense understandings of morality, with the suggestion that there is no special moral merit attaching to actions informed by a more theoretically sophisticated understanding. On the contrary, the everyday non- or pre-theoretical moral understanding, which serves ordinary people as their guide, is perfectly adequate for moral purposes (see Kant 1996a, 58).

Whichever of these views we treat as the more representative of Kant's views, it remains clear that for Kant some knowledge/understanding of the nature of morality itself is an indispensable component of moral goodness. Can we push the point further perhaps, and attribute to Kant the view that moral knowledge/understanding is both a necessary and a sufficient condition of moral goodness? This would be view (2), mentioned earlier – the Socratic view of the theory/practice relation. The answer to this question will depend on whether Kant thinks that knowledge/understanding fundamentally determines the will, and on this his views seem to be at best unclear. According to Allen W. Wood, Kant holds that:

> 'To act from duty is to recognise the inherent moral value of the act, and that recognition gives rise to a direct desire to perform the act for its own sake.... the desire arises from freedom, from reason recognising the action as practically necessary.' (Wood 1999, 29)

On this account the desire to perform an act, the more immediate determinant of the will, is itself the product of a rational appreciation of the fact that that act is practically necessary. In this process the rational recognition of the action as practically necessary is the ultimate driving force. This process could reasonably be characterised as a case of knowledge/understanding determining the will. That would be a controversial conclusion. Nevertheless the fact that Kant holds that acts whose motives are desires not springing from reason's recognition of those acts as practically necessary are morally worthless entitles us, in my view, to permit us to speak of a Kantian/Socratic conception of the theory/practice relation. On such a view it is either knowledge/understanding alone, or some desire born of knowledge/understanding, which determines us to act morally. And this Kantian/Socratic view offers us a further example of the way in which a particular conception of the theory/practice relation in ethics may lead to a dehumanisation of ethics.

Consider Michael Stocker's example of the friend who comes to visit you while you are recovering in hospital from a long illness (Stocker, 1997). You have been feeling bored and restless, and at first your friend's arrival cheers you up immensely. You tell him so, and what a good person he is - how grateful you are to have such a friend. He protests that he would have done the same for anyone in your position. You think he is engaging in polite self-deprecation, and you re-emphasise your gratitude. It then emerges that he was being quite sincere all along. He really would have done the same for anyone in your position. Stocker uses the example to show how while an individual's action can seem morally impeccable on a Kantian analysis, there can yet be something dreadfully awry, to the ordinary moral consciousness, in that individual's motives. In the case in question the Kantian reason for acting morally, that is obedience to the principle of obeying only universalisable maxims, founded on a rational appreciation of how such action is a requirement of autonomy, does not look like respectable moral motives. Surely, the ordinary moral consciousness wants to say, the correct moral motivation when visiting a friend in hospital must say something about them as an individual. It is crucial that you would not go and visit just anyone in a similar position, but that you go to visit a particular individual, because it is they who are in hospital, and because of the particular relationship you have with them.

Stocker's example suggests that the Kantian/Socratic view of moral motivation implies that moral agents must have a superhuman (or possibly a quite inhuman) commitment to the requirements of morality as such. Their motives, if they really do qualify as moral motives at all, do not strike us as *human* moral motives.

We have seen that both the view that moral knowledge/understanding is only contingently connected with moral goodness, and the view that moral knowledge/understanding is necessary and sufficient for moral goodness, seem to generate dehumanising forms of ethics. Where might we find an alternative to such views? One possibility would be to appeal to an Aristotelian conception of moral agency. It is, I shall argue, an unsung virtue of Aristotelian approach to ethics that it embodies a comparatively humanised conception of the relation between moral knowledge/understanding and moral practice.

In the Nicomachean ethics Aristotle famously states that we are studying ethics, 'not in order to know what excellence is, but in order to become good' (Aristotle, 1984, 1103b29). Unfortunately this remark suggests a rather anti-intellectualist programme – as if Aristotle felt that being good, as opposed to knowing what goodness is, were all that mattered. But contrary to appearances Aristotle is not moving toward the view of the theory/practice relation we find in consequentialism here. Aristotle certainly puts less emphasis on the role of the rational intellect in ethics than either Plato or Socrates apparently did. For Aristotle the virtuous person is not one who simply knows the good, or in whom the rational part of the soul simply rules the spirited and appetitive parts.[5] However, the idea that for Aristotle the rational intellect has little to do with ethics, as if the concerns of theoretical philosophy and practical philosophy had little to do with each other, is quite false.

When we consider the role that, according to Aristotle, the intellectual virtues play in ethics, it becomes clear that, for him, one cannot live a morally good life without possessing certain important intellectual qualities. Aristotle discusses the intellectual virtues in book VI of the *Nicomachean Ethics*. In distinguishing these virtues he makes it plain that some have, in and of themselves, little to do with what we would think of as moral practice. So for example the virtues of *episteme* ('scientific knowledge'); of *nous* ('intuitive reason'), and *sophia* ('wisdom'), which are concerned with the eternal and unchanging first principles of scientific enquiry, and the demonstration of conclusions derived from these, have little relevance to ethics (Aristotle, op cit. 1138b18–1142a30). *Techne* (art) is an intellectual virtue connected with production. It, too, is largely irrelevant to ethics however, because ethics is concerned not with the production of goods or effects, but with action which is an end in itself. (ibid. 1140a1-b6)

But while these virtues have little relevance to ethics, they are not entirely irrelevant to ethics. This is because, according to Aristotle, the cultivation of these virtues is part and parcel of a flourishing human life. Wisdom, for example, is related to human flourishing not as medicine is related to health – as something that helps us procure health - but as health is related to health (as for example 'mental health' is related to health per se): as constitutive of health (ibid. 1144a3-6). This means that the aforementioned intellectual virtues, while not being closely relevant to ethics, are nevertheless essentially connected with a flourishing human life.

Can we, on the strength of this, claim that for Aristotle there is an essential connection between theory and practice in ethics? Yes and no. Yes, if what is required for there to be such a connection is that it be impossible to live a morally admirable human life without possessing certain theoretical virtues. But no, if what is required thereby is that moral theory per se should be shown to have some essential connection with virtue. For it is perfectly possible that one could possess the virtue of *sophia* without having any significant grasp of moral theory. Aristotle emphasises that young men often excel in intellectual activities without evidencing any particular moral virtue (ibid. 1142a15-20). Thus while there is an essential connection between virtue per se and the various intellectual virtues mentioned so far, it is a somewhat distant relation, which sheds no particular light on the relation between moral theory and virtue.

However, the intellectual virtue that has most relevance for ethics is that of *phronesis* ('prudence' or 'practical wisdom'). This is a virtue of the deliberative faculty, which is concerned with changing things rather than the eternal and unchanging things that are the object of *nous*. The virtue of *phronesis* makes it possible for us to deliberate well with regard to the end of human life *eudaimonia* ('happiness'), and the various 'means' by which that end may be attained. *Phronesis* is:

> '[A] true and reasoned state of capacity to act with regard to the things that are good and bad for man.' (ibid. 1140b4-6)

It is possible to downplay the more intellectual-seeming side of *phronesis*, by focussing on the role Aristotle considers this virtue to play in our ability to apply general rules to particular cases (see ibid 1141b14-20: 1142a23-30). Notoriously, this is an ability that cannot in principle be held to be rule-governed. And undue emphasis on this can make *phronesis* can seem almost like a practical skill or an intuitive ability, rather than a specifically intellectual virtue. A more balanced view is obtained however by bearing in mind that *phronesis* is also held to include the ability to grasp the relevant general principles.[6] Thus while it includes an element that in principle resists codification, it also has a much more straightforwardly intellectual dimension: it is the foundation of our ability to grasp and deliberatively employ general ethical principles.

The fact that *phronesis* is the basis of our ability to engage in deliberation on ethical matters makes it sound very similar to *euboulia*, 'good deliberation' (see ibid. 1142a31-b33). However, since it is also possible to deliberate well with respect to ends that are not unqualifiedly good for human beings, 'good deliberation' is broader than *phronesis*. What is distinctive about *phronesis* is that it is not simply the skill of deliberating well, but the virtue of properly grasping the ends towards which deliberation must be directed if we are to deliberate well in the full moral sense of that phrase. *Phronesis* is not then simply about deliberating well with respect to some given end, but of 'seeing' the proper ends for human beings, and deliberating well in respect of them (ibid. 1142b30-35).

The intellectual virtue of *phronesis* then marks the place at which, for Aristotle, moral theory and moral practice intersect. It isn't simply that this virtue is constitutive of a flourishing human life – for the same could be said of *sophia*, which has little relevance to ethics. Rather, *phronesis* is the virtue that specifically enables us to act well. Morally good action, according to Aristotle, requires a particular state of mind in the one carrying out the act:

> '[T]he products of the arts have their goodness in themselves, so that it is enough that they should have a certain character, but if the acts that are in accordance with the excellences have themselves a certain character it does not follow that they are done justly or temperately. The agent must also be in a certain condition when he does them; in the first place he must have knowledge, secondly he must choose the acts, and choose them for their own sakes, and thirdly his action must proceed from a firm and unchangeable character.' (ibid. 1105a27-32)

The final point, that the act must reflect an abiding disposition on the agent's part – that one good act does not make a virtuous person, any more than one swallow makes a summer – is a familiar one. What seems to be less often emphasised in discussions of Aristotelian ethics is the importance of the first two points. The agent must know what s/he is doing, and must choose the act in question for its own sake. And the intellectual virtue of *phronesis* explains the agents ability to do this. So important does *phronesis* turn out to be that, as Aristotle concedes, one might easily be led to think that all of the virtues are forms of *phronesis* (ibid. 1144b17). Still, he corrects, it is not right to identify phronesis with virtue. This was Socrates mistake. Everyone agrees, according to Aristotle, that to act virtuously is to act in accordance with the right principle (ibid. 1144b21-25). And the right principle, he insists, is that given by *phronesis* (ibid). However, virtuous activity is more than just action in accordance with the right principle (which is why it is possible to be law abiding yet unjust – to do what the law requires and still not be a good man). Moreover virtuous action is not reducible to *phronesis*, *episteme*, or indeed any rational principles or set of principles (as Socrates had suggested). Rather, according to Aristotle, the virtues are reasoned dispositions to act which imply or involve *phronesis* (ibid. 1144b27).

Aristotle then offers us a middle way between the alternative views of the theory/practice relation we considered earlier. Moral knowledge/ understanding, in the form of the virtue of *phronesis*, is essentially connected with, but not identical with, moral goodness. It is necessary for, but not sufficient for, moral goodness. That is a rather formal way of putting the point. There is also however some merit in putting the matter less formally. What Aristotle manages to do by locating the point of interaction between moral knowledge/understanding and moral practice in an *intellectual disposition* is to permit such understanding to take its place alongside a range of other human virtues, intellectual and non-intellectual, within a remarkably vivid and rounded picture of a flourishing human life. (Though given the historical gulf that separates us from Aristotle there are naturally some parts of his view that we should not accept). This picture of the virtues as part of a flourishing human life displays both diversity and unity. On the one hand it is sufficiently multi-faceted as to avoid appearing reductionistic. On the other hand the functional centrality of the virtue of *phronesis* means that any implicit tensions between the various virtues are never permitted to bulk too large. We might well feel moved to ask whether one can really have courage without magnanimity, or truthfulness without wisdom, but the apparent urgency of these questions recedes somewhat when we appreciate that 'with the possession of the one virtue of *phronesis* will be given the possession of them all.' (ibid. 1145a1)

The great merit of the Aristotelian view for present purposes is that it points the way to an intellectually satisfying picture of the role of theory in ethics, which avoids the dehumanising tendencies of the consequentialist and the Socratic/Kantian picture of the theory/practice relation. Aristotle develops a robust and vivid picture of human flourishing, while at the same time placing knowledge/understanding and intellectual virtue at centre stage. That picture suggests both plausible reasons and plausible motives to be moral.

NOTES

1. By a teacher of nursing ethics in a large UK university
2. See e.g. Plato, *Protagoras*
3. I shall ignore the further possibility that moral knowledge/understanding might be sufficient but not necessary for virtue, as I am not at all sure what it would mean in practice.
4. The student essay that seeks, for example, to set the ethical principle of respect for autonomy on consequentialist foundations is depressingly familiar. (The argument might run: preference satisfaction is good in itself, and since a principle of respect for individual autonomy ensures that individual preferences are respected, we should do our utmost to respect individual autonomy.)
5. Cf. Plato, *Protagoras, Republic* books VIII & IX.
6. Aristotle says repeatedly that *phronesis* is not concerned 'with universals only'; 'is concerned not *only* with universals' (Ibid., 1141b14;1142b14, my emphases).

REFERENCES

Aristotle (1984) *Nicomachean Ethics*. Trans. Ross/Urmson/Barnes Oxford: Oxford University Press

Kant, I. (1996a) *Groundwork of the Metaphysics of Morals*. In Gregor, M. J. (ed.) *Immanuel Kant: Practical Philosophy*. Cambridge: Cambridge University Press, 49-60

Kant, I. (1996b) On the common saying: That may be correct in theory, but it is of not use for practice. In Gregor, M. J. (ed.) *Immanuel Kant: Practical Philosophy*. Cambridge: Cambridge University Press, 280

Stocker, M. (1997) The Schizophrenia of Modern Ethical Theories. In Crisp and Slote (eds.) *Virtue Ethics*. Oxford, Oxford University Press

Williams, B. (1973) A Critique of Utilitarianism. In Smart J.C.C. and Williams B. (eds.), *Utilitarianism: For and Against*. Cambridge: Cambridge University Press

Wood, A. W. (1999) *Kant's Ethical Thought*. Cambridge: Cambridge University Press.

4
Learning and earning in the knowledge society
Some ethical considerations

Peter Jarvis

Traditionally the universities have been the place for research and the production of new knowledge. The research conducted in universities produced knowledge that was public and one way of disseminating it was through teaching it to students and another has been through publication. In a sense the universities were the first knowledge organisations – whether they have been learning organisations is a much more debatable point. As society developed, and co-incidentally the professions, some of the large manufacturers, especially those in pharmaceutical and similar industries, established their own research laboratories, producing private knowledge that could be used in the production of medicines that were seen as for the public good. Gradually, however, over the past half a century, as society has used more sophisticated commodities and people have been living longer, more organisations have established their own research sections and pharmaceutical companies have been engaged in even greater amounts of research. This has meant that no longer are universities the main locus of research and knowledge production.

Now knowledge is an important element in the production of new commodities in a very competitive worldwide market, and some societies in the West and elsewhere have become knowledge societies. The ownership of that knowledge, therefore, also assumes considerable significance, as Lyotard (1984, 5) was amongst the first to see:

'Knowledge in the form of an informational commodity indispensable to productive power is already, and will continue to be, a major – perhaps *the* major – stake in the worldwide competition for power. It is not inconceivable that the nation-states will one day fight for control of information, just as they have battled in the past for the control over territory, and afterwards, for control of access to and exploitation of raw materials and cheap labor.' (*italics in the original*)

Lyotard was wrong about the nation-states as now some of the large corporations are more powerful than many of the nation states (Korten, 1995), but he was perfectly correct about the significance of knowledge. The relationship between knowledge and power has also been explored by Foucault in a variety of writings (see Sheridan, 1980 for an overview), and it is one to which we shall return in this chapter. The chapter itself falls into four parts: the knowledge society; the learning process – from novice to expert; managing knowledge (learning and data); ethical considerations. We shall conclude with a brief discussion of the place of the universities in relation to the knowledge society.

THE KNOWLEDGE SOCIETY

There is a sense in which the knowledge society is a product of the global economic developments of the past half a century, something that I have written about elsewhere (Jarvis, 2001) and so I do not want to rehearse that argument here; suffice to note that I argued that power in global society now lies in a global sub-structure: those who have power control financial and intellectual capital and the use of these which is facilitated by technology – especially information technology. The global superstructure is everything else, including the State. However, the State will perhaps be able to play a more significant role in the power structures of the globe since the events of 11th September, 2001 in the USA because it has the legitimate control of military force whereas the corporations do not. This is, however, by no means certain. Globalisation does not mean that every society has become standardised because each is in a different stage of development in relation to the globalisation process and each has its own individual history and culture. Nevertheless, there are standardising tendencies throughout the world, as we are all aware.

It is those societies that are at the centre of economic globalisation and can be seen as the knowledge societies, referred to by Daniel Bell (1973) as the post-industrial societies. For him, knowledge is the fundamental resource for such societies, especially theoretical knowledge (Bell, 1973, 14), and as Stehr (1994, 10) pointed out that when these societies emerge they signal a fundamental shift in the structure of the economy, since the primacy of manufacturing is replaced by knowledge. It is not knowledge *per se* that is significant to the knowledge society but scientific – including social scientific - knowledge (Stehr, 1994, 99-103) since it underlies production of new commodities and services and, consequently, has economic value. Knowledge in itself has no intrinsic value, it is only its use-value as a scarce resource which is significant. Indeed, new knowledge is a scarce resource. Every marginal addition to the body of scientific knowledge is potentially valuable in the knowledge economy.

As Stehr indicates, it is scientific knowledge that underlies the knowledge society and it is this which changes rapidly. As early as 1926 Scheler (1980, 76) tried to classify types of knowledge according to the speed by which they change. He produced seven categories, of which the final two were positive knowledge of mathematics and natural sciences and humanities and technological knowledge. The other five were: myth and legend; knowledge of natural language; religious knowledge; mystical knowledge; philosophical-metaphysical knowledge. The final two, he regarded as artificial since they changed so rapidly and never had time to become embodied in a society's culture before they disappeared, while the other forms of knowledge changed more slowly. These other forms of knowledge have, consequently, been relegated to a less significant place in capitalist knowledge societies, something that was very apparent in Kerr *et al.*'s (1973, 47) discussion of the nature of higher education in the contemporary society:

> 'The higher education of industrial society stresses the natural sciences, engineering, medicine, managerial training – whether private or public – and administrative law. It must steadily adapt to new disciplines and new fields of specialization. There is a relatively smaller place for the humanities and the arts, while the social sciences are strongly related to the training of managerial groups and technicians for the enterprise and the government. The increased leisure time of industrialism, however, can afford a broader public appreciation of the humanities and the arts.'

Of course, they were wrong about the nature of society but they were right about the emphasis being placed on scientific subjects, albeit in the post-industrial society. The dominant discourse about knowledge in knowledge societies is scientific, so that it appears that all knowledge has to be scientific, or at least social scientific.

However, if knowledge changes so rapidly, how can we decide whether it is true? Traditionally, there have been three ways of legitimating knowledge: by rational argument, empirical discovery and pragmatism (Scheffler, 1965). Underlying both modernity and, therefore, science is the idea of instrumental rationality, of which pragmatism is an important articulation. Indeed, Tuomi (1999,101), writing about corporate knowledge claims that 'Knowledge is more true if it solves more important problems than some previous knowledge'. Whilst I find the concept of 'more true' unacceptable since truth is truth, the point is that in corporations in global capitalism pragmatic knowledge is crucial, or as Lyotard (1984, 41-53) puts it 'performative'.

Once we recognise that knowledge changes rapidly, it is more difficult to view it as something objective. Indeed, Lyotard (1984) sees it as narrative, which is necessarily subjective. Consequently, the subjectivism of knowledge has to be distinguished from something that is changing less rapidly and can therefore be regarded as objective, and so for the purposes of clarification we will view objective knowledge as data and information and subjective knowledge as knowledge and wisdom, a concept I will discuss below.

THE LEARNING PROCESS: FROM NOVICE TO EXPERT

For many people in the knowledge society, the work place is the primary source of learning, either through the production of new knowledge or through having to react to innovative changes that occur in it. It is hardly surprising, therefore, that learning has assumed a dominant place in the educational vocabulary, and the learning society has become part of that discourse. Indeed, there is a sense in which the terms 'knowledge society' and 'learning society' are almost interchangeable.

Learning is increasingly being seen as an experiential process, and in recent years there have been many learning theorists who have focused on experiential learning (Kolb, 1984; Jarvis 1987, 1992,1995 etc; Weil and McGill 1989, *inter alia*). My own definition of learning is that:

> 'Learning is the combination of processes whereby we construct and transform our experience into knowledge, skills, attitudes, values, beliefs, emotions and the senses.'

My own model of the learning processes, which has gone through a number of amendments since I first researched it in the mid-1980s, is illustrated below. While it is impossible to discuss this model in full here since there many different forms of learning which have a variety of implications (see Jarvis, 1987, 1992, 1995 *inter alia*), it can be seen from it that the social situation provides the location for experiences which are potential learning situations, although not all experiences result in learning. Consequently, the work place is a dominant site for learning. We learn from actively doing our work but we also learn from colleagues with whom we work. There is a sense then that we can share each other's knowledge and expertise.

In the complex model shown in Figure 1, the persons (the learners) (box 1) take their own biography (their life experience) into any social situation (box 2) in which they may have an experience (box 3) which is itself socially constructed. Since work is a social activity, there are many opportunities for individuals to have such a learning experience. This may occur through actually performing the work tasks at hand, or from reflecting on the experience of practice, or from sharing ideas and knowledge with fellow workers. From the social situation (box 3) it is possible to learn by memorising (box 7), through practice (box 5) or from reflection (box 8). Through these learning experiences, novices might to move towards the status of expert, a process which was first discussed by Dreyfus and Dreyfus (1980). They posited that a learner goes through five stages in becoming an expert: novice, advanced beginner, competent, proficient and expert (cited from Benner, 1984,13 – see also Tuomi, 1999, 285-340). This, then, is a role for managers of human resources – to develop staff so that they may acquire a greater degree of expertise. In precisely the same way, more experienced

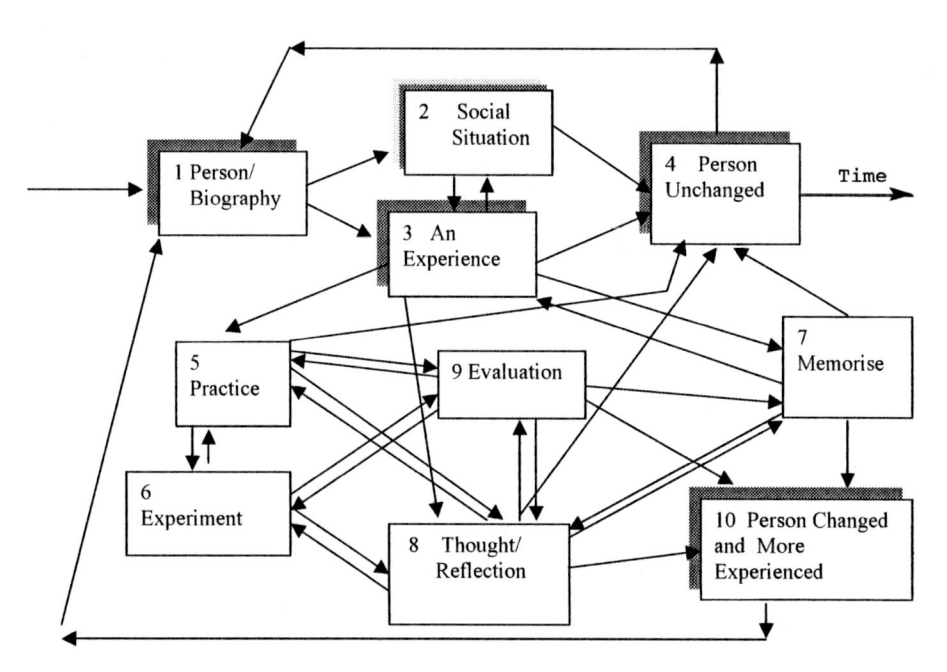

Figure I A Model of the Processes of Learning

workers might continue to learn and continue to develop new knowledge through the process.

The expertise gained is in pragmatic practical knowledge as the experts have both knowledge and the skills to practise their expertise, learned in practice, since these three learning processes mentioned above, that is from box 3 to boxes 5, 7 and 8, occur simultaneously. This expertise gained is not all conscious learning, for this model allows for pre-conscious learning, which means that some of the expertise gained is tacit rather than explicit. I shall return to the concept of tacitness below.

Nevertheless, the work situation has to be so structured and organised that it can both provide an opportunity to learn and be flexible enough to respond to the learning that occurs. By contrast, in my own doctoral research (Jarvis, 1977), I discovered that the more bureaucratic the organisational context the lower the job satisfaction and the greater the role strain of individuals who had a professional ideology towards their work. Consequently, one of the tasks of management is to ensure that both the conditions are right for learning and flexible enough to respond to it. Stahle (2001) made a similar point when she described organisations as being mechanistic, organic or dynamic (see also Frenkel et al., 1999). Many of them are not dynamic enough to respond to the changes needed because of the learning that has taken place in the work force. Nevertheless, as Thompson et al. (2000, 125) remind us, a great many service workers do work in highly routinised and stringently monitored work situations (see also Frenkel et al., 1999), so that they are by no means all knowledge workers. Indeed, the number of people who actually work with knowledge which demands this degree of organisational flexibility may be much smaller than the number of people who might be viewed as knowledge workers.

Given the right conditions, workers can acquire the knowledge, skills, attitudes, values, beliefs, and so forth to progress from novice to expert. Not all will do so, since they may cease to learn from their work, as the learning model above indicates (from box 1 through 2 to 4, or from box 1 to box 4). In these cases, their practice will remain static or even deteriorate. However, some will continue to learn and to move along the path to become experts, and expertise of this type is an important resource for corporations operating in the knowledge economy. Experts are, therefore, to be used not only because of their expertise but because they can also provide information and become role models for less skilled or less knowledgeable workers. Additionally, there is another sense in which organisations seek to capture that knowledge and expertise, and that is through getting the experts to articulate it and share it in a variety of different forms, such as reports and so on. This becomes a problematic exercise since a great deal of the experts' knowledge is tacit (Polanyi, 1968). Nyiri (1988, 20-21) highlights this problem:

'One becomes an expert not simply by absorbing explicit knowledge of the type found in text-books, but through experience, that is, through repeated trials, 'failing, succeeding, wasting time and effort...getting a feel for the problem, learning when to go by the book and when to break the rules'. Human experts gradually absorb 'a repertory of working rules of thumb, or "heuristics", that, combined with book knowledge, make them expert practitioners. This practical, heuristic knowledge, as attempts to simulate it on the machine have shown, is 'hardest to get at because experts – or anyone else – rarely have the self-awareness to recognize what it is. So it must be mined out of their heads painstakingly, one jewel at a time.' (All quotations from Feigenbaum and McCorduck, 1984)

As the years go by the experts not only gain knowledge and skills, they gain wisdom, which can be regarded as:

'...the ego's increasing capacity to tolerate paradox. This same capacity characterizes the mature defenses, which can maintain a creative and flexible tension between irreconcilables and allow conscience, impulse, reality, and attachment all to have places at the center stage.' (Vaillant, 1993, 328)

This wisdom only comes as a result of learning through experience and it is something that no novice can have. It is almost as if it becomes part of the expert's being.

MANAGING KNOWLEDGE (LEARNING AND DATA)

However, the idea of mining such knowledge from their heads, as Nyiri suggests, or as Tuomi (1999, 325) explains in the process that he sees as moving from tacit knowledge to explicit knowledge. More significantly, it is also about corporations seeking to capture the wisdom of the experts. These processes raise ethical questions of ownership, control, and management. In addition, we also confronted with the traditional potential antagonism between employer and employee.

Clearly a number of issues arise in seeking to manage knowledge and these revolve around the problems of its location and ownership. Yahklef and Salzer-Morling (2000, 21) neatly summarise this problem:

'What is knowledge? Where does it reside? How to secure it, spread it, develop it, manage it, measure it, etc? The ultimate aim – which can be traced to Taylor – is to displace knowledge from the body it inhabits to the balance sheet, where it is meant to feature as a new type of capital, commonly referred to as 'intellectual capital', rivalling and eclipsing the traditional concept of financial capital...... Hence, within the terms of the discourse on 'intellectual capital', knowledge has fallen prey to the vocabulary and practices of accounting. Knowledge has become the target of management, of control, of rational calculative thinking and of the practices of accounting.'

These authors divide intellectual capital into two forms: human capital and structural capital. The former resides in the employees, so that it can be either individual or shared, and the latter in the corporation's structures and databases. Since the latter are either elements of the company culture or in organisation's ownership, they present it with no problems. However, it is the human capital that is uncertain as far as the corporation is concerned since this is not entirely controlled by the corporation, and so one major element in the managing of human capital is 'to enforce routines of documentation, of transferring knowledge from humans to machines where it can be articulated into more endurable and stable forms' (Yahklef and Salzer-Morling, 2000, 30). These can then be more easily controlled and measured. It will be recalled that earlier we suggested that data and information are objective, so that what actually happens is that knowledge is transformed into data, or subjectivity is replaced by objectivity. However, it can be seen that data are inanimate whereas knowledge is something that is changing and developing along with the employees who are generating it. There are, therefore, two broad issues for management: managing human capital both to create and share knowledge, and extracting knowledge from practitioners in order to create data and information. The former may be epitomised as managing people's learning and the latter as managing data.

In the former, if we return to the model of learning above, we can see that human learning occurs from the meeting of individual's biography and the experience that is created in social situations. While the learning is an individual process, the situations within which a great deal of the learning occurs are social. Management, then, needs to create working situations – teams, small groups - where individuals can exchange knowledge and learn from each other. Consequently we see communities of practice, of interaction and learning emerging, both with experts working together to generate new knowledge by sharing their own expertise with each other, and with experts working with novices so that the latter can learn from the former. In one sense this might be seen as human resource development but, in another, it might be seen as the corporation ensuring that the experts' knowledge, both explicit and tacit, is retained within the organisation through the next generation of workers, even if experts leave and go elsewhere. These structures help to generate and sustain the company's culture and, at the same time, ensure that its intellectual capital continues to expand and be retained.

In the latter form of management, knowledge is documented and stored. In some transnational organisations these data and information are actually stored in a centralised computer system, often based at the corporation's own headquarters. They contain reports and extracts from documents and reports about good practices, procedures, consultations, and so on. Companies, therefore, develop their own body of specialist data, which is the basis of their operations – data which may become a commercial secret. Companies, such as the consulting firm McKinsey, require employees to sign a pledge that they will not reveal the knowledge that they have learned in the company for the rest of their lives (Rastel, 1998) because it might be commercially sensitive. Not only are there ethical questions about these practices that we will discuss in the next section, but as we have implied earlier, there are major epistemological ones. For instance, once the knowledge has become data it is static, although it can be updated by ensuing reports, as so on – but it is no longer really directly applicable to new and developing situations. Some procedures might still be applicable but the data will always have to be treated with care and used by some one who already has considerable knowledge. Young and inexperienced consultants cannot just be provided with data and left to apply it. There was, for instance, a case (reported on British television. Channel 4, *Managers of the World*), where a young consultant took out a set of procedures stored on the database of her corporation to a foreign country only to find that the Muslim women with whom she was consulting did not learn in the same way or at the same pace as she had been led to believe, and she was having severe difficulties. The company had over-valued the data that it had stored, treating them as if they were universalisable knowledge. Not only was the company wrong to treat data as if they were knowledge, it might also have been making claims about its database that were incorrect.

ETHICAL CONSIDERATIONS

McInerney and LeFervre (2000, 15) claim that

> 'Knowledge management (KM) is more than just a technology or a software. It is a sophisticated way for an organisation to share intellectual assets. KM is best practised in situations that are

collaborative and team-oriented. Effective knowledge management calls on those who are experienced to provide the knowledge that they have gained to those who develop the firm's knowledge repositories. It is up to the information specialists, then, to treat the knowledge and the people responsible for it in a fair and just ways that engender trust and confidence in the systems that have been established.'

It may be seen from the above discussion, however, that this might be a statement about an idealised situation rather than an actual one, but there are a considerable number of ethical concerns that might arise about the way that knowledge and knowledge workers are treated in the knowledge society, but also in the way that some knowledge workers treat their company. I want to focus briefly on five here: the ownership of intellectual capital; respect of the workers' rights by the employers; respect for the firm's rights by the workers; the right use of knowledge and databases; the ethic of the discourse of scientific knowledge in the knowledge society.

The ownership of intellectual capital. If we look at the processes of learning, we can see that a great deal of it is individual, although it happens because the employing organisation has provided the opportunity for it to occur. It has provided the situation, the colleagues and so on, so that there has been shared learning. This is the more so if workers do work in teams or small groups. The outcome of this is that neither the individual nor the employing company has the right to claim total ownership of the intellectual capital. Since there has been an emphasis on individualism in modern society, it is easy to see how such a claim of individual ownership might arise. At the same time it does not mean that the company has the right to claim that it owns all the knowledge learned by all its workers, since this would effectively mean that the company would be claiming ownership of its employees' minds, not only from the time that they began their employment but since they were born. But as the company is paying its employees to work with knowledge it does have some rights to some of that intellectual capital. There is a sense in which the company has made an investment in its employees. Consequently, there is a case to be made for entering some form of contract or agreement between employers and employees about the rightful ownership and use of that knowledge.

Respect for the Workers' Rights by the Employers. This point emerges from the last: the company might actually be trying to extract all the personal knowledge and expertise from the experts and store it in databases, and so on. It might do this openly or in much less obvious ways. In these cases, the company is seeking to deny some rights of ownership of the knowledge to those people who have produced it. While this procedure might be immoral, there is another sense in which the epistemological changes that the knowledge undergoes do make this less significant than it might otherwise have been. Even so, there are situations where expert workers develop their own practices and skills that are more efficient than those procedures laid down by the company, and in these situations it could be argued that if corporations appropriate them without recognition or reward they are stealing from the intellectual property of their employees.

Respect for the Corporation's Rights by the Employees. When employees treat all their learning on the job as their own, there is a tendency for some to use their expert knowledge to change companies and move to their employer's competitors in order to improve their salary or working conditions, and so on. This is either job-hopping or company poaching. But as we have just argued, there is a mutual ownership of that knowledge so that job-hopping and employee poaching are, in a sense, cases of the employee stealing some of the intellectual rights from the corporation. Hence, there is a need for a specified work contract that can help overcome this problem.

However, there is another legitimate attitude to take about job-hopping which is that since companies are always seeking to extract and document the expertise of its practitioners, even without rewarding them appropriately, job-hopping is an employee right. This situation, then, reflects the distrust that frequently exists between employers and employees.

The Right Use of Knowledge and Databases. Throughout this discussion we have made a distinction between so-called 'objective knowledge', such as data and information, and 'subjective knowledge', such as expert knowledge and wisdom. The latter cannot be totally captured on a database or through documents. Much of the expert knowledge and wisdom concerns knowing how to act in specific situations, and so on, rather than following specific procedures, as Nyiri (1988) pointed out above. Consequently, for corporations to claim that they have captured all the intellectual capital about specific procedures on databases, so that they can use less experienced and less costly personnel is to make false claims about the knowledge and expertise that the company has. And if they then send out inexperienced employees or consultants claiming to offer the companies' expertise and charging the type of fee that the few experts might demand, it is either ignorant or immoral – or both.

The Discourse of Scientific Knowledge. The discourse of rational and scientific knowledge has emerged in this period, rather like the Protestant Ethic emerged in a previous age (Stehr, 1994, 81). This instrumentality of rational pragmatism seems to be the dominant discourse, and yet we are highlighting the need for another form of rationality here, since we are advocating that expert wisdom is more than rational knowledge. Indeed, cognitive knowledge is not all we learn in the knowledge society, and as my own definition of learning suggests – we learn knowledge, skills, attitudes, values, beliefs, emotions and senses. In addition, we know that there are irrationalities in human behaviour. Consequently, we are suggesting that there is another form of rationality that has a significant place in these deliberations – a value-rationality that stems from one of those slower moving categories of knowledge that Scheler (1980) discussed – moral philosophy. The discourse of scientific knowledge does not do justice to either the whole of knowledge nor the nature of our humanity; in this sense, it depersonalises what is fundamentally human. The power of scientific discourse must be recognised but also undermined, and perhaps this is one of the functions that universities should assume.

CONCLUDING DISCUSSION

We began this paper by pointing out that research and the transmission of knowledge used to be performed primarily by the universities. This dominance has disappeared in the knowledge society, although they are still very important research organisations – and so, finally, we need to address the question about the place of the university in this contemporary knowledge society.

Apart from research, universities do have a major place in the preparation and continuing education of the work force, but this should not be their only function. Education is not only for work, but for living. Learning is not only life-long, but it is also life-wide. Learning is about the whole of our humanity. Universities remain the only knowledge-intensive organisations that seek to incorporate all branches of knowledge within their sphere of activities. By their very existence, therefore, they should symbolise the narrowness and lack of balance of the prominence of scientific knowledge. This breadth is also both an advantage and a disadvantage; an advantage because it enables universities to offer a wider population the opportunities to learn but a disadvantage because universities tend not have the finances to act independently of those corporations that need a more narrow curriculum, as Kerr *et al.* (1973) pointed out, and which support them in a variety of different ways. Yet we do need a university system that can generate opportunities for people both to learn about and to question the type of society in which we live. In so doing they will broaden the debate about the nature of the human life in the knowledge society, but failure to do this will help create a less moral society.

REFERENCES

Bell, D. (1973) *The Coming of Post-Industrial Society.* New York: Basic Books

Benner, P. (1984) *From Novice to Expert.* Menlo Park, Calif: Addison Wesley

Dreyfus, S. and Dreyfus, H.L. (1980) *A five stage model of the mental activities involved in directed skill acquisition* Unpublished Report: University of California at Berkeley

Feigenbaum, E. A. and McCorduck, P. (1984) *The Fifth Generation.* New York: Signet

Frenkel, S.J., Korczyske, M., Shire, K. and Tam, M. (1999) *On the Front Line: organization and work in the Information Society.* Ithaca: Cornell University Press

Jarvis, P. (1977) *A Profession in Process: the relationship between occupational ideology, occupational position and the role strain, satisfaction and commitment of Protestant and Reformed Ministers* unpublished PhD: University of Aston

Jarvis, P. (1987) *Adult Learning in the Social Context.* London: Croom Helm

Jarvis, P. (1992) *Paradoxes of Learning.* San Francisco: Jossey-Bass

Jarvis, P. (1995) *Adult and Continuing Education: Theory and Practice.* London: Routledeg (Second edition)

Jarvis, P. (2001) *Universities and Corporate Universities: the higher learning industry in global society.* London: Kogan Page

Kerr, C., Dunlop, J. T., Harbison, F. and Myers, C. A. (1973) *Industrialism and Industrial Man.* Harmondsworth: Penguin (Second edition)

Kolb, D. A. (1984) *Experiential Learning.* Englewood Cliffs, NJ: Prentice Hall

Korten, D. C. (1995) *When Corporations Rule the World.* London: Earthscan

Lyotard, J-F. (1984) *The Postmodern Condition: A Report on Knowledge,* trans. Bennington, G. and Massumi, B. Manchester: University of Manchester Press

McInerney, C. and LeFervre, D. (2000) Knowledge Managers: History and Challenges. In Prichard, C., Hull, R., Chumer, M. and Willmott, H. (eds.) *Managing Knowledge: critical investigations of work and learning.* London: MacMillan

Nyiri, J. C. (1988) Tradition and Practical Knowledge. In Nyiri, J. C. and Smith, B. (eds) *Practical Knowledge: outlines of a theory of traditions and skills.* London: Croom Helm

Polanyi, M. (1968) *The Tacit Dimension.* London: Routledge and Kegan Paul

Rastel, E. (1998) *The McKinsey Way.* New York: McGraw Hill

Scheffler, I. (1965) *Conditions of Knowledge.* Chicago: University of Chicago Press

Scheler, M. (1980) *Problems of a Sociology of Knowledge* trans Frings, M.S. London: Routledge and Kegan Paul

Sheridan, A. (1980) *Michael Foucault: The Will to Truth*. London: Tavistock
Stahle, P. (2001) *Knowledge Management as a Learning Challenge*. Paper presented at conference on Creating Human Capital, Helsinki (September)
Stehr, N. (1994) *Knowledge Societies*. London: Sage
Thompson, P., Warhurst, C. and Gallahan, G. (2000) Human Capital or Capitalising on Humanity. In Prichard, C., Hull, R., Chumer, M. and Willmott, H. (eds.) *Managing Knowledge: critical investigations of work and learning*. London: MacMillan
Tuomi, I. (1999) *Corporate Knowledge; theory and practice of intelligent organizations*. Helsinki: Metaxis
Vaillant, G. E. (1993) *The Wisdom of the Ego*. Cambridge Mass: Harvard University Press
Weil, S. W. and McGill, I. eds.(1989) *Making Sense of Experiential Learning*. Buckingham: Open University Press and Society for Research into Higher Education
Yakhlef, A. and Salzer-Morling (2000) Intellectual Capital: Managing by Numbers. In Prichard, C., Hull, R., Chumer, M. and Willmott, H. (eds.) *Managing Knowledge: critical investigations of work and learning*. London: MacMillan

5

"Academics at the coal face"

Ethical dilemmas in the real world – lessons from research into social exclusion

Nicholas Walters, Linda Townsend and Florina Zoltan

Students are encouraged into higher education (HE) with expectations of future careers offering high salaries. The current estimated premium for graduates is that over the course of their working lives they will on average be £400,000 better off than their non-graduate peers. In this there is a blind leap of faith that the 'knowledge society' will deliver a prosperous and successful future, both for the UK and the enlarged European Union. If labour in the developed world can no longer be seen as competitive in global terms then a highly educated and highly skilled workforce will deliver a bright future, by securing a competitive advantage. To ensure this, the political rhetoric is to enforce the importance of education, and in particular the acquisition of high skills. The practical result is the construction of ever higher numerical targets for HE and so move to a workforce in which 50% have qualifications at first degree level. The pressing problem for HE is how to fund this. This misses the importance of questioning the supposition behind the policy. There is a cause and effect issue, in that there is no guarantee that the one will automatically follow the other. University pay scales themselves question the assumption. A previous example of a similar kind of failed rhetoric was the claim from proponents of computerisation that the introduction of computers would lead to the paperless office. The policy promises do not magically deliver. The real world of employment is complex and tougher than a simple linear upward progression to success and wealth generation. How far is it right to train future professionals without an understanding of broken career paths, periods of unemployment and social exclusion in and out of the workplace?

What is the nature of exclusion and how can those in HE deal with this structural reality? This is made even more urgent as HE itself is not immune from these processes. There is a constant demand for enhanced collaboration with employers and the labour market, for relevant teaching and applied research. Financial pressures on the HE sector itself make it far from a safe employment haven with tenured jobs for life and resources to discharge those jobs. We know too well that job insecurity, and the stress that follows, is a commonplace experience in HE.

It is therefore appropriate that issues of unemployment and social exclusion are a legitimate concern of HE and integral to its understanding of both its own role and responsibilities, and its analysis of the real world. The Department of Political, International and Policy Studies at the University of Surrey has a small team researching issues of social exclusion and developing appropriate political and policy responses to promote inclusion (www.surrey.ac.uk/politics/cse/index).

The concept of social exclusion is rapidly developing. Its French origin (Evans, Paugham and Prelis, 1995) was taken up in European Union policy (Klasen, 1998) and so, like the EU itself, has a strong economic bias. During the 1980s it became clear that unemployment was a structural problem for the EU, and for many years social exclusion was used as a synonym for unemployment. This prompted a policy initiative to reinforce and renew efforts to train unemployed people to compete in the labour market. In the UK the introduction of the Manpower Services Commission responsible to the Department for Employment rather than the Department of Education and Science poured resources into mass training programmes for unemployed people, on the belief that training magically led to jobs. This neo- vocationalism is largely discredited, 'There is general agreement in the EU that this approach does not work' (Lambert, 2002).

Social exclusion is not simply unemployment, nor is it synonymous with poverty. The Organisation for Economic Cooperation and Development and the World Bank discussion on poverty tend to restrict the discourse to relative income measures. Duffy (1995, 5), defined social exclusion as 'low material means and inability to participate effectively in economic, social and cultural life and, in some characteristics, alienation and distance from mainstream society', while Berghman (1995, 19) adds 'the denial or non realisation of civil, political and social rights of citizenship'.

More recently the UK government has paid increased attention to social exclusion issues. The most well known is the establishment of the Social

Exclusion Unit, but this is only one manifestation of a much more wide ranging policy interest, from the introduction of Tax Credits by the Treasury to the Widening Participation activities in Higher Education. This new interest is producing a range of different approaches in terms of a variety of responses. There are now different discourses dependent on the perspectives of lifelong learning, economic regeneration, community development, specific professions, (such as the health profession), and Information and Communication Technology (Walters, 2003, 244). The most recent development is the discourse on the relationship between social exclusion and environmental concerns (Adebowale, 2003). In terms of ethics, the most significant new discourse has been prompted by the impact of the EU Treaty of Amsterdam (1997) and its subsequent impact on national legislation relating to The Human Rights Act 1998 (HRA) which came into force on 2 October 2000.

A useful distinction in understanding the notion of social exclusion can be made between external and internal factors. External factors include a lack of social infrastructure, poor quality housing, inadequate public transport and a dearth of social amenities. Internal factors are usually, but not exclusively, personal, such as low self esteem, loss of confidence, low expectations, continued benefit dependency, but can include loss of community cohesion and community trust, at its most extreme leading to civil unrest.

Most practical responses, actions to combat exclusion and to enhance social cohesion and inclusion, are promoted on a fixed-term project basis. In the UK this is usually targeted towards a particular social group of beneficiaries, for example projects funded by the European Social Fund, and frequently located in neighbourhoods that rank highly on Indices of Multiple Deprivation. Examples of this are the Neighbourhood Renewal programme and the former Single Regeneration Budget initiatives:

> 'The policy vision is to narrow the gap between deprived neighbourhoods and the rest of the country, so that within 10-20 years, no one should be seriously disadvantaged by where they live. This commitment has been made in the light of sustained research by the Social Exclusion Unit culminating in its report, "Bringing people together: a national strategy for neighbourhood renewal" (1998), and the follow up work by 18 Policy Action Teams in a range of areas including housing, education, crime and health'. (White 2002, 3)

Three Case Studies of projects illustrate the ethical dilemmas within work related to combating social exclusion and have been chosen to illustrate the range of ethical challenges that this work uncovers.

The first Case concerns working with former substance abusers, who are a recognised social group who find particular difficulty re-entering the labour market. Widespread fear, suspicion and ignorance surround the issue of drug and alcohol misuse. Employers, despite their Equal Opportunities policies and frequent declarations that they always employ the best person for the job, see anyone with a history of addiction as a person who is a high risk. Providers of services – treatment and rehabilitation - are themselves split between harm reduction and maintenance, and abstinence programmes. CVs of former abusers are distorted. At first sight this is a target group that would appear as very unattractive in terms of employment prospects. However, it proved possible to set the legal issues and judgemental responses aside, and a new reality for this group began to emerge. Addiction is not the result of moral failure, nor of social class or levels of educational qualification. Those who experience dependency on mood altering chemicals have indeed learned a range of transferable skills that are attractive to the labour market. Such people are often creative, but have added skills in negotiation, enterprise, problem solving, social interaction and team work, all acquired while they were active addicts. Once the negative personal context, where these skills were learned, is effectively addressed, there is a real opportunity to relate recovery beyond the well being of the individual to wider societal relationships including re-employment. 'Addictive experience need not be seen as a closed book which is best forgotten and discarded or disguised in CVs or interviews. The experience is then used as a human resource of benefit to the individual and society as a whole'. (Walters and Winter, 2001, 18)

The second Case is that of a project that addressed the employment situation of Gypsies. With the enlargement of the EU that now includes new Accession States in eastern Europe, Gypsies are the largest minority ethnic group in the EU. There is an abundance of research undertaken by Roma and non-Roma in terms of language, group classifications, education, health and culture. It is all too easy to design and create programmes and policies that are considered to be ethical from a non-Roma standpoint without even being aware that for other ethnic groups 'the shared norms of the community' are distinctively different. Recognition of 'difference' throws up issues and ethical dilemmas.

On one traveller site, a sixteen year old woman explained that she did not read and write and saw no need for such a skill. This statement compels researchers to examine how constructed our own assumptions are, overlaid and justified by systems of educational and personal world views. The Workalo project, led by the University of Barcelona, funded under the EU Fifth Framework programme, addressed the changing working patterns of

Gypsies across the EU. The traditional jobs of the Gypsy communities are disappearing, so is it possible to suggest new potential working patterns based on researching these changes and their impact on Gypsy communities?

The project has adopted a research methodology based on communicative dialogue for its enquiries with Gypsy people. Communicative dialogue encourages participants to offer their own meanings and understandings surrounding their statements. Egalitarian dialogue implies the recognition of everyone's voice on the basis of the arguments that they make and not on their position of power. So when talking of racism and education and work, we listened. Previous research has created little or no positive change for Gypsies, just catalogued the disadvantages they face.

This communicative method is based on the traditions of Freire and Habermas. Freire defines praxis as using 'reflection and action on the world in order to transform it' (1972, 28). Habermas argues for the need of 'ideal speech situations' in fostering both understanding and 'reciprocal and unforcedly egalitarian everyday communication' (1986, 82). This focuses on addressing diversity and working with a notion of 'equality of differences'. This principle is part of dialogic learning and is based on the idea of egalitarian intervention that considers differences on equal terms. In the project's examination of the institutionalisation of policies, the objective was dialogue aimed at understanding prejudices so that they are overcome. Anti-racist alternatives have to make possible the creation of spaces for dialogue and coexistence as, without this, transformational proposals are impossible to frame.

This research was challenging, as it was not a simple analysis of data and information, and is especially problematic as it was accessing and working with the most excluded minority ethnic community. The fieldwork component of the project involved the creation of dialogue with a wide range of Gypsy communities and social policy recommendations were based on what Gypsies say they need themselves. The data collated from them was key to the work. From the analysis of fieldwork, it was possible to look at transformational proposals for the definition of guidelines that will better inform policy.

The collection of data has been complicated because it is difficult to have a straightforward interpretation. The project had to use interviews as a way of elaborating on the mechanisms and thought processes of people from a strong oral rather than written culture. The sensitivities within these communities demanded concise communication skills, where language itself had to be framed in a way to capture essential personal testimony.

The project team included both Roma and non-Roma researchers, so adding to the ability to engage with these socially excluded communities and so to build trust. Our ethical premise was to understand that these communities are themselves emerging from many years' of oppression and marginalisation. Their historical exclusion has created within the traveller communities a real and tangible fear of assimilation and this became acutely clear when trying to build relationships. Two extracts from field visit reports illustrate the relationship between researcher and those researched:

> 'I met to discuss our findings with a large community in Darlington, five caravans travelled south from Scotland to meet me. They had just begun their summer travel, when I requested a meeting. I knew just Matt and his wife Helen but I was really surprised to see the elders of the community together with younger members. I did not expect them to want to meet me, but I understood they needed other Gypsy people who might give to them a more objective perspective of the outside world though a Roma eye. These Gypsies are real horse sellers, so I had to exchange opinions about my skills in horses and methods of selling, and so this provided them evidence that I am one belonging to them and this developed a bigger trust atmosphere and pride. In our discussions it was clear how an educated Gypsy could prove that the non-Gypsy world is not such a dangerous place for them and a new world of Gypsy dialogue and empowerment can start in the educational system without the fear of assimilation.'

'As a Roma researcher, I can see a chance for people from my ethnic group to reach emancipation, but it is necessary for mainstream society to understand their attitudes. It is too easy for policy to ask Roma groups to go into the educational system and too easy, correspondingly, to conclude that they refuse to be educated or integrated into mainstream society. If we as Roma researchers want to create positive change then the dominant discourse must include the voice and viewpoints of members of these communities.'

The research was based on the premise that Roma face many barriers in terms of education, training and employment, which in turn have a profound impact on their present and future paths. This has created for Roma an image of the non-Roma mainstream community that they may not want, and indeed they may choose themselves deliberately to be excluded.

The third Case is the EU Community Initiative EQUAL funded project, which created the SEQUAL Development Partnership of eight Universities in Great Britain, engaged in community education and lifelong learning. This partnership has researched the question of the relationship between discrimination and employability.

The UK has experienced a significant fall in unemployment rates and in comparison with other EU member states is enjoying prolonged periods of economic stability. The central issue for this research is that, despite the fact there are now vacancies in the labour market, which creates a potential for fuller employment, the reality is that many still find real difficulty in finding employment and sustaining themselves in work. Many experience prolonged episodes of unemployment and worklessness. Are there other factors related to discrimination that have little or nothing to do with economic cycles that are excluding such people? This work has divided the grounds of discrimination as reflected in legislation between the partners, who then used their community based networks to analyse the community level experiences of discrimination in terms of race, gender and class, political and religious belief, ethnicity, age, and disability. This was supplemented by a series of studies of perceived cross cutting issues including those related to health, both physical and mental, language and geographical isolation and rurality.

The methodology included the analysis of actual community experience, identifying the significance of evidence, and its relevance for policy formation. Current policy is promoting Human Rights and Equal Opportunity, and EU policy is particularly promoting participative citizenship reflected in a policy of a labour market that is 'open to all', in the context of a Single Market, offering mobility of labour. The voices of those experiencing exclusion need to be heard with understanding, so they can have impact directly on mainstream thought and policy. The Partnership's role in this was to use its established academic resources to act as an intermediary for this process to happen.

CONCLUSION

Within these Case Studies themselves there is a plethora of ethical dilemmas, which are confronted on a day to day basis by those researchers and staff engaged in this work. Addiction confronts the rightness of current law on narcotics, the work with Gypsies challenges even the most liberal concepts of integration, and the discrimination work questions the current analysis and categorisation of Human Rights.

However, there are further ethical challenges. This area of work has been criticised as "first aid", in that it is perceived as a series of remedial measures for individuals in crisis, and therefore should be consigned to yet another attempt to address deficits. Yet we argue that there is no intention of promoting an ethical "grand plan", if the notion of a grand plan implies an ideology constructed from ethical universals. The moral obligation is that the experience of exclusion is real, and the academic obligation is to develop an understanding of the processes and outcomes of the phenomena. In addressing this, there is a challenge to the traditional mainstream processes of both Higher Education teaching and research in that traditional academic knowledge and research methodology has not produced the answers to these societal problems. The charge is that traditional research has failed to deliver, and innovation is now vital. Without innovation, the experience of social exclusion will have to be accepted as a necessary evil, and one to which there are no ethically or societal answers. For HE, the ultimate result of this will be a further marginalisation from the real world, and expose HE to charges of irrelevance.

From Plato onwards, education has been accepted as an intrinsic good. Is this work simply an extension and reapplication of this principle to new client groups and non-traditional learners? As such, it would then become an extension of widening participation policy, based on outreach, access and institutional change. The Case Studies illustrate that this is far from a series of altruistic "good works" provided to benefit the disadvantaged, rather they are illustrations of attempts to unravel the complexities of the experiences. Above all, these are seen as shared experiences, whether at any one time we ourselves find we are excluded or included and whether or not we are part of an academic community. The categorisation itself is fluid, in that individuals, communities, organisations and states move in and out of exclusion. It would be an arrogant assumption to assume HE was the permanent repository of the good, and so an ivory tower of inclusion.

It is too easy to stereotype those who are excluded as morally weak or academically deficient. Others working in the social exclusion field when asked about their ethical position see the excluded as victims of structural processes, but not necessarily innocent victims. When asked about their professional ethics, they reply that they simply want a "better chance for these people". Behind these statement may lie ethical values that have their origin in traditions of supporting the side of the less favoured "underdog", in terms of promoting natural justice, through intervention based on principles of fairness.

If this is so, are we then forced back to a pragmatic ethic that is a knee-jerk reaction to social and personal crisis and dysfunction? It is possible to go beyond principles of good practice in terms of approaches to social exclusion by pointing to an ancient Celtic ethical tradition encapsulated in the phrase, 'it is under the shelter of each other that the people live'. This notion has within it both societal and individual implications. For work with the socially excluded, there is an extension of the notion that can perhaps best be described in metaphor. The idea of shelter implies hierarchy rather than a shared responsibility. There is a tile at the top of a roof. The ethical emphasis in combating social exclusion is the attempt to construct the tiles on as flat a roof as possible, to promote equity, empowerment and equality of opportunity.

Traditionally HE has developed and promoted canons of knowledge of the good. Social exclusion does not fit neatly into this model. This work looks again at the real world which is itself searching for meaning and problem solving proposals.

REFERENCES

Adebowale M. and Schwate, C. (2003) *Integrating social exclusion and environment*. London: Capacity Global

Berghman, J. (1995) *Social Exclusion in Europe: Policy Context and Analytical Framework*, in Room, G. (ed.), *Beyond the Threshold: The Measurement and Analysis of Social Exclusion*. Bristol: Polity Press, p 10

Duffy K. (1995) *Social Exclusion and Human Dignity in Europe*, Report for the Steering Committee on Social Policy, Council of Europe, Strasbourg

Freire P. (1972) *Pedagogy of the Oppressed*, Harmondsworth, Penguin

Habermas J. (1986) *The Theory of Communicative Action Volume 1*, Cambridge, Polity Press

Human Rights Act 1998

Klasen S. (1998) *Social exclusion and children in OECD countries: some conceptual issues*. Paper presented at OECD experts seminar, January 22-23 1998, Centre for Educational Research and Innovation, http//www.oecd.org/els/edu.ceri.conf220299.htm

Lambert J. (2002) Member of the European Parliament (MEP) and EP Committee for Employment and Social Affairs, Opening remarks, SEQUAL project launch, London Metropolitan University, London, 20 September 2002

Room G. ed. (1995) *Beyond the Threshold: The Measurement and Analysis of Social Exclusion*. Bristol: Polity Press

White L. (2001) *Neighbourhood Renewal, Case Studies and Conversations, focusing on adult and community learning*. Leicester: NIACE

Winter, N. and Walters N. (2001) Work to recover, *Addiction Today*, Vol. 12, No. 69

Walters N. (2003) Social exclusion discourses, rhetoric or the Tower of Babel? In *Speaking in tongues: languages of lifelong learning*. Bangor: SCUTREA, University of Wales

6
Is there space for 'moral development' in education?

Anna Abram

INTRODUCTION

Is there a space for 'moral development' in education? If education, as several English dictionaries seem to suggest, is the process of teaching, training or learning of specific skills in a *prescribed* or customary course of study in a school or college, then we may hesitate to say that there is a space for moral development in education. Can we prescribe moral development? If so, how? What is the *prima facie* problem here? Are we nervous about teaching any specific moral doctrine and giving specific set of answers to moral issues as the content of our teaching? Such a concern would seem legitimate, especially in our increasingly multi-cultural and multi-religious society.

The argument I want to develop in this chapter is that giving space for moral development in education or, to put it more directly, teaching moral development, is not about teaching specific moral doctrines or giving simple answers to the type of questions as 'is it right or wrong to do x?' It is rather about developing skills, attitudes, techniques and certain types of habits that will enable one not only to know and act rightly in a single sphere of life, let us say, professional life, but to realize the right living and behave in the way that would promote the overall moral good.

In the context of higher education, there are other issues to be considered: do we need to teach all ethics, its history, its different schools, approaches or simply focus on ethics that relates to what students are training for, in terms of their professional life, so students of law study the ethics of law, nurses - bioethics, journalists – media ethics, economists – business ethics, and so forth.

If by 'education' we mean not simply teaching the specific skills or moral doctrines or codes of professional ethics but also the imparting of knowledge, good judgement, discipline of character and wisdom, then our answer may be a more affirmative 'yes' or, at least, 'it should be so'. Imparting of knowledge, good judgement, discipline of character and wisdom requires more than focusing on issues related to one narrow area.

There may be another reason for 'moral development' not being taught. It may well be because we do not know exactly what moral development is. We do not teach it because we do not know how to articulate it. The aim of this chapter is to find ways of defining and articulating the concept of moral development. To achieve this aim, I will turn to two disciplines, moral psychology and virtue ethics. I will take four steps towards a constructive grasping of this concept: the first two steps will be an exploration of the insights that each discipline offers regarding moral development, the third and fourth steps step will be attempting to combine and extend the interdisciplinary insights. In the concluding part I shall propose to recognize 'moral development' as the key concept in education. Firstly, I suggest we clarify the linguistic meaning of 'moral development.

MORAL DEVELOPMENT

'Moral development' is often interchanged with terms like 'moral growth', 'moral maturation', moral progress' and 'moral formation'. 'Growth', 'maturation', 'progress', 'development' and 'formation' are words from the same 'family'. They all imply change and some sort of open-endedness in such change. 'Formation' can have a negative meaning, since it can be programmed in such a way that it prevents growth or progress. In my experience of being brought up to a certain degree under a communist regime in Poland, this term was employed to 'form' a certain type of citizen in accordance with political (Leninist) propaganda. Such programmed formation prevented development. In Western educational circles, there is a more positive use of this term.

The main problem with the term 'moral development' arises from the lack of precise definition[1]: of 'moral' and of 'development'. I suggest that 'moral' can be articulated (not defined) as about becoming a better, rightly ordered and more authentic human being. 'Development' as translated from Latin *'dis'* means 'apart' and the French *'voloper'* means to 'unwrap'. The *Oxford English Dictionary* (1992, 563) has as its third meaning (the closest one to the theme of moral development) "to unfold more fully, bring out all that is potentially contained in". Thus, I propose to define the term 'development' as 'unfolding the potential' and the term '*moral* development' as unfolding of the potential of the moral self.

EXPLORING MORAL DEVELOPMENT

Although the topic of moral development is widely considered, especially by developmental psychologists, it is not adequately understood. Outside developmental psychology, within the area of philosophy of education 'moral development' is not a 'number one' concept[2]. Besides, the whole field of philosophy of education is one of the weakest subfields of both philosophy and education[3]. Therefore, since developmental psychology does deal directly with the concept of moral development, let us briefly explore what we can learn from it.

DEVELOPMENTAL PSYCHOLOGY

There are three main schools or styles within developmental psychology that deal with ego development (see Freud, 1961 ed.; Erikson, 1980, 1968, 1964), cognitive development (see Piaget, 1972; Kohlberg, 1984; Gilligan, 1982; Flavell, 1977), social development (see Turiel, 1975; Selman, 1980; Damon, 1977), affective development (see Dupont, 1979; Rogers, 1959), and affective/interpersonal development (see Loevinger, 1977; Heath, 1977). They are: the Freudian school with the focus on how a person's identity as a whole is formed, the Piagetian and the Flavellian schools, both with the focus on cognition. In my studies of psychological developmental theories I chose one or two representatives of each school: Erik Erikson as a representative of the Freudian school, Laurence Kohlberg and Carol Gilligan as representative of the Piagetian school and Jane Loevinger as a representative of the Flavellian school. The space here does not permit for even sketching each theory. Hence, the only alternative is to briefly summarize the findings of my study.

Developmental psychology contributes towards a better understanding of the self. It points to the nature of the human person as relational. Human relationality is essential to successful moral development. It insists on a movement from self-absorption to self-transcendence. It emphasizes the role of cognition in moral growth. It points to the relationship between childhood development and later (adult) growth. It stresses the developmental dimension of a person. It helps us to understand the meaning of *epikeia* in moral growth – a capacity to make reasonable and responsible exceptions to rules. By using the term 'postconventional' we are reminded that there is more to moral growth than simply following the rules which prevail in a society.

Psychological theories help us understand that moral development is about skilful living of our relational lives. They articulate what precisely is involved in the skilful living so that our cognitive, affective and interpersonal human capacities can grow. The growth of human capacities is presented in a form of progressive-hierarchical steps: each theory defines development in terms of structure, organization, and process, and expresses it in the form of stages. However, the approach to stages differs from theory to theory, and most notably, between the theories of Erikson and Loevinger on the one hand, and those of Kohlberg and Gilligan on the other. These (structural) differences are not especially significant for us, and present no great difficulty. Harder to handle is the issue of the different contents ascribed to each stage by the different theorists, especially the higher stages. The lower stages are easier to describe and their boundaries are more clear-cut, and the movement from one stage to another is relatively straightforward. By contrast, adult life is usually much more complicated and difficult to describe than life during childhood and adolescence. The content of lower stages is similar in each theory but there is no overlap in the content of the higher stages. Each theory aims to describe the path to moral maturity.

Moral development, in the context of the four psychological theories, is a process of expanding self-awareness and of the more conscious exploration of the self – the self as relational – so that the self successfully meets the demands of the relational life.

VIRTUE ETHICS

Another discipline that contributes to the understanding of moral development is virtue ethics[4]. Although virtue ethics unlike developmental psychology does not operate with the developmental terminology, it too stresses the importance of skilful living, but skilful living is realized through the practice of virtue(s). Virtue refers to the human disposition that involves the judgment of intellect, leads to right action and directs towards the attainment of the moral good. Virtue ethics focuses on the individual virtues (such as prudence, justice, temperance, courage) that are essential for moral growth which characterize a well-developed human being. It stresses that the acquisition of these virtues takes place through participation in practices. This insight of virtue ethics complements the deficiency of psychological accounts seen in the fact that the latter pay little attention to practical aspects of the moral life – they presume rather a straightforward link between mind and action. Participation in virtuous practices is not simply mechanical motion, but it is purposeful and chosen doing. Virtue ethics tells us that, if we want to live in a morally right way, we not only need to develop our reasoning skills, shape our identity and realize relational nature. We, also, and most of all, need to act intelligibly and promote the moral good. Virtue ethics views a person as moral agent. A moral agent is one who not only possesses the capacity to act, but one who has a capacity to choose which actions to perform, because he or she has moral understanding. Virtue ethics engages the self much more than the psychological theories. Human beings are not simply formed by the interaction of psychological and environmental forces. The overall idea of moral agency helps us to understand that, despite the limits of the world in which one lives, one is still able to shape responsibly the image of the person one ought to become.

COMBINING THE INSIGHTS OF MORAL PSYCHOLOGY AND VIRTUE ETHICS

So far, we have been dealing with the insights of two disciplines separately. Now I will attempt to offer a combined account of these insights. Both disciplines communicate that moral development as the unfolding of the potential of the moral self is expressed in moral behaviour.

Moral behaviour

The psychological theories claim that if we are able to understand what the demands of our relational life are and if we are able to resolve successfully any tensions that occur, then we will be able to live rightly. Virtue ethics conceives the developed self as the one that behaves in a virtuous way. Such behaviour is produced by virtues, that is, by dispositions of our mind that direct us to the moral good. It is expressed in intelligible actions and it is characterised by consistency and continuity. This does not mean that 'virtuous behaviour' is not concerned with the fulfilling of relational demands. The two approaches, developmental psychology and virtue-centred ethics, are not concerned with two different realities but with the same reality expressed in two different ways. Virtuous behaviour is displayed by people whose characters are rightly ordered; characters cannot be rightly ordered without fulfilling the demands of relationships. Although character is a person's individual identity, it is shaped by interactions with other people. By pointing to virtues, virtue ethics suggests that right behaviour is not just about resolving tensions (as in Erikson's theory) and finding solutions to dilemmas so that parties representing both sides of the tensions and dilemmas are satisfied with the outcomes (as in Kohlberg's and Gilligan's theories). Virtue ethics goes a step further by suggesting that right behaviour must not simply be about settling down and being content with the smooth running of our relational lives. Right behaviour is the type that constantly examines (through the virtue of prudence) whether one's living promotes the moral good and finds ways of improving one's behaviour so that one can move closer to the *telos* (underlying purpose), and truly live the best kind of life for a human being to live. The point that needs to be realized here is the distinction between smooth running and what is truly best. Virtue ethics is clearly concerned with the latter. Psychological accounts tend to be concerned with the former. However, they help us to recognize that, in realizing what is truly best, we need to be fully aware of our relational nature and display certain personal characteristics.

For approaches grounded in developmental psychology, it seems that to have these characteristics means to have a certain kind of attitude, a certain level of reasoning or emotional integrity. For virtue ethics, to have these characteristics means to have virtues and to express them in behaviour. This is where the two disciplines complement each other.

What both disciplines have in common is a certain dynamism that suggests the need for improvement of our behaviour, and growth towards moral maturity. Therefore, in what follows I shall synthesize the accounts of moral maturity (that is, the different ideas of the culmination of moral growth) that each discipline provides.

Right living is more than just a sum total of singular actions, understood narrowly in terms of external performances. It is, most of all, a continuous (habitual) and skilful combination of right attitudes and emotions, and the internalization of values and principles.

Culmination of moral development

Does moral development have a culmination? If so, what is its culmination point or a goal. If not, how best can we describe its endless (though not aimless[5]) journey. My preference here is to adopt the first approach and seek to identify and describe the culmination of moral development.

While developmental psychological theories communicate their account of maturity by the content of the highest stages of psychological theories, virtue ethics articulates such an account by attempting to answer the following question: 'how do I achieve my ideal moral self?' This question is formulated on the basis of the three-question structure: 'who am I?', 'who I ought to become?' and 'how do I get there?' Psychological theories see moral maturity in terms of relational maturity and virtue-centred ethics sees it in terms of individual attributes – that is, virtues. In spite of the fact that each discipline sees the culmination of moral development in a different way, I think it is plausible to combine these two ways in order to have a richer account of the culmination of moral development.

According to our four psychological theories, if a person moves successfully through the stages of growth, he or she will not only effectively resolve dilemmas (both real and hypothetical), and sort out conflicts and tensions that are caused by living with others, but will also reach a state of overall relational maturity. Such a state would be a sum total of what each psychologist proposes as the culmination point of his or her theory. Erikson calls this point integrity. Kohlberg sees it in terms of autonomy based on the internalisation of the principle of justice. Gilligan understands it in terms of care and responsibility. Loevinger (like Erikson) views this state as integrity, by which she means something like a mixture of identity, autonomy and responsibility. Thus, according to the psychological theories, a person who reached the final stages and hence has developed integrity, autonomy and care would be able to live a successful relational life.

Unlike psychological theories virtue ethics does not have a culmination point as such. Instead, it suggests that virtues as personal attributes can make a person morally mature. Such a person would have a set of related virtues like prudence, justice, temperance, courage, that would enable him or her to act in a way that promotes the moral good and achieve internal goods (like friendship, solidarity, honesty, fairness). These goods can only be reached, as Alasdair MacIntyre (1981) suggests through the practice of virtues.

If we combine relational maturity of the psychological theories with virtue ethics, we can say that a morally mature person, through the virtue of prudence, which involves skilful reasoning, would understand how society functions. He or she would know and understand its laws and regulations and the strengths and limitations; he or she would act in way that is best for others (those distant ones– in the light of justice, as well as those with whom one is bonded in a special way– in the light of fidelity); he or she would be able to exercise courage and self-restraint and would take into account one's individual needs (through the virtue of self-care).

Moreover, virtue-centred ethics with its use of the concept of the *telos*- a moral goal that can be viewed as a culminating point of virtue-centred ethics, but not as a definite one as it is presented in psychological theories- can deepen developmental psychological theories. Virtue ethics contributes a sense of the variety of ways in which this can be realized and asserts that the good of the *telos* is internal.

Having established the link between the relational maturity emphasized in the psychological theories, individual attributes and the idea of the *telos* stressed in virtue ethics, I suggest we now consider the structure of the process of moral development.

The process of development

To a large extent, the psychological theories see the process of moral development, but by no means exclusively, in terms of adjustment, whilst virtue ethics stresses the importance of creativity, especially the working out of the *telos*. Thus, the two disciplines make a complementary contribution. Both disciplines see the process of moral development in terms of progress, even though their understandings of the idea of progress are not the same.

Basic to the psychological theories is a sense of an ordered sequence of invariant stages. These stages are in general quite exact, measurable and dependable. 'Exact' means that the content of each stage is different and easily distinguishable; 'measurable' expresses the possibility of assessing to which stage an individual belongs; 'progressively attained' means that the higher stages depend on the successful completion of the lower stages. These accounts of moral development, structurally logical and systematized, are useful as a starting point. They offer a general framework for analysing an individual's moral growth. However, they do not leave much space for individual differences[6]. Here virtue ethics offers complementary insights. Through offering us a structure of moral growth. It views it as a passage from 'who we are' to 'who we ought to become'; a transfer from good to better or from worse to less bad.

The dynamics of the developmental process in virtue-centred ethics implies that, although progress is a kind of a movement that leads towards becoming a more rightly ordered person, this movement may be intermittent, subject both to regression.

With regard to the content of the process of moral development, the two disciplines help us to see that this process is about improving our moral self: psychological theories express this as growth in our understanding of our relationality; virtue ethics expresses it in terms of development of the self. In the former it is expressed as a greater ability to co-ordinate different relational tasks so that the demands of different kinds of relationships are met and fulfilled. In the latter it is expressed in the choice and performance of action that, in line with one's virtues, promotes the moral good.

While the psychological theories indicate that in the process of moral development we adjust our selves to the external realities of our relational life, virtue-centred ethics points to two inter-related aspects of this process:

participation in virtuous practices, and the subsequent acceptance of a general principle[7], on the basis of one's prudent judgment, because of the value of these practices for the whole of the moral life. How can these three facets (adjustment, participation and acceptance) of the reality of moral growth be translated into the language of moral development?

First of all, 'adjustment' suggests that, to a large extent, we are not creators of our external realities. We find ourselves in the midst of realities in which we need to discover how best we can interact with others who share these realities with us. But even if we do influence our relational realities by our own choices, as when we choose friends or marriage partners, there are still things in these realities to which we need to adjust. Thus, adjustment is a process of adapting ourselves to different relational experiences of our life, taking responsibility for those with whom we share our life (in an intimate, global and unique way) and managing and meeting the demands of these relationships. In order to progress in the moral life we constantly need to adapt to relational spheres of our lives. Adjustment requires from us both partiality and impartiality, so that we can reach and maintain our integrity. Adjustment, as the psychological theories hold, is a developmental and not a static reality: the more we adjust the fuller will the relational life that we will be able to live. Adjustment is never fully accomplished, as there are always new situations of life to which we will have to adjust. Nevertheless, having successfully adjusted to the realities of the past we will be better equipped to adjust to the realities of the future.

The stress of virtue ethics on participation in practices means that growth in the moral life is not possible without taking part in different kinds of activities that make human life flourish. Though this ethics stresses the importance of *individual* involvement in activities that engage other people, it does not deal in detail with the relational dimensions of this participation. The relationality that virtue-centred ethics adumbrates can be filled out in much more detail if we introduce the insights of our psychological authors. Although the psychological theories do not consider the idea of participation in practices, they remind us that participation in practices should not simply refer to the sphere of civil activities (to which MacIntyre primarily refers), but it should include the participation in the narrower sphere of our personal relationships. For example, we cannot be good husbands or wives if we devote our whole time to just caring for values in our workplace. Conversely, we will not be of much use for the wider society if the only thing we really care about in life is our own family. Moreover, the psychological theories stress the need to find the right balance among conflicting realities. We constantly need to work out in which activities we should get involved so that the poise in our lives is sustained, and the virtue of prudence has an important role to play. Our participation in practices does not merely serve the smooth running of our relational life but also helps us to realize that we need to improve constantly and continuously so that we can lead the best kind of life for a human being to live. Through our participation in virtuous practices we can consciously discover the values of these practices as our general principles and, on the basis of these activities, plan our further moral activities.

Accepting values as our general principles means adopting these principles as our own. We are aware of what we are doing and we recognize that this activity is right. We are not doing something because someone has forced us to do it but we are recognizing the importance of our activity. Accepting values as our own also entails occasional rejection of types of activities which we consider to be not worthy of engaging in. At this point we can see that moral development is a conscious process.[8] It fully involves an engagement of our cognitive capacities. This development involves a continuous expanding of self-awareness and a more conscious exploration of the self. However, it also involves our affective domain: relational interactions touch our emotions.

On the basis of the above synthesis we can say that the process of moral development is not a one off-activity, but a series of movements that take place within us and which are expressed externally. Both psychology and virtue ethics imply that moral growth proceeds from ego-centred orientation to other-centred orientation, but without the exclusion of the self. It proceeds from the unconscious to the conscious, in terms of a lack of self-understanding to a better self-understanding. It proceeds from dependence on external sources of reinforcement and lack of insight about oneself towards a progressive interiorization of one's experience and responsibility for oneself and the other.

The process of moral development is a relational journey which leads towards the improvement of the moral self. 'Moral development' is the means by which we integrate our life activities (such as different kinds of practices) into purposeful behaviour. It is a continuing, dynamic and always-new process that realistically and truly has to be open-ended. There are always new situations to which one has to adjust, new practices to promote and new principles to adopt. Although there are relational patterns that are common to us all, this journey is always creative. Only such a process can be called developmental.

Although moral development is about progress, it is not always straightforward. It can be broken, irregular and regressive. However, growth can take place even when there is disruption and brokenness – growth in those situations, in particular growth through moral failure, can be profound. I will return to this point.

The understanding of the 'self'

I suggest we understand the self as the innermost[9] dimension - the core of a person. The two disciplines conceive the self in terms of consciousness. Moral growth, as we noted earlier, is, largely but not exclusively, a conscious reality. But although both disciplines view the self as conscious, the psychological theories view the self as the self-in-relation, virtue ethics understands the self-as-moral-agent.

Psychological accounts stress that one's true selfhood allows mutuality and connectedness with others. They hold that to know oneself is to know one's desires, needs and reasons, and that this knowledge entails the ability to assume the roles of others: to see oneself as others do; to construct a sense of self that is modelled on others' expectations and on roles that one has to fulfil; to organize one's experiences mentally – experiences that always involve interactions with others. The self and others are always connected. Each of our four psychological theories sees development in terms of the movement from self-absorption to self-transcendence. Self-transcendence is understood in terms of other-regarding concern– concern for those who are close as well as for distant others.

Virtue ethics is also concerned with self-transcendence, but in a different sense. It is concerned with the movement from the self as at present to the self in the future. Although the present is the outcome of one's past, virtue ethics does not pay great attention, as do the psychological theories, to the past part of one's moral history. The self, in this context, denotes the capacity to act intelligibly, that is, to choose which actions to perform on the basis of one's moral understanding. A person is able to shape his or her future by becoming the kind of person he or she wants to become, because he or she has worked out his or her ideal moral self (who he or she ought to become). Virtue ethics concentrates primarily on the future of the moral agent. (Note that this ethics is often labelled 'teleological').

The idea of moral development, as the two approaches emphasize, implies that the self is developmental. The ideal moral self needs to be worked out on the basis of our relational nature. In order to develop morally one needs to accept 'who one is' in the light of one's moral history. The self is conditioned by the past, but it is not determined by it. This means that our past immoral behaviour does not determine our future behaviour. Conversely, our rightly ordered behaviour of the past does not guarantee moral success in the future.

Both disciplines, although with different emphases, stress the importance of having self-understanding. To have self-understanding is to have a realistic view of one's own self. To have a realistic self-understanding means to understand one's moral history on the basis of experiences.

Experiences, as the psychological theories emphasize (especially those of Kohlberg and Gilligan), involve other people. Self-understanding and experiences are necessarily connected. We cannot reach moral maturity without integrating the former with the latter. Different experiences shed different light on the way we understand ourselves (a point stressed by Gilligan). I want now to look at two aspects of such different experiences as a way of extending insights of developmental psychology and virtue ethics: 'growth through moral failure' and 'growth through unpredictable reality'.

'GROWTH THROUGH MORAL FAILURE'

Although the two disciplines indirectly refer to moral failure, they don't really deal with it. However, moral failure is part of life, and this cannot be neglected in our educational systems. To neglect the concept of moral failure would be a failure in itself. Moral failure should not be simply acknowledged, but must be understood and viewed as a growth-furthering experience. Knowing where we went wrong disposes us to understand better how to avoid making similar mistakes in future. A person who fails morally can have a better practical understanding of the area of life in which moral failure has occurred. Understanding the reality of moral failure can help us to develop compassion and a kind of sensitivity to the plight of those with whom we share our relational lives. It is not just moral success but also moral failure that can enable us to look more deeply what our relational demands and living rightly are about. On the basis of this understanding we can plan our behaviour and constantly examine it in the context of the moral good. Behaving rightly as the outcome of moral failure enables us to be more committed to issues as well as to people.

Thus, although moral failure is an obstacle to a regular pattern of growth, it can still be incorporated within the structure of moral development. Even if we operate with the vocabulary of psychological stages it may still be plausible to bring moral failure into developmental patterns of growth. It may be impossible to predict precisely where (at which stage) and what (the kind and depth of) moral failure will occur and how exactly we can grow out of it. Moral failure can be an awakening experience. It can enable one to see things that, without moral failure, would never have occurred (such as the power of forgiveness)[10].

'GROWTH THROUGH UNPREDICTABLE REALITY'

Another point that psychological theories do not include is the relationships in which we find ourselves totally unpredictably, and they too as much or as little as the other types affect our moral life and moral growth. The question that arises here is how the unpredictable other, which by nature is unpredictable, can be conducive to moral behaviour? Obviously, a clear-cut answer to that question, given that the growth is of its nature unpredictable, is impossible. However growth that results from an encounter with the unpredictable can be truly profound and the demands of relationships can be met in a more powerful way than when the unpredictable does happen. The unpredictable situation, such an illness of a close one, can be an opportunity to develop virtues that otherwise may have not been developed. Moreover, it can give new meaning to our existing virtues. Unexpected realities involve other people, either directly (as when one falls in love with another person) or by means of an event that involves a human being (like a car accident that involves someone's injury or death). There is always a relational reality. Therefore, bringing this reality to our consciousness can lead us to a fuller realization of our connectedness with others; we can begin to act in a way that expresses our deep concern for others and for ourselves. It is the particular qualities of persons whom we encounter in our lives that shape the process of moral growth. It is not simply their existence but their talents, problems, their whole life histories, that can help us to unfold our potentials. The unexpected reality can wake us into finding the fuller meaning of the moral life. Contingent relationships change the moral landscape of our imagination and broaden the view of our own moral selves. They are the means to self-discovery; discovery of who we are now and who we are capable of becoming. The unpredictable other can improve our understanding of self as moral agent, influence the practice of virtue and give new meaning to activities that promote the moral good. It can restructure our cognitive capacities and emotional engagements. Unexpected realities mark changes in us. This theme can help us to take into account a variety of our experiences that influence our moral outlook and moral behaviour and empower us to a new self-understanding. Through contingent relationships we can unfold our potential – a potential that would not have been realized if we had not encountered the unpredictable other.

SUMMARY

The idea of moral development is not intended to give the impression that moral growth is an easy enterprise. This idea implies that we are subject to change, and that this change is inaugurated in the self – here lies its dynamic character. John Henry Newman (1973 ed., 100) said: 'To live is to change and to be perfect is to have changed often'. Thus, the moral development is a process that is never completed, because there is always something that needs to be to be unfolded more fully. A person can always become more just, more temperate, more brave, more compassionate, more faithful and so forth.

Moral development is *cumulative*. On the model of moral development sketched here, human capacities (cognitive, affective, interpersonal) play a central role. Also, this model of moral development takes into account who we are and who we ought to become in the context of our past.

The process of moral development starts at the point of 'who we are' and leads to the point of 'who we ought to become'. However, a person's character is his or her moral history. That is why the past is also important. We can reflect on it and learn from it. We can see how well we are moving towards the moral good. Thus, the past – 'already', in terms of 'who we have been' is linked to the now, in terms of 'who we are' at present and gives us a background for the future – 'not yet', in terms of 'who we ought to become' (our own *telos*). The *telos* is not a static point – something that can be achieved as in a race. There are many unexpected realities that make the *telos* open to redefinition, reformulation and unfolding, even though the basic idea of the moral good remains the same.

The concept of moral development belongs to the language that has a significance independently from the specific contents of the values of specific cultures. It is an essentially tolerant concept. This means that every culture at every moment of history would have an idea of moral growth and moral maturity and will be able to list some basic virtues that constitute right behaviour. And even though the list of virtues, values and moral outlooks do change in their contents, the lists themselves do not really change. For example, if we take patience, we could say that patience has different meanings in New York and San Salvador. However, both New Yorkers and San Salvadorians would know whether their fellow citizens are patient or not. And it is here where different cultures and religions can find a common ground for providing space for 'moral development'.

SOME FURTHER POINTS AND CONCLUDING REMARKS

If education is more than a form of 'child-farming for the sake of the state' as proposed by Plato (even if we agree that the desired outcome of education is – to put it in Greek philosophical terms – a just society), it is rather a form of 'unfolding of the human potential' for the benefit of both the state and the individual, then 'moral development' – a process that enables the unfolding of human potential – seems to be not only a concept compatible with education but a key concept within it. This concept, in spite of its generic character, allows us to focus on a person – a subject of education – as a whole. In contemporary moral and pedagogical theorizing there is a tendency to focus on one or two aspects of moral growth. Some writers concentrate exclusively on, for example, the rightness of moral action, others on detachment from actions. Bringing the concept of moral development to education allows us to integrate different concerns into one, namely, the concern for moral maturity of people and focus less on 'what academic results our students ought to achieve' and more on 'what sort of persons we ought to have as the result of our educational system'.

The achievement of clearly specified results and learning outcomes is the main agenda of our educational system. The contemporary understanding of teaching or pedagogy is preoccupied with methods of teaching. By bringing in 'moral development' to our teaching we are not making a revolution, but promoting a somewhat different attitude – an attitude of openness and redefinition, adjustment, participation and acceptance. In this kind of education 'what is to be learned is something to be attended to rather than grasped, in a spirit of humility and reserve, and not in a view that everything is a 'resource' which can be endlessly remoulded or manipulated to satisfy immediate needs and in a series of problems to which mere cleverness and expediency can always find solutions' (Hemming and Parsons, 2003).

In this chapter, having at the beginning acknowledged the lack of a clear and precise understanding of moral development, I was trying to present ways of utilizing and extending the knowledge and the studies available to us so that we can construct an account of moral development that is both illuminating and promising. A successful approach to moral development has to be inter-disciplinary. Moreover, in order to be plausible, it has to go beyond what the developmental psychology and virtue ethics suggest and find ways of incorporating ideas, such as 'moral failure' and 'unpredictability of life'.

A further obvious question is: 'how to translate all that has been said so far to the sphere of higher education?' Teaching ethics in a diverse society includes means, and requires formulation and teaching professional ethics. However, before we articulate ethical codes for different professions we must make available to our students explorations of more basic, round and generic concepts that have to do with imparting of knowledge, good judgement, discipline of character and wisdom. Hence, my general proposition is that prior to teaching professional and applied ethics comes the teaching of moral development. By definition, of both 'education' and of 'moral development', there is space for the former in the latter. In practice, we may have to work out how much space we can or should give.

NOTES

1. For example, The *Encyclopedia of Ethics*, although it presents a variety of views by different scholars, fails to give a clear single explanation of moral development. See 'Moral Development', in Becker Lawrence C., and Becker Charlotte B. (eds), *Encyclopedia of Ethics*, Chicago and London: St. James Press, 1992, pp. 828-835.
2. Philosophy of education is the study of such questions as: what education is and what its purpose is; the nature of the knowing mind and the human subject; problems of authority; the relationship between education and society; and democratic education. Such study obviously includes issues related to the idea of moral development, but does not deal with this idea directly.
3. Philosophy of education seems to be both unpopular and disconnected from philosophy (by being insufficiently rigorous for the tastes of many "real" philosophers) and from the broader study and practice of education (by being too philosophical and theoretical).
4. In this very brief presentation of virtue ethics, I intentionally avoid reference to the specific virtue writers – the body of literature is too vast – my understanding of virtue ethics is influenced by classical writers such as Aristotle and Aquinas and contemporary scholars such as Alisdair MacIntyre, James Keenan and Jean Porter.
5. Although the aim of moral development is to grow, in the context of this approach we cannot go any further in defining the goal. This approach would only go as far as to say that moral development aims at furthering moral growth, becoming more and more skilful in the moral life. The approach I am adopting seeks to identify characteristics that constitute a well developed person.
6. This may suggest to an individual that, if he or she does not progress on the moral ladder designed by the psychological theories, he or she may be morally underdeveloped. In most situations this would be the right 'moral diagnosis' but this may not apply to all cases. Psychological theorists may well be right in claiming that most human beings share the same developmental pattern. However, there are also variations to this process and psychological theories do not accommodate these variations.
7. 'Principle' in this context means a guide or signpost for one's future behaviour. It is derived out of the recognition of the value of practice.
8. There is also an unconscious side to this process which renders us unaware of what we have inherited. However, it would be beyond the scope of this thesis to consider this aspect.
9. By 'inner' I mean first-person experiences – knowable to me. 'Inner' is not an opposite to the 'outer'. Although both categories are unique, I view them as closely linked with each other, to the extent that the outer is the expression of the inner.
10. It is important to stress here that what energizes moral growth is not only moral disequilibrium, but real moral failure – something that can only be fully understood when it is experienced.

REFERENCES

Damon, W. (1977) *The Social World of the Child*, San Francisco: Jossey-Bass
Dupont, H. (1979) Affective Development: Stage and Sequence. In, Moscher, R. R. (ed.), *Adolescents' Development and Education: A Janus Knot*. Berkeley: McCutchan
Erikson, E.H. (1980) *Identity and the Life Cycle*. New York: W.W. Norton
Erikson, E.H. (1968) *Identity: Youth and Crisis*. New York: W.W. Norton
Erikson, E.H. (1964) *Insight and Responsibility*. New York: W.W. Norton
Flavell, J.H. (1977) *Cognitive Development*. Englewood Cliffs NY: Prentice-Hall
Freud, S. (1961) *The Standard Edition of the Complete Works of Sigmund Freud*, trans. and ed. James Strachey, London: The Hogarth Press, especially vol. XIX, *The Ego and the Id and Other Works*
Gilligan, C. (1982) *In a Different Voice: Psychological Theory and Women's Development*. Cambridge MA: Harvard University Press
Heath, H.H. (1977) *Maturity and Competence: A Transcultural View*. New York: Gardner
Hemming, P. and Parsons, S. (2003) 'The Vocation and Formation of Theologians and the Teaching Office of the Bishop in the British Context', paper presented to the Catholic Theological Association, 27 August 2003
Kohlberg, L., (1984) *The Psychology of Moral Development: The Nature and Validity of Moral Stages*. San Francisco: Harper and Row Publishers
Loevinger, J. (1977) *Ego Development: Conceptions and Theories*. San Francisco: Jossey-Bass
McIntyre, A. (1981) *After Virtue*. London: Duckworth
Newman, J.H. (1973 ed.) *Essay on the Development of Christian Doctrine*, Harmondsworth: Penguin
Oxford English Dictionary (1989) 'Development' in the *Oxford English Dictionary*, Oxford: Clarendon Press, vol. IV, 563
Piaget, J. (1972) *The Moral Judgment of the Child*. London: Routledge and Kegan Paul
Rogers, C. (1959) A Theory of Therapy, Personality, and Interpersonal Relationships, as Developed in the Client-Centred Framework. In Koch S., (ed.), *Psychology: A Study of Science*, Vol. III, New York: McGraw-Hill
Selman, R. (1980) *The Growth of Interpersonal Understanding*. New York: Academic Press
Turiel, E. (1975) The development of social concepts. In De Palma, D. and Foley, J. (eds.) *Moral Development: Current Theory and Research*. New York: L. Erlbaum Associates

7
Ethics and the teaching profession

Ron Best and David Rose

INTRODUCTION

The concern of this paper is with teaching, by which we mean those practices, and the attitudes which they express, which are intended to bring about occasions of learning in another human being. Following the analyses of Peters and others (Peters,1967), teaching is concerned with something more than (mere) instruction and training, and is undertaken in ways which accord with such moral principles as those of truth-telling and respect for persons. This chapter seeks to illuminate the significance of ethics for the practice of primary and secondary school teaching, and to consider the impact of the political and social context of the late 20th Century on the teaching profession in the UK.

ETHICS, TEACHING AND THE PROFESSION

In her recent book on *The Ethical School*, Felicity Haynes argues that,

> '...ethics is relevant to anyone who ever asks the question 'what ought I to do? or 'would this be right?' It is of relevance to anyone who ever makes moral judgments about others, who ever praises or condemns people's actions. It is of particular importance in education because not only are teachers and administrators beset with moral questions, but now, more than ever, they are responsible for the moral well-being and education of their pupils, the future generation.' (Haynes, 1998, 3)

She goes on to distinguish ethics from morality on the grounds that ethics goes beyond the consideration of 'the practical question "What ought I to do here and now?" to examine such moral questions within a broader, more schematic or theoretical perspective' (ibid, 4-5). No doubt there are grounds for such a distinction. However, as Haynes' own book demonstrates, what are of concern to teachers in their daily work are the practical questions of what to do here, now, with this child or this class.

Such questions may be asked in a technical manner, as (for example) with regard to the sequence in which material might be presented to a class, or what activity the children should be engaged in next. But in the context of education, such questions can never be exclusively practical or technical, because education is defined in terms of its moral purpose. Whether we accept Peters' notion of education as 'initiation into intrinsically worthwhile activities', or John White's (1990) view of education as concerned with the individual well-being, or, indeed, the views of those like Lawrence Stenhouse who see education as empowering and emancipatory (Stenhouse, 1983), a concept of education which is not in some sense developmental, enriching and of worth to the learner seems a contradiction in terms. Those who question whether education is an intrinsic good, such as Wilson (2002), seem to us to be more influenced by empirical questions about how some adults 'see' education, or what pupils actually experience in schools, than with establishing what, conceptually, education is in terms of its relationship with human development. Similarly, the 'de-schoolers' of the 1970s (such as Illich, Goodman, and Holt) had a point, but it was that schooling simply was not education, rather than that education, properly understood, was 'a bad thing'.

The practical questions teachers ask therefore have an intrinsic moral dimension, and may be illuminated by ethical considerations as much as by pedagogy (thought of as 'the science of teaching'). However, it has become questionable whether teachers are any more permitted the authority to answer such questions for themselves, either in terms of practicalities of technique, or in terms of genuine moral choices between courses of action (or between action and *in*action). Posing of the question 'what ought I to do?' entails freedom of choice. If the regulation of teaching by the state constitutes a restriction on teachers' capacity to exercise either the 'craft knowledge' of their vocation or the moral judgment entailed in decisions about what is for 'the good' of their students, it may be seen as a limit to morality.

The idea of teaching as a profession is important here, for it is arguable that the exercise of both technical expertise and moral judgement in the context of practice is a defining feature of a profession (as opposed to other forms of labour). According to Sayer (1996), the characteristics essential to a profession are that:

a. it performs an essential public service
b. its practices are founded on a distinctive body of knowledge and research
c. its members undergo a lengthy period of initial education and training both in mastering that knowledge and in developing the skills to exercise it
d. this initial acquisition of knowledge and skill is complemented by continuing professional growth and development
e. it exercises a high degree of responsibility for the way it fulfils the objectives formed by the community of which it is a part
f. its members act with integrity and conscience primarily in the interests of their clients
g. its members accept and are governed by a code of ethics underwritten by its organizations
h. it is well organized, with disciplinary powers to enforce ethical practice
i. careful control is exercised over entry, training, certification and standards of practice (Sayer, 1996, 18).

It is arguable that teaching has never, at least in the UK, achieved sufficient of these characteristics to qualify for the title, although such societies as the College of Preceptors (renamed the College of Teachers in 1998) have attempted to create the necessary conditions over the years. We shall ask below whether this state of affairs has been changed significantly by the advent of the General Teaching Council (GTC). At this stage we should note that characteristic (f) would entail individual teachers exercising moral autonomy, while characteristics (g) and (h) would entail teachers' compliance to a code of ethics determined by someone else. These criteria appear to reduce the latitude for individuals to reach their own answers to the question 'what ought I to do?', but this depends on the individual's participation in the formulation (or adoption) of the code of ethics and the degree to which a code permits more than one possible course of action in any situation. Members of a profession may freely and whole-heartedly embrace a code of ethics expressed in generalizations without being denied the right to decide what precisely to do in any specific situation. Nor might they escape responsibility for the moral reasoning required in reaching a decision to act.

There are grounds for arguing that social and political developments over the last quarter of a century have militated against the exercise of such professional and moral autonomy, and these are considered later in regard to the policies of successive governments.

DISCOURSES

The manner in which policies find expression may be seen in the discourses engaged at various stages in the implementation and justification of government programmes.

> 'A Discourse is composed of ways of talking, listening, reading, writing, acting, interacting, believing, valuing, and using tools and objects in particular settings at specific times, so as to display or to recognize a particular social identity .... The Discourse creates social positions (or perspectives) from which people are 'invited' ('summoned') to speak, listen, act, read, write, think, feel, believe, and value in certain characteristic, historically recognizable ways, in combination with their own individual style and creativity ... Discourses create, produce, and reproduce opportunities for people to be and recognize certain kinds of people'. (Gee et al., 1996, 10)

In establishing and exercising identity, discourses exercise an inclusive-exclusive function, identifying particular groups as 'in' or 'out'. Therein lies (at least some of) their power as Ball (following Foucault) notes:

> 'Discourses are, therefore, about what can be said, and thought, but also about who can speak, when, where and with what authority. Discourses embody meaning and social relationships, they constitute both subjectivity and power relations'. (Ball, 1990, 17)

Professional discourses both embody power relations and express aspirations. However, professional discourses may have little impact where the power relations and structures of dominance and accountability are imposed from elsewhere: where political discourse, expressing and extending the hegemony of a particular social group, party or government, negates, silences or 'scrambles' the professional 'voice'.

We suggest that, in the following consideration of the policies of the Tory and Labour Governments since 1988, a number of discourses can be discerned. Some of these derive from economics; others from political philosophies of liberalism and pragmatism; yet others hark back to periods of idealism and imperialism. One may even identify a certain nationalism which from time to time runs through the competitive rhetoric of a country which is almost part of Europe, but still profoundly 'British'.

THE TORY YEARS: CENTRALISING TRENDS AND SHIFTING PATTERNS OF POWER

The period of Conservative Government 1979 – 1997 was marked by the publication of 20 Education Acts. The 1988 Education Reform Act (ERA) resulted in 418 new powers being vested centrally in the Secretary of State, whilst the Education Act of 1993 gave a further 299 powers to the Secretary of State. It has been argued that "both the volume and prescriptive nature of this legislation can be seen as dramatically circumscribing teachers' autonomy, and [this] has led critics to argue that teaching is becoming 'deprofessionalised' or 'reprofessionalised' despite the rhetoric of 'professionalism' contained in official policy documents". (Welch and Mahony, 2000, 139)

The radical reforming nature of the ERA affected most of the key areas of education. In particular, it included a redistribution of powers from LEAs to schools via LMS (Local Management of Schools); the appropriation by central government of the power to determine the curriculum; the introduction of a national system of assessment; and the development under OFSTED of a draconian inspection regime. These changes constituted a dramatic shift from past consensus politics to a more radical, centralised and (some would say) dictatorial style of educational politics. Feintuck (1994) notes that Labour/Liberal Democrats were, as expected, opposed to this centralisation, but significantly, it was the former Conservative Prime Minister Edward Heath who was the biggest critic:

> 'The Secretary of State has taken more power under this Bill than any other member of the cabinet. The extent of the Secretary of State's power will be overwhelming. Within the parliamentary system, no Secretary of State should ever be allowed to hold such a degree of power.' (Hansard, Commons, Vol.123, Col.792)

The ERA can be seen as an expression of the New Right and the Neo-Liberal philosophy of education (Green 1990). It may be perceived as part of the struggle to reverse the social democratic policies of the post-war Welfare State, but it may also be seen as an attempt to reconstruct a new social order based on free-market principles. As Green comments:

> 'Education has been one of the principal targets for radical reconstruction, and, although it is not without its contradictions, the 1988 Education Act represents in some parts of it at least, a first stage in the construction of a market education system.' (Green, 1990, viii)

The (then) Secretary of State, Kenneth Baker, expressed it in these terms:

> '(W)e had to shift power towards the parents and children who were the consumers of education and away from the education administrators and vested interests who were the producers of education...the curriculum had to be made more relevant to Britain's national needs and the future employment opportunities for young people.' (Baker, 1993, 177).

The paradoxical juxtaposition of ideology is clearly evident here. The language of consumerism and the world of economics has increasingly become the dominant discourse within the educational arena. This market force mentality has been readily criticised by prominent educationalists such as Wragg, who note the prevalence in the language of contemporary educational politics of such terms as market-forces, competition, privatisation, efficiency, cost-effectiveness, value for money, choice, performance, standards, testing and accountability (Wragg, 1988, 5).

For some, this is not so much a matter of a philosophy as of dogma. Kelly (1990, quoted in Docking, 1996, 46) argues that within the ERA 'there is no statement of philosophy or underlying ideals' apart from that of 'raising standards'. However, others have argued that the policy was underpinned by a framework of right-wing sentiments, such that the ERA is characterised by the values of instrumentalism, commercialism and elitism. Basini argues that such commentators as Wragg, Lawton, White and Ball are in essence objecting to what Kelly has described as a 'factory-farming approach to schooling' (Basini, 1996, 70). According to its advocates, such a market-led approach to education should make it easily discernible whether it is successful or not through consideration of its output. Feintuck (1994, 53) sees the implications of such an approach as fairly obvious: if the policy maker decides that the input will be choice, the output will be competition. If the outcome is to be higher educational standards, policy choices cannot be justified unless they point towards improved standards.

In the Britain of the mid- to late-1980s, the excesses of the market-place economy began to impact on the educational system when those consumers who could choose exercised their choice. But this had a detrimental impact on those from the poorer sectors where real choice did not exist. This outcome does not seem to have been seen as wrong or even undesirable, but as an inescapable but tolerable consequence of competition from which all would benefit in the end. Market values were bolstered by reference to the traditional values, notably of 'self-help', entrepreneurship and the laissez-faire society. A sense of inevitability emerged which was divorced from moral conscience. The notion of one society, or one country, was replaced by self-interest, self-advancement and self-gain. Reform and tradition became bed-partners in educational policy making and implementation.

Ball (1994, 30) argues that 'the theoretical and the innovative in education have been replaced, as the signifiers of reform, by tradition'. Clearly, there was a tension within Tory politics between an emphasis on continuity and that on planned change; that is, between those who may be categorised as either traditionalists or modernisers. While the traditionalists emphasise the old ideas of the freedom of the market and the protection of individual liberty from bureaucratic interference, the modernisers may be described as being intent on creating an enterprise economy allied to a reducing of union influence, thus borrowing much from the free-market programme. As Jones (1991) comments:

> The free marketeers and cultural right see the State's role as essentially negative, in putting down all those forces - bureaucratic or insurgent - which in Scruton's words 'threaten ancient shackles which now chain down the potential for economic, and for individual, development'. (Jones, 1991, 87)

whereas for the modernizers, 'the reality is the calculated deployment of material resources and regulatory power to construct new class alliances favourable to capital' (Rustin, 1989, 62).

Right wing ideologues were very influential in articulating the Tory educational agenda. For example, the Centre for Policy Studies always pushed for radical reform. That their aims were never fully achieved should not detract from the scale of their influence; whenever they set the pendulum in motion it never returned all the way to its original position. This point is reinforced by Thomas who argues that:

> 'we should not set aside the ideological aspect of policies for reducing the size of the public sector, as the British have a government which believes that private ownership and markets are normally not only more economically efficient but socially and politically superior to publicly provided services.' (Thomas, 1993, 44)

According to Carr and Hartnett (1996), this position reflects some core assumptions in a national culture which includes ideas of:

> 'racial and national superiority; a deferential attitude towards authority; a preference for secrecy in the practice of high politics; an anti-egalitarian ethos; and the awarding of status and respect to

hierarchies.' (Carr and Hartnett, 1996, 153)

In their view, the New Right re-state and re-invent the ideas of selection, privilege and excellence: 'It is not just a return to old values but re-constructing the old values' (ibid, 158). Using the example of selection, they argue that there is a 'political' refashioning of language into acceptable and unacceptable usage. Some terms are 'good' others are 'bad' in their common usage post-1988. The 'good' or best' words include excellence, quality, core subjects, traditional discipline, standards, examinations, parents, freedom, market, choice and local autonomy. The 'bad' or 'worst' words, which have formed part of the 'discourse of derision' (Ball, 1994) include equality, experts, expertise, educationalists, militant teachers, loony-left councils, ill-discipline, falling standards, progressive education, clutter on the curriculum, anti-racism, anti-sexism, local bureaucrats, and political indoctrination (ibid).

1997: NEW LABOUR'S EDUCATIONAL POLICIES

It is arguable that virtually all of the key Tory policies remain intact and that the differences between the policies of New Labour and their predecessors are far more apparent than real. The 1997 White Paper *Excellence in Schools* began by listing six principles which were to underlie the agenda for the new Government. These have been summarised as follows:

- Education will be at the heart of Government
- Policies will be designed to benefit the many, not just the few
- The focus will be on standards, not structures
- Intervention will be in inverse proportion to success
- There will be zero tolerance for under-performance
- Government will work in partnership with those committed to raising standards. (Chitty, 1999, 93)

And it is true that many of the steps taken in honouring these principles - such as the introduction of public awards for teachers, the designation of 'beacon' schools, the creation of education action zones ('EAZs') and (at long last) the establishment of General Teaching Councils - had a new 'ring' to them. But other outcomes had a less novel appearance, such as the proliferation of targets for schools and their pupils and greater parental and community involvement in school governance (see Docking, 2000, 24-28).

At the end of the day, while there is a change of emphasis in the discourse of Labour's 'Third Way'(for example, from 'structures' to 'standards', and from 'selection' to 'specialization'), the majority of the 'good' and 'bad' words of the Conservative era have stayed in their categories. Moreover, some changes were by no means what they seemed. In particular, the apparent rehabilitation of LEAs has been accompanied by a significant alteration in their function. No longer are they the manifestation of the local and democratic administration of a national system of schooling, but as the chief agents of central government initiatives, policing the 'reforms' rather than initiating or leading them. As Chitty has concluded:

> '... it would seem clear that the Third Way in education is about far more than 'stretching' pupils and raising standards. It is, as many critics fear, about marginalising local education authorities and speeding up the process of privatization. It is perhaps, after all, simply a fine phrase designed to disguise an underlying continuity between Thatcherism and New Labour.' (Chitty, 1999, 107)

TRAINING AND REGULATION WITHIN THE PROFESSION

We have argued so far, that the policies of successive governments have embodied values and set up procedures which are inimical to those we associate with professional autonomy and with the morality which should underpin education. This can be seen also in regard to the training of teachers, but here, too, it is essential to see the history of what has happened and not take the current situation at face value.

Qualifying to Teach, the handbook of guidance for initial teacher training published by the Teacher Training Agency (TTA, 2003) gives pride of place to professional values and practice. In a change from the preceding guidance, the professionalism of teachers is the first section after the Introduction in this document. This section asserts that those qualifying to teach should 'understand, and uphold the professional code of the General Teaching Council by demonstrating' (*inter alia*) that,

> '.... they have high expectations of all pupils; respect their social, cultural, linguistic and ethnic backgrounds ....; treat pupils consistently with respect and consideration ...; (and) demonstrate and promote positive values, attitudes and behaviour that they expect from their pupils....'[TTA, 2003, p.7]

However, to conclude that ethical practice and positive values in teachers' autonomy are now the highest priorities in teacher training would be quite unwarranted. This is at best an attempt to soften what has happened in the previous 20 years, during which the training of teachers had become centrally determined in ways which are the antithesis of professional freedom. From the advent of the Council for the Accreditation of Teacher Education (CATE) in the mid '80s, through the development of a national curriculum in teacher training, dominated by check-lists of competencies, heavily weighted towards core subjects, class control and paperwork requirements, the professional wisdom and autonomy of those involved in teacher education has been whittled away. In the process, the time available for students to seriously consider moral questions underpinning their practice as teachers has all but disappeared.

The annual visitations of OFSTED inspectors on training providers, linked to the TTA's control of allocated student numbers (and the funding which goes with them) has entirely dominated the scene. There is little room for students or their tutors to be creative or reflective when overwhelmed by the tick-box mentality of outcomes-driven training. This is perfectly in tune with both the 'discourse of derision' (Ball, op cit) which characterizes educational 'debate' today. This discourse serves to discredit an 'educational establishment' which holds out against such instrumental and imposed models of training. Against this backcloth, the location so early in the document, of the section of the Handbook which deals with professionalism seems cosmetic. When looked at closely, these values become yet more standards, supposedly observable in some behaviouristic way, and imposed without real discussion or reflection on the next generation of teachers.

Others might argue that the advent of the General Teaching Council, to which these standards refer, is itself evidence that ethical issues are, after all, falling within the jurisdiction of the profession itself. But is this so?

General Teaching Councils in England and Wales were set up under *The Teaching and Higher Education Act 1998.* The GTC for England began its work in September 2000, with 25 of the 64 members being elected teachers, 17 members representing other bodies and 13 appointed by the Secretary of State (who also appoints the Chairperson). Welch and Mahony (2000, 146) summarise its key responsibilities as 'to maintain a register of qualified teachers, discipline teachers for serious misconduct or incompetence, and advise the Government on issues such as the recruitment and supply of teachers, initial training and induction, and professional development.' In her introduction to the GTC's first corporate plan (for 2001/2), the Chief Executive (Carol Adams) stated its 'key commitments' as 'raising the status of the profession'; 'providing a professional voice for teachers'; 'listening to and working for teachers'; and 'guaranteeing high standards.' (GTC, 2001, 07)

The advent of the GTC is clearly a significant event. For the first time, the teaching profession as a whole has some say in the determination of teachers' work and, indeed, who is eligible to undertake that work. The GTC's brief seems to meet some of the criteria for full professional status quoted earlier (Sayer, op cit, 18), notably a degree of government through a code of ethics and disciplinary procedures. However, given the emphasis on advice to the Government (rather than executive powers) its impact remains small. In terms of the setting of standards of practice, certification and control of entry to the profession, these responsibilities lie elsewhere in such government (or quasi-government) bodies as OFSTED and the Teacher Training Agency. Docking (2000, 34-5) considers that 'the powers of the GTC fall far short of those enjoyed by the General Medical Council', while Welch and Mahony conclude:

> 'If we take the most basic sociological definition of a profession ... there is little basis for viewing the GTC as comparable with professional bodies in other occupational sectors.' (Welch and Mahony, 2000, 153)

WHAT ISSUES FOR ETHICS AND THE TEACHING PROFESSION ARE RAISED BY THIS DISCUSSION?

We began this paper with a declaration of our primary concern as *teaching*. What we have tried to do is to show that the political context within which state schooling operates has enormous consequences for what teachers are both expected and allowed to do. Whether teachers are permitted to exercise moral judgement in the context of their professional work is a matter of the degree of central control and the way it is exercised. We have suggested that such developments as the creation of General Teaching Councils may have little real effect on teachers' professional freedom since they are outweighed by much more wide-reaching policies of centralisation and accountability. Moreover, the morality of the government policies themselves can over-ride both the moral values of individual teachers and the codes of ethics of an entire profession.

The issues confronting those who wish to enhance the professionalism of teaching are therefore matters of national policy, the manner in which it is expressed through discourse, and the way in which it is implemented and policed. To conclude, we wish to focus attention on four such issues and the questions they raise for teachers:

- The manner in which central government assumes power and exercises control over education. The replacement of the 'national system locally administered' through LEAs which had been in place since 1944, with a combination of central imposition and powers devolved to individual schools, and 'policed' by LEAs as agents of central government, makes the autonomy of the profession highly problematic. Within the last month (February, 2005) the Secretary of State for Education, following the clear lead given by the Prime Minister, has refused to accept the central recommendations of the Tomlinson Report on 14-19 education, i.e. the replacement of GCSE and 'gold standard' A-levels with a diploma which might once-and-for-all have resolved the academic/vocational divide. The consensus amongst academics, practitioners, teachers' unions and professional associations, was clearly in favour of the Report's proposals and the Secretary of State has been heckled about her decision to reject them at recent meetings of teachers' representatives. How should the teaching profession respond to situations which are a retreat from democracy, a refusal to take the evidence of research and consultation seriously, and an abnegation of the professional judgment of teachers and educationalists?

- The exploitation of the media in shaping the public consciousness with regard to education. The last two decades have seen the replacement of educational debate with the dominance of a discourse which pits 'common-sense' against rational and professional argument. Thus, slogans like "Education, Education, Education", soundbites about 'driving up standards' and appeals to common-sense notions like 'desirable outcomes' are clearly in evidence when politicians speak through the popular media. Those who have attempted to be heard through a 'voice' of reason, and who appeal to wider educational concerns, have been ridiculed and all but silenced. Ball's (1994) phrase: the 'discourse of derision' sums up perfectly the means by which this is achieved. How should the profession fight the power of media which are fast becoming an ideological apparatus for the imposition of educational dogma?
- The stratification and diversification of institutions. It is New Labour and not the Conservative Party which has sounded the death-knell of the comprehensive school, an institution which, since the mid-1960s, came to epitomise the principles of social justice and equality of educational opportunity. The advent of 'specialist' schools and colleges in the context of public-private partnership, the creation of city academies, pump-primed by private capital but heavily subsidized and maintained in perpetuity by the tax-payer, and the ranking of schools in numerous 'league tables', is no less than a moral crisis for those who embraced the comprehensive ideal. So, too, for those who believe in a

secular system, is the current policy of state support for Faith schools. What is a reasonable ethical response for those who eschewed the private sector on grounds of conscience and for those whose beliefs make faith schools abhorrent?

- The promotion and extension of a quasi-market for education. The principle of consumer sovereignty ('parent power') in which schools compete for pupils, the setting of 'sales' targets, the introduction of performance-related pay and the commodification of curriculum knowledge are strikingly at odds with the idea of universal entitlement to education as a social good. What should be the response to the marketisation of education of a profession motivated less by the profit motive than by a sense of moral duty and social service?

Any talk of the teaching of professional ethics in the context of teacher education has a hollow ring while such questions remain to be answered.

REFERENCES

Baker, K. (1993) *The Turbulent Years. My Life in Politics.* London: Faber & Faber
Ball, S. J. (1990) *Politics and Policy Making in Education.* London: Routledge
Ball, S. J. (1994) *Education Reform.* Buckingham: Open University Press
Basini, A. (1997) The National Curriculum: Foundation Subjects. In Docking, J. (ed.) *National School Policy.* London: David Fulton, 1-14
Carr, W. and Hartnett, A. (1996) *Education and the Struggle for Democracy.* Buckingham: Open University Press
Chitty, C. (1989) *Towards a New Education System: The Victory of the Right.* London: Falmer
Chitty, C. (1999) *The Education System Transformed.* Tisbury: Baseline
Docking, J. ed. (2000) What is the Solution? An Overview of National Policies for Schools, 1979-99. In J Docking (ed) *New Labour's Policies for Schools. Raising the Standard?* London: Fulton, 21-42
Feintuck, M. (1994) *Accountability and Choice in Schooling.* Buckingham: Open University Press
Gee, J. P., Hull, G. and Lanksheare, C. (1996) *The New World Order: Behind the language of the new capitalism.* Sydney: Allen & Unwin
Green, A. (1990) *Education and State Formation.* London: Macmillan
GTC (2001) *Working for Teachers. First corporate plan for 2001/2.* London: General Teaching Council
Haynes, F. (1998)*The Ethical School.* London: Routledge
Jones, K. (1991) Conservative Modernization. In Moore, R. and Ozga, J. eds. *Curriculum Policy.* Oxford: Pergamon, 87-103
Peters, R. S. (1966) *Ethics and Education.* London: Allen & Unwin
Peters, R. S. ed. (1967) *The Concept of Education.* London: RKP

Rustin, M. (1989) 'The Politics of Post-Fordism, or The Trouble with "New Times"', *New Left Review*, No, 175, 45-77

Sayer, J. (1996) The Need for Recognition and Professional Status. In McClelland, A.V. and Varma, V. eds. *The Needs of Teachers*. London: Cassell, 10-26

Stenhouse, L. (1983) *Authority, Education and Emancipation*. London: Heinemann

Thomas, H. (1993) The Education Reform Movement in England and Wales. In Beare, H. and Boyd L. eds. *Restructuring Schools*. London: Falmer

TTA (2000) *Qualifying to Teach. Handbook of Guidance*. London: Teacher Training Agency

Welch, G. and Mahony, P. (2000) The Teaching Profession, in Docking, J. (ed) *New Labour's Policies for Schools. Raising the Standard?* London: Fulton, 139-157

White, J. (1990) *Education and the Good Life – Beyond the National Curriculum*. London: Kogan Page

Wilson, J. (2002) 'Is Education a Good Thing?' *British Journal of Educational Studies*, 50(3), 327-338

Wragg, E. (1988) *Education in the Market Place: The Ideology Behind the 1988 Bill*. London: National Union of Teachers

8
Responsibility for nature
A challenge to reflect critically on cultural values

Jens Christensen

INTRODUCTION

Discussions about responsibility for nature are important for all practitioners whose technical and social practice affects the natural world, particularly engineers, in the broad sense of technical and social engineers. In this broad sense, the term 'engineer' encompasses all professionals who contribute to forming technical practices, including the formation of the social conditions of these practices.

Responsibility may be defined as acting in a way that responds to problems through the consideration of values. If professionals are to develop into ethical responsible agents, it is important that they acquire the qualifications allowing them to identify and manage problems and values, not merely as they appear , but also at a more basic level, including the cultural context. During their education, they should achieve the ability to understand this context, both as culturally specific, and as a result of a historical process, in which they take part. They should obtain the ability to reflect their own way of thinking and acting critically, as culturally and historically influenced agents.

With the aim of contributing to this reflection, this chapter shows what may be involved in facing problems and values on a cultural level. The paper is centred around two images. The first image gives a view of the problems in man's relation to nature, and the second image serves as a reference for promoting the discussion of values to be considered in responsible action. The discussion of the second image ends up with a focus on ethical tensions and dilemmas. Responsibility implies a challenge to understand and manage such tensions.

PROBLEMS IN MAN'S RELATION TO NATURE

Current problems

How can we conceptualise problems in the relationships between human beings and nature? In the search to answer this question, it is important to realise that the problems have different levels.

On the level of appearance, problems most obviously occur as a direct pressure on nature, caused by the human exploitation of nature. However, understanding the causes involves many factors. As a conceptualisation of this complexity, we may imagine a global extension of a 'technosystem', rooted in Western culture, centred around science and technology, and aiming at economic production and consumption of material goods.[1] The concept of a 'technosystem' includes not only the material technology, but also the dominating motive powers of technological development, socially, economically, and ideologically. The dominating base of knowledge, the Western conception of scientific knowledge, is part of the technosystem, too. In a broader sense, the technosystem expresses a cultural and historical specific type of consciousness and practice. Already by introducing the concept of a technosystem, it becomes clear that the actual pressure on nature is deeply rooted in culture and critical reflections on culture are important.

Less obvious, the extension of this technosystem also causes an indirect pressure on nature. The dominating global development tends to marginalize cultures other than the Western; including cultures with traditions which relate to nature. On a basic level, and in spite of many various expressions of the technosystem, the earth tends to become subject to a one-sided culture. The more cultural plurality is eroded, the more the technosystem looses cultural competition, and the more open is the space for a continued expansion of the technosystem together with its values. The indirect pressure does not only have a cultural aspect, but also a material aspect. The dominating technology and economy provide benefits to some of the global social groups, while the materially poor groups are often forced to over-exploit their natural conditions, in order to satisfy their basic needs.[2]

A meta-problem

Behind the appearance of these problems, attention should be paid to the existence of a more fundamental problem, a meta-problem. This meta-problem is the tendency to remain within a context, even when basic premises of this context are parts of the problem. Changes at the surface level may show a persistence on a more fundamental level. Facing the surface level only, without attention to the meta-level, is equal to reacting on symptoms rather than on problems.

The meta-problem can be found in all human life (see Watzlawick, 1974). As human beings we behave according to a life-orientation, embedded in our way of thinking and acting, and directing the course of our thoughts and actions. It seems to be a common disposition in human life that we persist in what we have once learned, in spite of crucial changes in the circumstances that form the conditions of our life. If we are faced with new types of problems, different from the former, and if we meet the problems with an unchanged life-orientation, then an inadequacy between the current problems and the efforts to solve them will occur.

What happens at a personal level, can also happen at a cultural level. During the course of history, cultures face new problems, while the cultural orientation in some respects remains unchanged. As culturally influenced beings, professionals as well as laymen continue to think and act on the premises of a cultural orientation, handed down by historical tradition. At the time of its origin, an orientation may have been adequate to the problems faced but it is not necessarily capable of responding adequately to new problems.

The globally extended environmental problems that we face today form a historically new situation. On a global level, a lot of work is put into problem solving, both politically and practically. However, and in spite of many alternatives, the main tendency is that both the methods to interpret environmental problems and the efforts to solve these problems remain within the context of the technosystem causing the problems. Practitioners within the fields of technical and social engineering often tend to interpret and solve environmental problems within the same frame of instrumentality, which forms the technological and social development. When this is the case, the practitioners do not handle the technosystem as external agents, but as a part of the technosystem, as internal agents. It means that their operations are conditioned by the premises of the operated system.

Associated with this trend, ethics may be perceived merely as an additional instrumental skill. There are dangers if ethics is taught only as a subject among other subjects, as one skill amongst many, rather than as a critique that critically challenges the context-level. Especially within the field of engineering, centred around instrumental sciences, ethics may very easily become interpreted instrumentally, as 'ethical rules'. Hence, ethics are interpreted as a corrective to the instrumental sciences, but within the context of instrumentality. When interpreted in this way, the critical potential of ethics will be weakened.

The challenge of a critical reflection is a challenge to reflect the cultural orientation embedded in the operated system. A precondition of reflecting a cultural orientation is to make this orientation visible.

The cultural orientation in the technosystem

A framework for analysing practice-oriented systems of knowledge (hereafter abbreviated as knowledge systems) may contribute to the visibility of the cultural orientation in the technosystem. The framework consists of four closely interconnected components: A process of acknowledging and acting, in its connection with a basic interpretation of nature (what is nature?), and a basic value (what is the role of human beings in relation to nature?).

The basic ideas of the instrumentality, forming the technosystem, can briefly be summed up as:

Acknowledgement: The technical sciences are fundamentally based on the idea of acknowledging what happens in nature through instrumental observation in combination with rationally developed theories about cause and effect.

Action: Technical science is not only for the purpose of explaining nature, but it is mainly for the purpose of making use of nature, and in a way that is directed towards technical and economic progress.

Interpretation: The relationship between acknowledgement and action refers to a specific interpretation of nature. Nature is not only perceived from a human perspective, but man and nature are separated in a dualistic way. Nature is the object, while man is the subject.

Value: The dominating value is that man has the role to play as a master of nature, and nature functions as a resource for human purposes.

Historically, the relationship between acknowledgement and action is rooted in the view of science formulated four hundred years ago by Francis Bacon. Also, the basic interpretation and the basic values lead back to the enlightenment, but with deeper historical roots; among others, the earlier theological interpretations of the Judeo-Christian religion (see White, 1967).

The knowledge system can be perceived as a specific expression of an even deeper orientation towards meaning, described by a relationship between freedom and interdependence.

During western history, particularly during the latest centuries and with reference to the enlightenment, freedom has been a dominating concept. However, the concept of freedom has also been interpreted in a way that is closely connected to power. As a master of nature man has the freedom to exploit nature. Nothing in nature, or in the relationship between man and nature, commits man to an attentive practice with nature. Protection of nature is predominantly argued from a human perspective. This is true also when the issue of sustainable development is in focus. Sustainability is mainly perceived as a commitment to future generations, not as a commitment towards nature.

Fundamentally, Western culture stresses human freedom at the expense of interdependence with nature. Nature is reified. Just as we might not feel responsible to other people, if we define them just as 'things' or 'objects', neither do we feel responsible to a reified nature, a nature which does not really mean anything to us. This is a fundamental problem, which challenges us to search for knowledge systems based on values committing human beings in a relationship with nature.

VALUES IN PEOPLE'S RELATION TO NATURE

Freedom and interdependence

Whenever alternatives are formulated, it seems important to avoid the risk of going into one of two opposites. One risk is to formulate the alternative so widely that it is likely to become interpreted at one's own convenience. Another risk is to formulate the alternative so rigidly that it very easily may become refuted as an arbitrary and subjective view only. The following is an attempt at a more balanced approach.

This involves two aspects. Firstly, there is a challenge to search for ways to develop an attentive relation to nature within Western culture. Secondly, there is a challenge to respect and appreciate cultures different from the Western, especially such cultures which have a tradition of relating to nature. The keywords in this are freedom and interdependence.

It has been argued that the persistence of some cultural constituents in Western culture is problematic, compared with the problems in people's relation to nature. This is, however, not to imply that all cultural constituents of the West are problematic A specific interpretation of the concept of freedom might be problematic, namely freedom perceived as man's right to exploit nature without obligation for nature. But this is not to deny the value of the aspiration and striving for human freedom as such. The orientation towards meaning in Western culture is based on the concept of freedom so fundamentally that denial of freedom would be the same as to disclaim Western culture in its roots. Freedom is not only an important concept, it is a symbol. As a symbol, the concept of freedom is a carrier of meaning, and this implies that the concept is emotionally charged. Moreover, the concept of freedom is one of the most crucial carriers of meaning in the Western culture. Questioning freedom goes straight into the heart of Western culture. Rather than questioning the very concept of freedom, it is a challenge to redefine the content of the concept, in a way that includes an interdependent relationship to nature.

Here a comment on the term 'interdependence' is necessary. The term is used to conceive an emotionally charged interrelation, symbolic in its character, and embedded with meaning. The term refers not only to reason, but also to the heart. Commitment is an important content of an interdependent relationship. 'Interdependence' is translated from the Danish concept 'samhørighed', with such connotations, cf. the connotations of German 'Gemeinschaftsgefühl'. The English words 'concordance' or 'affinity' may contribute to the intended connotations.

Furthermore, two points ought to be emphasised. First, the technosystem is not Western culture in its totality, even if it has its origin in this culture. Second, the criticism of the technosystem is directed only towards the problematic aspects of the cultural orientation of this system.

The criticism should be connected to a search for potentials within the Western culture, including potentials of the concept of freedom. The search is for an interdependent relationship with nature, emotionally charged, as a counterpart to the one-sided focus on freedom from nature, but in respect of the very aspiration towards human freedom. A crucial issue for further discussion is, how to unify freedom and interdependence as a base for a responsible approach to the way of forming the technical and social practice with nature.

A multiplicity of expressions of freedom and interdependence

How can we understand freedom and interdependence, neither as contradictions, nor as two separate concepts that are interrelated, but as parts of the same orientation towards meaning?

As a response to the one-sided expression of the technosystem, a first step is to adopt an open attitude towards a multiplicity of expressions of freedom as well as interdependence. Freedom may be said to be equal to realising the many-sided potentials of human beings for entering into a process of getting insight and expressing oneself. With reference to the framework used above, the realisation of potentials involves the interconnection between acknowledgement and action (keeping in mind that the distinction between four components is only for analytical purposes, and that a knowledge system should be perceived as an entity).

Acknowledgement: As humans, we can get insight in a multiplicity of ways, different from instrumental observation and rational reasoning, for instance by means of intuition and empathy.

Action: As humans, we can express ourselves in a multiplicity of ways, different from technical and economic progress, for instance artistically. Interdependence may be said to be equal to entering into a meaningful relation to an otherness, meaning something else than oneself, including the non-human nature. A meaningful relationship involves the interconnection between interpretation and value.

Interpretation: As humans, we can interpret nature in a multiplicity of ways, not only as an object, separated from the human subject. Interpretations of nature as spiritual, as divine, or as akin to the soul of man, are known from cultures that are different than Western cultures. On the basis of Western culture, we may think in terms of man's origin in nature or in terms of an inextricable interconnection between man and nature.

Value: As humans, we can enter into a meaningful relationship with nature in a multiplicity of ways, different from the role of man as a master of nature. Different kinds of interpretations involve different meanings, for instance spiritual or divine. In Western culture, a respectful attitude towards nature may be perceived in terms of a dialogical relation between man and nature.

A unifying concept may be 'the meaning of man as a whole human being in its whole and meaningful connections'. 'Man as a whole human being' refers to the realisation of human potentials to get insight and to express oneself. The realisation of potentials of human life take place in the world, and the term of 'connection' includes everything that influences and is influenced by the life of man on earth, as an incarnated being. Thus, 'connections' include all relations within mankind, as well as relations between mankind and non-mankind, including nature.

The existence of a multiplicity of cultures on earth, as well as subcultures, indicates that by nature, as human beings, we have potential for a huge variation of cultural orientations, expressed as knowledge systems. Every culture is expressive of a specific system. Every culture is expressive of an interpretation of: what 'man as a whole human being' is, and what 'meaningful connections' are, as well as a specified interpretation of the concepts of freedom and interdependence (even if the culture does not have such concepts in its vocabulary).

As the first step, the *leitmotif* of unifying freedom and interdependence is a challenge to be open-minded and respectful towards the plurality of cultural life and worldviews. However, an open-minded approach is not sufficient to ensure responsibility for nature. As a second step, a search for a decisive approach is needed.

Responsibility: a challenge to understand and manage dilemmas

The decisive approach should respond to the meta-problem, discussed above. The meta-problem was emphasised as a gap between the current problems and the cultural orientation, on which the efforts to solve the problems are based. Responding to this meta-problem should involve a search for cultural orientations, adequate to the historical circumstances, including the historically new problems, to which the culture has not developed any adequate 'compass' for orientation.

Here, we need to take a step backwards and reflect the result of the argumentation so far. Linkage between freedom and interdependence is a leitmotif, and a leitmotif is open for discussion of its specific implications. Also, adequacy between current problems and cultural orientations is a leitmotif, open for discussion. Leitmotifs are not the same as rules, and the indication of a leitmotif is not the same as operative guidelines for action. . When we stand before leitmotifs, we need to realise that we have not obtained an applicable answer to the question that was asked, ready made for implementation. We have only reached the stage of formulating entries into continued discussions, hopefully on a more qualified level than earlier.

At this stage, we also need to realise that we face crucial tensions and that responsibility requires the ability to identify and manage these. On a more general level there is a tension between open-mindedness and decisiveness and a challenge to manage the movement in between. More specifically and only for the purpose of exemplifying, three tensions will be indicated.

One tension is between theoretical concepts and symbols. Unification of freedom and interdependence may be introduced as a leitmotif on a theoretical level. Also, it may be exemplified how freedom and interdependence are interpreted differently in the various cultures and subcultures (see Christensen 2004). However, in order to function as a leitmotif in the practical life, among people, the symbolic character of the concepts is important, including emotive connotations. Concepts do not achieve the character of symbols, carrying meaning and guiding action, by means of rational thinking only. The development of symbolism is subject to human interaction.

Another tension is between the ability to orient oneself as a cultural being and the ability to solve problems; especially with regard to new historical problems. The perception of a phenomenon as problematic is influenced by the cultural perspective, and at the same time new phenomena challenge this. From this view there is no fixed standpoint for deciding 'adequate' problem solving.

The second tension becomes clearer by focusing also on a third one, between being part of a culture and reflecting this culture critically. Essentially, reflection is an activity from an external position compared with the reflected issue. However, the critical reflection of one's own culture will always take its starting point within this culture. The search for possible changes will interfere with the culture to be changed. Outlooks to different cultures may inspire, but the inspiration will be influenced by the cultural perspective, from which an outlook is taken.

THE NEED OF EXISTENTIAL ENLIGHTENMENT

It has been argued that responsibility for nature should consider problems and values in a cultural perspective. As individuals, of course, critically reflecting agents cannot change the cultural constituents of the globalised practise with nature. However, professionals with considerable influence on the development of the technical and social practice, especially engineers of all kinds, may have an important role to play by contributing in a professional manner to reflections on the basic aspects of a responsible practice with nature. The precondition is that their education gives them a foundation for fulfilling this role. During their professional education, engineers should not only achieve scientific enlightenment, but also existential enlightenment.[3] At least two aspects are important here.

Firstly, existential enlightenment goes far beyond ethics as a specific discipline. Knowledge about the history and the fundaments of one's own culture is needed, combined with an attitude towards this culture as only one among a variety of cultures on earth. Based on historical and cultural knowledge professionals in the fields of technical and social engineering should acquire the ability to identify and reflect two interrelated aspects of their professional work critically: a) The cultural constituents of the issue, with which they deal, the technical and social practice, and b) The cultural constituents embedded in their own way of thinking and acting, and on the basis of which they deal with technology and society.

Secondly, existential enlightenment also goes far beyond instrumentalism. A crucial point is the acquisition of an ability to identify, reflect, and manage basic tensions, including the ability to manage situations with no fixed answers.

NOTES

1. The term of a technosystem is inspired by the Finnish philosopher Georg Henrik von Wright, but I use the concept more comprehensively than von Wright. G.H. von Wright (1994) *Myten om fremskridtet (The Myth of Progress)*. Copenhagen, Denmark. - To a certain extent, the 'technosystem' is akin to Heideggers concept 'Das Gestell'. Martin Heidegger. "The Question concerning Technology". Pp. 283-317 in David Farrell Krell ed. (1978) *Martin Heidegger, Basic Writings*. Routledge & Kegan Paul, London and Henley, Great Britain.
2. An indirect pressure as described, both culturally and materially, can be observed for instance in the Indian Himalayas.
3. I owe thanks to Jesper Garsdal, Ph.D. from Aalborg University, Denmark, for the distinction between existential enlightenment and scientific enlightenment.

REFERENCES

Christensen, J. (2004) Frihed og samhørighed i menneskers forhold til naturen. In Niels Jakob Harbo *et al.* (ed.s). *Det gode liv – mere end dig selv*. Forlaget Philosophia, 213-246

Watzlawick, P. *et al.* (1974) *Change. Principles of Problem Formation and Problem Resolution*. Grand Rapids: Baker

White, L. Jr. (1967) "The Historical Roots of Our Ecologic Crisis." *Science*, Vol. 155, No. 3767, 10 March

PART TWO

TEACHING PROFESSIONAL ETHICS

9
Beyond unilateralism in ethics

A South African multilateral ethics education experiment 1997–2003

Martin Prozesky

This chapter rests on two main contentions. The first one is that it is educationally and ethically insufficient to treat ethics, understood both as an academic discipline and as moral practice, as if it were no more than the ethics of the west and north, especially in contexts where there is cultural diversity. This policy can be called a policy of moving beyond unilateralism in ethics, unilateralism being defined as any approach to ethics that is based on a single, dominant ethical tradition in a situation where others are followed. Secondly, I propose that in contexts marked by problems of social injustice, rising crime, violence, corruption and other grave problems, academic ethicists are challenged to move beyond theory to ways of enhancing the moral fibre of those contexts. These two contentions have strongly influenced the work of a new Ethics Centre set up under my direction at the University of Natal in South Africa in 1997 (now renamed as the University of KwaZulu-Natal), giving that work a distinctive character but also presenting it with fresh challenges. They have their origins in some defining experiences in the decade preceding the founding of the new ethics centre. To understand the nature, achievements and difficulties of the Centre, it is necessary to know something of those experiences.

PRECEDING EVENTS

The last decade of apartheid brought with it much state violence against those who were struggling to overthrow that system. One such episode began on the campus of the University of Natal in Pietermaritzburg. Police had entered the Durban campus of the same university a day or two before and had opened fire. Angered by this violation of the academic space of an institution that had by then already been defying the law and admitting African and Indian students, a column of about 200 staff and students formed near the main entrance to our campus. In defiance of yet another apartheid law we moved forward to the nearest city road. There we were met and stopped by a large number of heavily armed police, forced to sit on the ground and then ordered at gun-point on to waiting police lorries and driven off to be held at the premises of the Murder and Robbery Squad.

I well remember the fear I felt. People had died in such situations, like an academic colleague and student friend of mine at another South African university who was murdered by state agents outside his own house. We tried singing protest songs but were told that we would be held with no further action unless we stopped. Some of our captors seemed particularly to relish making things difficult when anybody needed to use a toilet. One in particular, a powerfully built man in plain clothes with an automatic pistol stuck under his belt, would swagger around as if just waiting to smash somebody's teeth in. I remember thinking that if a group of white, middle-aged professors was being treated with such contempt, what hope would there be for young black people who defied the apartheid system and its enforcers. No wonder Steve Biko and so many others were killed in their custody.

But the reality that struck me most strongly that tense and fearful day was not the utter injustice and inhumanity of one side and the courage and commitment of the other, but the sight of Muslim, Hindu, Christian, African and secular staff and students united against the evil of apartheid, shoulder to shoulder ethically despite all our differences of creed and culture. For somebody with my interest in religion and ethics, the single most important lesson of 20th century South African experience is therefore that while the creation and violent maintaining of apartheid was largely the work of a culture steeped in a single Christian ethos, its defeat was the shared project of morally committed people from many belief- and value-systems, secular as well as religious. It was a lesson experienced by everybody who lived through and took some part in the struggle against apartheid, and it embodied, so I believed, a vital principle for the future, namely the imperative of moving beyond the kind of political, cultural and religious unilateralism that characterized the apartheid period.

A first objective in translating this imperative into practice was groundwork for the constitution of a post-apartheid South Africa. The objective towards which I and others worked was that the constitutional privileging of so-called Christian values had to end and be replaced by recognition on an equal footing of all our belief and value systems. This objective was achieved in the Bill of Rights of the 1996 South African constitution, and would, as the supreme law of the land, be the basis of similar moves beyond unilateralism in other aspects of society (SA Constitution, 1996, sections 9 and 15).

A few years after the police experience described above, which led to a late night court appearance followed by a midnight release on bail provided by the University and to the eventual dropping of charges, and with the walls of apartheid finally collapsing, I became Dean of Humanities at my campus. My term of office therefore coincided with the birth of a democratic, non-racial South Africa and thus with a time of what I can only call total immersion in the work of planning for a new kind of society and a new kind of university in which the privileges and injustices of the apartheid period would have to go and new initiatives develop.

For me, one particular issue emerged as critical for our future: the need to revisit and interrogate our values and our assumptions about ethics itself. Here too the apartheid period had caused damage and distortion, mostly unnoticed. In society at large, values for most people seemed to mean Christian values and within our universities, ethics meant either the moral theology of the churches or the moral philosophy of the west. Having studied both of these and having been very strongly influenced by the faith-based ethics of the late Daantjie Oosthuizen, my philosophy professor at Rhodes University in Grahamstown, South Africa in the 1960s, I was and remain deeply aware of their importance, but I had also become convinced that more would be needed if ethics in South Africa was to be reflective of the values of all our communities. It would have to be both ethically and academically more inclusive and practically effective, as well as intellectually powerful, drawing on but not limited to our existing resources in philosophical and theological ethics.

For my academic life after being a Dean I therefore proposed the setting up of an Ethics Centre as an academic base for the initiative I had in mind. Greatly aided by Professor Brenda Gourley, a Vice-Chancellor for whom ethics was also a priority and who is now Vice-Chancellor of the Open University in Britain, and a bit later by generous donor funding from the Unilever Foundation for Education and Development, the new Ethics Centre became a reality in 1997. One of its main briefs was to develop an applied ethics course that would give effect to the principles just mentioned. A multi-disciplinary group comprising myself with a mainly Religious

Studies background, a philosopher, a Christian ethicist and a classicist with interests in African and Chinese cultures, all of us sharing a strong interest in ethics, was convened to plan the project.

ETHICS AS AN INCLUSIVE, MULTIDISCIPLINARY FIELD OF STUDY

The course that emerged has four distinguishing features. The first is to conceive of ethics as a field of study rather than as a discipline, involving a complex, historically developing dimension of human existence occurring in some form in all known cultures, aspects of which form part of our consciousness and aspects of which are open to empirical observation in the same way as economic, religious and political activity.

Secondly, this view of the subject-matter of ethics immediately meant including all the main value-systems or moral traditions found in our society and the wider world, especially those of Africa which were so marginalized and even demonised under apartheid. Thus our course design began with a short introduction to the ethical dimension of human existence, immediately presenting the subject as something culturally diverse, and then proceeded to give short introductions to the emergence, development, main values and present situations of the ethics of traditional Africa, Judaism, Christianity, Islam, Hinduism, China and of secular humanism in the west, followed by a short introduction to the main philosophical theories about ethics in the west. We use the term Comparative Ethics for this section of the course.

There are indications that this comparative, inclusive approach has very few counterparts elsewhere in academic approaches to ethics, so it is necessary to explain its importance further. In a rapidly globalizing world which is also marked by very deep-seated cultural differences, there is a clear case for fostering a comprehensive, multi-traditional grasp of human morality. Already, such powerful aspects of life as the economy, pollution and information have taken on global proportions. These trends have enormous implications for the future quality of life, and there is no way that an essentially provincial view of ethics can be sufficient in such a situation (Kung, 1997). The only alternative is to widen the approach to ethics. At the very least this means covering the main ethical traditions of one's own society. But with an eye on the rise of a global era, I for one prefer to work towards an even more inclusive coverage that would embrace the world's most widely-followed value-systems past and present.

To prevent this from becoming impossibly complex, the approach used at the University of KwaZulu-Natal uses the following classification of these value-systems, presenting them where appropriate in the order of their appearance in world history: (1) Surviving traditional ethnic moralities, such as those of Africa, America and Australia; (2) the ethics of Judaism, Christianity and Islam as the three Abrahamic moralities; (3) Hindu and Buddhist ethics; (4) the Chinese moralities; (5) the ethics of the western philosophical tradition going back to Ancient Greece; (6) the secularistic moralities of the modern west, including secular humanism and Marxism; and (7) new ethical movements such as feminist ethics and the search for a global ethic which have both religious and secular forms and exponents.

For those who are used to a secular, western philosophical approach to ethics it is important to say something more about the importance of a knowledge of faith-based value-systems. On one hand we must surely acknowledge the great social benefit that has been fostered by the emphasis in all the great faiths on active compassion for those who suffer. Not for nothing did Humphrey Carpenter, a secular historian, end his study of Jesus of Nazareth by saying that in the field of morality his influence has had no equal, at least in what we call the West (Carpenter 1980, 95; Theissen and Merz 1998, 347ff) Similar things could be said about the prophet Muhammed, Confucius and the Buddha in their strands of history. Another important point is that while religion is now treated as a private and even marginal matter in some countries, others, including the USA, have a much stronger religious presence. In them the religions are a force to be reckoned with, often playing an important part in fostering a more caring, more honest society because they can get through to large numbers of people and influence their moral values in socially valuable ways, but also sometimes playing a much more questionable role. A sound grasp of morality must surely include awareness of this reality.

But on the other hand there are also problems to be faced. For one thing, the religions do not give us an agreed set of moral values, though they do all seem to have something like the Golden Rule in common as a core value. Then there is the fact that much religion, though not all, functions in top-down ways that seem more at home in pre-democratic days than in a democracy, not to speak of the status of women in some widely followed faiths. In addition, the track record of our religions is not always ethically admirable, as we in South Africa know better than most from our apartheid past. There is, alas, such a thing as harmful religion, not only when judged from the standpoint of democratic values, human equality and gender justice but also when judged by the best ethical norms of religion itself like the passion for justice. If we are to understand the ethical dimension of life adequately as well as inclusively, a critical awareness of this problematical side of religious ethics must also be cultivated in the academy, for there is not much evidence of it in some forms of religion, especially the very conservative kinds.

The component in Comparative Ethics from western moral philosophy, as it sometimes called, was included not just because of its importance as one of the great strands of ethical thought that influence a society like ours, but also for the valuable reasoning skills it can provide in seeking to resolve ethical dilemmas. But because the intention was (and is) to offer students something that complements rather than competes with the ethics taught by our philosophy colleagues (and also those from theology and religious studies) in their own ethics courses, the coverage has been kept quite short, as with the faith-based value-systems listed above. This enables us to encourage our students to take philosophy and religious studies courses as well as ours, without an unacceptable amount of overlap or encroachment on their spheres of expertise, a policy given further effect by making use wherever possible of lecturers from those two disciplines. Clearly this differs from the usual subject matter of conventional theological and philosophical ethics.

The third feature of our handling of the study of ethics was to see it as a field of study requiring a multi-disciplinary approach, rather than as a discipline with a single main method. Given my background in comparative religious studies, it was natural for me use the same phenomenological and historical methods in presenting the various value-systems to students, with special emphasis on empathy and bracketed personal value-judgements. (De Gruchy and Prozesky, 1991, 3). As has already been explained, philosophy has from the start been seen as another essential discipline, and as the course developed and led to others, the disciplines of psychology and some of the life sciences, such as genetics, animal science and human neurobiology, among others, have added their approaches to our work.

While few would doubt the ethical relevance of these life sciences, I believe that we must cast the scientific net much wider in our quest for the most comphrensive understanding of the ethical domain, for it would be of great interest and value if findings supportive of morality were also present in other sciences. The one that strikes me as particularly interesting and significant is physics, especially in connection with cosmology - the attempt to understand the large-scale nature of the universe. No less an authority than George Ellis has carefully explored this field in relation to ethics, and has concluded in a recent, co-authored book with the revealing title *On the Moral Nature of the Universe*, that there are good grounds for holding that the cosmos itself at a profound level is structured so as to give point and purpose to morality. Let me quote from this book:

> '....physical reality constrains the moral sphere by shaping the context in which it operates....This shaping happens, first, by making moral activity possible at all...by allowing for life, intelligence, free will and predictability....but also through

determining basic features of the physical world such as the conservation of matter. This conservation is needed for the temporary stability of our existence, but it also causes the scarcities of resources that shape much of our physical and social lives....This is the context in which generosity and sharing are needed; if we could conjure such resources out of nowhere, such behaviour would not be required. If we could reconstitute and repair injured bodies merely by thought, medicine would not be necessary and bodily harm would not be a crime.' (Murphy and Ellis, 1996, 219)

Similarly Danah Zohar, whose work I have already mentioned, uses her knowledge of quantum physics to develop a new and richer understanding of what it means to be ethical in her book *The Quantum Self*. Comparing our ethical decisions to "an electron's virtual transitions", she sees them as "experiments in reality creation" some of which can lastingly enrich the world of the future (Zohar, 1991, 183).

In this chapter I can do no more than mention this interesting new frontier of the multidisciplinary exploration of ethics. It reminds me of A.N. Whitehead's bold claim, prophetically made in 1938, that the 'energetic activity considered in physics is the emotional intensity entertained in life.' (Whitehead, 1968 ed., 168) That would mean that what is discovered in the laboratory and what is discerned by our moral sense are in fact two doorways into the self-same space. I find profound attraction in the possibility of scientific grounds for holding that ours is a universe with an unbroken line between the Big Bang of 13 billion years ago when the story of the cosmos began, and the ballot box of a democratically ethical future; a universe where light and warmth, knowledge and ethics, might in some profound way be one.

The fourth defining feature of our approach to ethics is a very strong emphasis on applied or practical ethics. Thus the second half of our basic undergraduate course comprises a study of issues like the environment, law, wealth and poverty, and violence and war in the light of the philosophical theories and the main value-systems introduced earlier in the course. From the start, a commitment to what is sometimes called advocacy ethics was present, understood as seeking not just to offer knowledge and understanding of the subject matter and its methods, valuable though that it, but to promote what Rushworth Kidder calls greater ethical fitness (Kidder, 1995, 57ff). How could things responsibly be otherwise in the context of a massive and critical chapter of national transformation after apartheid?

Raising awareness of ethical issues in our own society and the wider world is in itself of very great value in pursuing this objective. So are the sharpened reasoning skills fostered by philosophy, and the enhanced empathy fostered by the phenomenological method in religious studies. These activities can be done without courting the risk of preaching or being perceived to want to inculcate a particular moral code, but the question remains whether they are enough. Should courses like ours not also include a range of strategies for making moral decisions and promoting best ethical practice in the life-choices and work-places to which our students are headed, above all at more advanced levels of study?

In view of these defining features it was necessary to name the new courses appropriately, respecting the terminology already associated with existing ways of studying ethics. This led to the adoption of the terms "Ethics Studies" and "Comparative and Applied Ethics."

ACHIEVEMENTS AND PROBLEMS

Such has been the approach to ethics devised in and largely continued since 1997 in our university courses and in a wide range of off-campus offerings to schools, professional bodies, medical bodies, businesses and sporting bodies. The response has been extremely favourable. Enrolments in our anchor course have risen every year from 8 at the first lecture in 1998 to around 300 in 2005, making it the semester course with the highest enrolment on our campus in the B.Soc.Sc. degree. In response to student requests for more such courses, others have been introduced at both undergraduate and post-graduate levels, developments that owe much to the outstanding work of the additional academic staff we have been able to appoint. Regular evaluations of these courses have also yielded student comments which underline the value of what we are attempting to offer, as well as helpful criticisms and suggestions for improvements.

The same is true of the work done in the wider community, some of it at national level, as the need for effective ethics education measures, tailored to both the practical ethical challenges of our society and to its strongly multi-cultural character, makes itself felt and as recourse to faith-based approaches to ethics remain confined to single-faith communities. This is especially evident in the work done by my colleagues in connection with professional ethics for school educators (Parker *et al.*, 2002), biomedical ethics and HIV/AIDS (Stobie, 2003) and the question of African values in the business world (Murove, 2003).

There are also problems. One of them is the absence of accessible published material in Applied Comparative Ethics which does justice to African values and experience. Another is the scarcity of academics in South Africa in the field of Comparative Ethics. A third and related problem is the fact that most black South African academic ethicists operate on a single-faith basis, usually Christianity, which greatly limits our ability to develop our experiment in Comparative Ethics in ways that advance the careers of black academics. A fourth challenge is more academic in nature, namely the lack of a theoretical framework or model with which to unify and do justice to the various strands of our work, with its comparative, philosophical and multi-disciplinary character. A fifth problem stems from the nature of transformation in South Africa as white control passes away and previously disadvantaged communities take their rightful and numerically preponderant place in the country. How credible can white academics in leadership positions, like myself, be in such a situations, above all in ethics, no matter how dedicated to the new, non-racial order? How free can people like me be – if ever - of perceptions of a Eurocentric, northern bias? Work is in progress in connection with each of these difficulties, but the fact remains that extremely healthy enrolments and highly favourable community responses are not in themselves sufficient to deem the experiment begun in 1997 an unqualified success. They do, however, seem to indicate that an innovation in South African ethics may well have come to stay.

REFERENCES

Carpenter, H. (1980) *Jesus.* Oxford: Oxford University Press
Constitution of the Republic of South Africa. Annotated version. Constitutional Assembly, 1996
De Gruchy, J.W. and Prozesky, M. (1991) *A Southern African Guide to World Religions.* Cape Town: David Philip
Kidder, R. (1995) *How Good People Make Tough Choices: Resolving the Dilemmas of Ethical Living.* New York: Fireside Books
Kung, Hans. (1997) *A Global Ethic for Global Politics ands Economics.* London: SCM
Murove, M. F. (2003) The Voice from the Periphery: Towards an African Business Ethics Beyond the Western Heritage. Paper presented at the *Third Annual Conference of the Business Ethics Network of Africa*, Livingstone, Zambia, July 2003
Murphy, N. and Ellis, G. F.R. (1996) *On the Moral Nature of the Universe: Theology, Cosmology and Ethics.* Minneapolis: Fortress Press
Parker, B. *et al.* (2002) *Handbook for the Code of Professional Ethics.* Capetown: South African Council for Educators
Prozesky, M. (1999) The Quest for Inclusive Well-Being: Groundwork for an Ethical Renaissance. Inaugural lecture, University of Natal, Pietermaritzburg, South Africa, 12 May 1999. Available: http://www.unp.ac.za/ethics/centre.htm
Stobie, M. and Slack, C. (2003) Should sponsors provide treatment for HIV infection to participants who become infected during HIV prevention trials?

A view from South Africa. Paper presented at Conferences in South Africa and Switzerland, 2003

Theissen, G. and Merz, A. (1998) *The Historical Jesus: A Comprehensive Guide.* London: SCM

Whitehead, A.N. (ed) (1966) *Modes of Thought.* New York: The Free Press

Zohar, D. (1991). *The Quantum Self.* London: Flamingo

10
Applied and professional ethics: a comparison

Susan A. Illingworth

INTRODUCTION

This chapter draws on a Learning and Teaching Support Network[1] sponsored initiative for the collective examination of professional and academic ethics teaching within a range of disciplines, namely: philosophy, theology and religious studies, bioscience, medicine, dentistry, veterinary medicine, psychology, health sciences and practice, and law.

A number of issues were identified as worthy of further investigation but one of the most striking was the extent to which professional ethics is evolving as a distinct subject area from applied ethics, with which it is often linked. The following discussion defines this distinction largely in terms of learning and teaching, but the issues raised also have implications for the content of professional ethics as an academic discipline.

I shall start with a review of the origins of professional ethics in professional codes of conduct and their impact on higher education benchmarks for ethics teaching. I shall then move on to a consideration of the following areas of divergence between applied and professional ethics:

- Learning and teaching objectives;
- Learning and teaching methodologies;
- Interests served.

The chapter will inevitably generate more questions than answers, but if it serves to stimulate debate about the role of professional ethics within higher education and beyond, it will have served its purpose.

WHY DO WE NEED BOTH APPLIED AND PROFESSIONAL ETHICS?

Anders Milton, then chair of the World Medical Association's Council, stated that '[a] profession is defined by two qualities: firstly, it defines its own area of work, and, secondly it has it own ethics" (Carnall, 1995, 620-622).

This places ethics at the heart of what it means to be a professional of any kind, but unless we can be clear about what is meant by ethics in this context, its implications for higher education will be difficult to determine. Ethics has a long history within departments of philosophy and theology, and students of law have also been expected to develop an understanding of the ethical context within which their subject operates. What these traditional approaches have in common is an emphasis on theory, conceptual analysis and reasoned argument. When students from these subject areas move on to a consideration of actual cases they do so via the application of theory, analysis and reasoned argument; a branch of study labelled applied ethics.

PROFESSIONAL CODES AND BENCHMARKS

Professional ethics, by contrast, has its origin in professional codes of conduct. The earliest of these codes were instituted mainly to protect the interests of their professions and accordingly had as much to do with the first of Milton's two defining qualities – the delineation of an area of work – as they did with ethics. However, over recent years the need to maintain (or in some cases regain) public confidence has pushed obligations to the service user into ever greater prominence and it is these obligations that are now stressed in higher education via the benchmarking academic standards issued by the Quality Assurance Agency for Higher Education. For example:

Dentistry: 'It is essential that all dentists understand the need to act at all times reasonably, responsibly and within the public interest, putting the interests of their patients before those of themselves' (QAA Benchmark for Dentistry, 3).
Midwifery: 'midwifery practice is moral and ethical with the rights, beliefs and values of others acknowledged and respected in a multi-dimensional society' (QAA Benchmark for Midwifery, 8).
Nursing: A registered nurse at the point of qualification should 'apply ethical and legal knowledge to practice ensuring the primacy of patients'/clients'/carers' interests' (QAA Benchmark for Nursing, 9).

While the benchmark statements for all registered professionals within health and social care services state that award holders must demonstrate an understanding of and commitment to their profession's code of conduct, this is supplemented by a requisite that they should:

- Understand the legal and ethical responsibilities of professional practice;
- Exercise a professional duty of care to patients/clients/carers.

What these standards indicate is that the primary function of ethics learning and teaching for health and social care graduates is to promote certain standards of behaviour; to produce alumni who possess not only the knowledge and skills appropriate to their discipline but a disposition to apply this knowledge and skill in accordance with a given set of values.

In some cases, the standards defined for healthcare workers are supplemented by an explicit requirement for graduates to acquire a facility with rational and critical evaluation, for example:

- *Veterinary Medicine*: 'graduates must ... be able to construct reasoned arguments to support their actions and positions on the ethical and social impact of veterinary science and the allied biosciences' (QAA Benchmark for Veterinary Science, 7);
- *Occupational Therapy*: 'The graduate occupational therapist must ... treat individuals with respect and draw on ethical principles in the process of reasoning' (QAA Benchmark for Occupational Therapy, 15).

The capacity for moral reasoning features most strongly in the benchmark statements on ethics within science and technology. For example,

- *Bioscience* graduates 'should expect to be confronted by some of the scientific, moral and ethical questions raised by their study discipline, to consider viewpoints other than their own, and to engage in critical assessment and intellectual argument' (QAA Benchmarks for Biosciences, 3).

The threshold requirement in these subject areas is normally an 'awareness' of relevant ethical issues but typical or modal students are expected to go beyond this, and acquire a deeper understanding, enabling them to offer a critical evaluation of the arguments and exercise their own judgement in discussing possible resolutions[2]. While this approach has much in common with the applied ethics tradition, the benchmarks link reasoning skills directly to their application to the graduate's own research activity or the implementation of a professional code. This suggests that the common underlying purpose of all professional ethics is to ensure that graduates work not only to high academic standards, but to appropriate moral standards too.

PUBLIC ACCOUNTABILITY

The dangers of losing public confidence have been highlighted in recent years by a number of well-publicised scandals in science and medicine[3], but these events took place against a background of an already changing relationship between public and professional in which the public can now access alternative resources via the internet such as Patient UK and the National Health Service's own NHS Direct Online.

Goodman (1998, 11) observes that:

> '[p]ublicly accessible health networks and off-the-shelf decision-support systems may be viewed as occupying a spectrum that ranges between ... 1) A great and democratising service that decentralises healthcare and empowers patients, or 2) a silly and dangerous way to allow people to practice medicine and nursing without licences'.

It is too early to say where on Goodman's spectrum the contribution of online services will lie. Much will depend on the number of users and the extent to which the resources become a replacement for, rather than a supplement to more traditional forms of service provision but at the very least, they offer an alternative to the face-to-face interactions which remain broadly under professional control.

In ethical terms, an increase in service-user autonomy should be welcomed. There might be limits on the contribution that can be expected from the non-specialist on technical and scientific matters but in the realm of value-judgements, especially those of a moral or spiritual nature, there is no reason to think that the professional's view should take precedence. As Gillon (1999, 69) observes:

> [the doctor] is not better trained professionally to make moral assessments than is his patient, and even if he were, many would object that it is not the doctor's role even to advise on his patient's moral decisions let alone make them.

The moral concerns of professionals outside healthcare usually focus on research ethics and the environmental/social impact of their work but here too, the internet is a medium through which the public can gain access to a wealth of information. From official sources such as the Home Office's pages on the use of Animals in Scientific Procedures through the research councils and bodies such as the Nuffield Council on Bioethics to national and international campaigning organisations such as Greenpeace and the Worldwide Fund for Nature, people can inform themselves on ethically sensitive matters and involve themselves in public debate more readily than ever before. A graduate entering a profession likely to attract public interest or concern must therefore be prepared to discuss ethical issues with those who do not share their professional perspective.

INTERPROFESSIONALISM

While benchmarking statements and public accountability provide sufficient reasons for the inclusion of professional ethics in higher education curricula, there is indirect support in the increasing interprofessionalism of work. This interprofessionalism can be overt and structured through the creation of multidisciplinary teams, or the result of a more diffuse requirement for increasing professional collaboration to secure public welfare.

Benchmark statements for registered professionals within health and social care services state that award holders should have a capacity for effective participation in inter-professional and multi-agency approaches and Malin *et al.* (2000, 105-114) have noted that 'professionals skilled at working across organisational boundaries are in high demand'.

Higher education is already beginning to incorporate multidisciplinary education and training provision into pre-registration programmes. For example, at the Dundee University School of Nursing, shared learning between nursing, midwifery and medical students in the field of healthcare ethics has been expanded to include students of social work. The use of interdisciplinary learning as a means to greater interprofessional cooperation is not limited to ethics but the Peach Report (1999, para. 5.39) concluded that the subjects seen to offer most scope for shared learning were ethics and communications skills.

LEARNING AND TEACHING OBJECTIVES

In the preceding section I have outlined some reasons for the emergence of professional ethics within faculties that have no tradition of applied ethics learning and teaching. I now want to look in more detail at they ways in which professional ethics is taught.

APPLIED ETHICS

When applied ethics is taught within a philosophy or theology department the primary learning and teaching objectives will normally include one or more of the following:

- Development of critical reasoning faculties;
- Application of moral theories such as rights, virtue ethics, Consequentialism or Kantian deontology to real-life situations;
- Identification and analysis of morally challenging situations;
- Acquisition of a facility with the language of moral discourse;
- Awareness of multiple perspectives on contested issues;
- Development of coherent principles of thought and action;
- Capacity for verbal and written presentation.

These abilities are deemed to be of benefit to anyone wishing to address ethical issues in a rational, transparent and consistent way, so that while students might be said to acquire a 'philosophical' approach to ethics, this would not be regarded as a barrier to discourse with people outside their discipline, but as a methodology designed to break down such barriers.

When we come to consider professional ethics as taught within faculties of science or heath and social care, it is not immediately apparent that perspectives on ethical issues should vary according to the primary discipline of the student but studies in the field have indicated that this is often the case.

For example, in a study of in-hospital ethics seminars carried out by Alderson *et al.* (2002, 508-521):

> '[a] haematologist noted the frequently discussed contrast between geneticists offering choice and other clinicians recommending best treatment: "The neonatal team have to think about best care, whereas in genetics the ethical goal is more informed choice, when you don't impose your view"'.

Differing perspectives need not be an obstacle to effective discussion, but Edward and Preece (1999, 299-307) report that conflict can arise within multi-disciplinary ethics seminars due to:

- Different perceptions of care;
- Different points of view concerning patients best interests;
- Variations in professional value systems;
- Variations in moral reasoning processes.

This might suggest that modules should adopt a philosophical approach as a way of superseding the values and methodologies of the students' primary disciplines but consideration should be given to the potential impact of such a move on student motivation. When ethics modules are offered on an optional basis, students can be assumed to have some interest in the subject but the increasing prevalence of benchmarked standards for ethics means that many students will attend a class because it is mandatory. This is of particular concern given that ethics can be a demanding area of study even for those with a thorough grounding and interest in moral theory, and must be doubly so for students for whom ethics (and in some cases the humanities as a whole) represent alien territory. Students of professional ethics might have personality types, skills, aptitudes and interests well suited to their primary area of study but less conducive to one based on theoretical reasoning and conceptual analysis. Levitt (1995, 70) observes that '[s]tudents may have a more instrumental attitude to their studies than expected by staff versed in the values of a liberal education'. These students will want to see the 'point' of devoting precious time and effort to an ethics module so attention must be paid to the learning and teaching objectives that it is intended to serve.

PROFESSIONAL ETHICS

Professional ethics teaching materials vary widely but they normally serve one or more of the following learning outcomes:

- The application of research guidelines or a professional code;
- Promotion of good professional conduct;
- Engagement in reflective practice;
- Exploration of background moral beliefs;
- Development of empathy.

More specifically, they aim to help students identify which choice or course of action is correct in a given set of circumstances, by reference to such things as:

- Government legislation and guidelines;
- Professional code(s) of conduct;
- Research guidelines;
- Canonical text(s).

These objectives have the merit of making clear to students the reasons for their obligation to study professional ethics, for it can be located in concrete advantages such as the formulation of research proposals that will gain ethics committee approval, the avoidance of professional censure and prosecution, and the ability to justify their conduct or area of research to the general public. However, in so far as these learning outcomes refer to morally desirable *behaviour* they would be considered inappropriate to the philosophical approach.

A teacher of applied ethics might hope that classes will help students gain a greater understanding of their own beliefs and their reasons for holding them. This might lead a student to develop or even transform their moral values and to modify their actions accordingly, but it is not an applied ethics learning objective to persuade students of the merits of a particular set of moral beliefs, or motivate them to attain predefined standards of behaviour.

McNulty (2002, 361-372) states that '[p]hilosophers are ill-suited to the role of moral guidance. Instead they should set out to instil in students the necessity of being able to formulate rational bases for moral views'. Similarly, within philosophical medical ethics Gillon (1999, 1) rules out the following concerns:

- The quoting or drawing up professional codes of conduct;
- An account of the legal constraints on doctors' behaviour;
- An effort to discover the attitudes of a particular community;
- The expression of religious rules or sentiments.

Instead, there is an emphasis on 'the analytic activity in which the concepts, assumptions, beliefs, attitudes, emotions, reasons, and arguments underlying medicomoral decision making are examined critically' (Gillon, 1999, 2).

By contrast, it is expected that students of professional ethics will allow their actions to be shaped and guided by the appropriate professional code or research guidelines, both in higher education and in their professional lives. Even where courses are not overtly prescriptive, there can be an implicit intention to go beyond the delivery of a body of knowledge by entering the realm of character development and the promotion of professional virtues.

The learning and teaching objectives of professional ethics can therefore be regarded as a significant expansion (and in some cases substitution) of what is normally covered by applied ethics. Modules structured around the enhancement of moral judgement alone will not suffice; learning environments capable of influencing moral behaviour will be required.

INFLUENCING MORAL BEHAVIOUR

Rest (1983, 556-629) defined a four-component model for moral behaviour comprising moral sensitivity, moral judgement, moral motivation and moral character.

Moral sensitivity is the ability to interpret a situation as moral. Students of both applied and professional ethics need to develop 'a practical skill that enables one to recognise when an act, situation or certain aspects of a situation have moral implications' (Jaegar, 2001, 131-142) but professional ethics students need to be able to do this in circumstances when their attention is being directed elsewhere.

Moral motivation involves prioritising the moral over other significant concerns, while moral character means being able to construct and implement actions that service the morally desirable choice. It has already been argued that motivation and character development are largely excluded from the learning and teaching objectives of applied philosophy, which focuses on moral judgement, but their importance within professional ethics highlights a further difference between the two approaches.

Applied ethics concentrates on what Seedhouse (1998, 39) terms specific or dramatic ethics such as end of life issues and the domain of the tragic choice. Professional ethics also prepares students to face moral dilemmas but is equally concerned with what Seedhouse calls persisting ethics; the underlying ethical issues that underpin daily working practice. Ashcroft (2000, 287-295) argues that '[m]edical ethical problems ... must be identified as features of an evolving medical Scenario'. These scenarios will involve a multiplicity of factors, only some of which will be morally significant and good ethical judgement will often be implicit – a way of acting rather than an interval of reflection and analysis. The professional must respond speedily, assessing the situation and 'seeing' how they should proceed without being aware of any deliberative procedure. Accordingly, their training must help them to reach a point where their knowledge and understanding is so firmly embedded that correct decision-making is a rapid and seamless process resulting in actions that feel like second nature. Moral clarity is one aspect of this preparedness and Pritchard (1995, 24) argues that a code of practice:

> 'will not be an effective tool for moral guidance unless those upon whom it is binding have had an effective opportunity to embrace its provisions ... and internalise the ethical principles embodied in them'.

CAN PROFESSIONAL ETHICS BE TAUGHT?

So far, I have suggested that professional ethics differs from applied ethics in two key areas. Firstly, a professional ethics teacher can expect their students to have interests and aptitudes appropriate to their primary discipline rather than those suited to a critical examination of applied moral theory. Secondly, professional ethics includes new objectives such as the shaping of character and the promotion of professional virtues, which require additional learning and teaching strategies. There is, however, a lack of consensus regarding the means through which standards of behaviour *can* be taught within higher education.

ROLE MODELS

Studies indicate that historically, professional conduct was learned mainly through example; the Pond Report (Boyd, 1987) found that medical students were heavily influenced by role models.

Ashcroft (2000, 287-295) describes this traditional method of professional inculcation as the vocational or V-model, in which the chief modes of instruction are:

> The emulation of senior professionals 'since right attitude cannot be formally taught but only acquired and developed, like a habit'.

> '[L]ectures providing a minimum of formal knowledge of the law and professional codes applying to medicine'.

The V-model is subject to a number of concerns. Firstly, the hierarchical nature of many professional environments means that ethical decisions can bring the agent into conflict with a superior from whom they would normally accept instruction. Milgram (1983) showed that heteronymous moral reasoning can occur in situations where adults perceive themselves as being under an obligation to accept the authority of another. Inequalities of power and authority within and between professions might inhibit junior or subordinate members of staff from expressing moral concerns (Alderson, Farsides & Williams (2002, 508-521). Secondly, there is a danger that students will not distinguish between scientific/technical judgements and ethical ones when learning from people whom they respect professionally. Pellegrino & Thomasma (1993, 177) state that:

> ' the faculty model's professional standing as a scientist or clinician often legitimates her personal ethical behaviour as well. That behaviour might be something the student previously had considered morally dubious'.

Unless senior role models are themselves habituated to behave in accordance with the values of their professional code, they will be unreliable as means of propagating that code to their students.

Thirdly, the rapidly changing nature of science in general and medicine in particular means that there are many cases in which there is either no precedent at all, or the precedents that do exist are too widely contested to function authoritatively.

ALTERNATIVES

Motivation and character have already been indicated as factors in determining a student's preference for their primary area of study and as a possible barrier to a facility with applied ethics. These factors find their counterpart in alternative approaches to professional ethics that start from the general characteristics and prevailing motivators of the profession as a whole, although all of these approaches have their critics.

The duty of care is a benchmarked requirement for all the healthcare professions and has been used as the basis for an ethics of care, which has been particularly strong in nursing, placing 'decision-making value on the feelings, attachment bonds, desires and constraints of the people involved' (Jaeger, 2001,131-142). Many nursing modules in higher education stress empathy as a desirable personal quality in applicants and it has also been advocated as a valuable professional skill in doctors (Halpern, 2003, 670-674). Gilligan (1982) defined the traditional view of morality as a 'masculine' position of justice and rights premised on equality and contrasted it with an allegedly 'female' morality of care premised on non-violence but this claim has not been vindicated by later research, much of which has suggested that 'both males and females reason based on justice and care' (Murray, 2002).

The use of exemplars and models is a key teaching method in this approach as 'it is only through a confrontation with images, stories and models of good care that nurses will be stimulated to evaluate and correct their own caring practice' (Gastmans 1998, 236-245). An emphasis on caring has been criticised for preventing nurses from becoming a properly scientific discipline (Paley 2002, 25-35)), but Gastmans rejects as false the dichotomy in which '..."care" stands for the soft, caring and existential involvement while "cure" represents the hard, scientific and clinical approach of medicine'.

A range of teaching strategies designed to enhance students' powers of empathy have been described, including the use of role-play (Barnbaum, 2001, 63-75), narrative (Greenhalgh & Hurwitz, 1999, 48-50) and experiential learning (Henry-Tillman, R. et al., 2002, 659-662).

One way of framing the importance of caring for a given profession is to define it as a professional virtue. While the ethics of care is largely confined to public-service professions, the professional virtue approach has a wider application and has figured significantly in recent literature (see Pellegrino & Thomasma (1993), Sellman (1997), Scott (1998), Forsberg (2001), Gould (2002) and Smith & Godfrey (2002)).

Pellegrino & Thomasma (1993, 179) state that when properly taught, virtue ethics can:

- Sensitise students to what constitutes an ethical issue or problem;
- Force self-criticism and examination of their values;
- Demand that reasons are given for moral choices;
- Demand that opposing viewpoints are given an adequate response;
- Encourage the laying bare of underlying pre-logical assumptions.

It is argued that these outcomes will, in turn, have some impact on the student's character.

MEASURING EFFECTIVENESS

One criticism of professional virtue ethics is that there are no reliable methods of selecting students or professionals on the basis of good or virtuous character. All the selection systems on offer (interviews, character references, psychological tests, record of public service etc.) have some deficiencies but Pellegrino & Thomasma (1993, 179) argue that there are many elements of medical education that do not yield to easy measurement. Indeed, assessment within professional ethics teaching is something of a moot point regardless of the discipline, although many methods have been proposed[4]).

A more fundamental criticism of this approach is that good character or professional virtue is not sufficient to ensure that professionals behave ethically. Gillon (1999, 33) compares the attempt to define the virtues of a good doctor 'without critical philosophical study of the moral assumptions and objectives of medical practice' to 'specifying the syllabus for therapeutics while claiming that neither medical students nor the doctors laying down the syllabus need to know any pharmacology'. A partial response to this criticism might be offered if advocates of professional virtue do not intend to rule out learning and teaching methods based on the enhancement of critical reasoning but rather to define criteria by which the success of those methods can be measured. However this will not meet the objections of those who oppose virtue ethics on the grounds that ethical sensitivity and moral reasoning are the only acceptable aims for ethics teaching (Clarkeburn, 2002).

REASONING SKILLS

None of the alternatives considered above are incompatible with the study of moral theory, but the question remains as to whether students can acquire the moral judgement skills essential to moral behaviour without it. Ashcroft (2000, 287-295) notes that a refined V-model within medical ethics, based on a medically approved bioethics, has the consequence that 'students may need to be taught at least some of its results, and perhaps also its methods, as an aid to making reliable judgements when they practice'. However he argues that this does not mean that every professional must be a skilled ethicist in the applied ethics tradition, for '[i]n teaching awareness of philosophical methods and materials, we are not trying to train philosophers, but practical reasoners'.

Practical reasoning skills will probably be taught and assessed most effectively when offered as part of a separate ethics module, but the development of moral motivation and moral character might be more readily acquired when embedded in a course with broader objectives. Course design must therefore take a full and rounded view of all the available methods of promoting professional virtues and standards, a view in which overt ethics learning and teaching might be the tip of the iceberg. However, transparency would require that embedded ethical training should be highlighted in course descriptions and handbooks, so that students are aware of values and principles promoted by implicit means. It is also incumbent on those responsible for course design to ensure consistency between overt and embedded ethics teaching.

Ethics teaching need not be uniform even within a given profession; the professional virtues of a theatre nurse might be different to those of a palliative care nurse. A variety of modules, based on a range of ethics learning and teaching approaches, would allow students to incorporate their choices in this aspect of their studies into broader decisions regarding their preferred role within their intended profession. If ethics options are linked to other aspects of specialism within the overarching structure of the course, students are more likely to experience it as supportive of their primary discipline and as an integral part of their fitness to practice.

CUI BONO

> 'The key feature in this statement ... is the explicit articulation of the academic and practitioner standards associated with the award in nursing. This duality reflects the significance of the academic award as the route to registration for professional practice' (QAA Benchmark for Nursing, 1).

I now come to the concluding section of my review of the key differences between applied and professional ethics, namely, the interests they serve. Higher education meets a number of social needs, but as the provider of a high quality learning and teaching environment, its service-users are the students and it is their interests that inform course structure and content. There is no reason to think that applied ethics is an exception to this rule but professional ethics includes disciplines for which graduation is a mark not only of academic attainment, but of fitness to practice.

When a professional carer is faced with a moral dilemma, there are many interests to consider:

- The needs of the service-user;
- The professional consequences for the service provider;
- The personal and emotional consequences for the service provider;
- Impact on colleagues;
- Impact on the service providing profession;
- Impact on society.

Conflict can arise between these competing interests and their relative weight has significant learning and teaching implications.

Scott (1998, 477–496) argues that:

> 'there is a real danger within the nursing context that ethical principles will be used as a stick with which to beat nurses, rather than as providing a potential framework within which to consider the real complexity of the issues that can arise in health care'.

A relationship between a professional and a service-user will always, however formalised, have at its heart an interaction between two people. Whilst it might be reasonable to think of the professional as an abstraction, one must consider whether current moves towards a more holistic interpretation of the service-user (Botes, 2000; Sanson-Fisher et al., 2002), should be accompanied by some recognition and respect for the service-provider's needs and beliefs. Henry (1995, 103) stresses the importance of 'psychological contracts' within caring organisations such as health and education. These relate to 'expectations, attitudes, self-esteem, self-value, loyalty, respect and opportunities' which, in addition to their instrumental importance to the organisation's ability to achieve its goals, 'are important for psychological well-being generally'.

Teachers must therefore identify their primary stakeholder before defining course structure and content. There are three main contenders for this role with differing implications for the module's primary learning objectives:

- *The Student*: modules would enhance the student's capacity to make moral choices that they can live with and reduce the stress caused by moral indecision and confusion.
- *The Service-User*: modules would promote conduct that serves the best interests of the service-user within the profession of which the graduate will be a registered practitioner.
- *The Profession*: modules would promote conduct that serves the best interests of the profession of which the graduate will be a registered practitioner.

It will sometimes be possible for an ethics module to serve all these interests simultaneously but where conflicts arise, teachers must decide where their priorities should lie.

ETHICS, CITIZENSHIP AND SUPRADISCIPLINARITY

It could be argued that while a professional has some non-reciprocal obligations towards service-users and the general public, the difference between the standards of moral behaviour to be expected of a professional and the public should not be exaggerated. Professional standards designed to ensure that the public is treated respectfully should, in theory, ensure that this respect is reciprocated but public attitudes are often influenced by external factors over which professional has little control. Public entitlements might therefore need to be correlated by public duties. Similarly, a professional's capacity to offer coherent and rational moral arguments will serve little purpose if the persons to whom those arguments are addressed are unable to understand their force or respond in kind.

Martha Nussbaum (Cornelius & Laurie, 2003) argues that all citizens should have the following three abilities:

- The ability to reason critically in Socratic fashion; to test and examine their beliefs, looking for flaws.
- The ability to think like a citizen of the entire world, not just of some one nation.
- Narrative imagination; the ability to think what it is like to be in the shoes of a person different from themselves.

If higher education were to adopt these abilities as learning objectives for all its students, professional ethics would have a sound basis on which to build. It would therefore be worth considering whether an appraisal of the ultimate objectives of professional ethics should recognise the supradisciplinarity of the subject, for ethics is fundamentally concerned with all human actions and agency, not merely those of the professional.

These wider concerns can be largely ignored by teachers of applied ethics, for whom the emphasis lies on the dissemination of a body of knowledge and the enhancement of the rational and analytical skills. Within professional ethics, the dynamism and immediacy of its relationship with external factors warrants a debate among all those involved in the subject, to ensure that the multiplicity of learning objectives, teaching methodologies and interests served are subject to proper scrutiny and debate. Applied ethics has much to offer professional ethics based on its long experience of the subject matter, but it can only contribute this expertise effectively in cooperation with those whose subject specific knowledge includes a profound understanding of the contexts in which professionals must bring theory to life.

NOTES

1. Now the Higher Education Academy. See <http://www.heacademy.ac.uk/> (Accessed 16/06/05)
2. See the benchmark statements for Agriculture, Forestry, Agricultural Sciences, Anthropology; Archaeology; Biosciences; Building and Surveying; Earth Sciences, Environmental Sciences and Environmental Studies; Engineering; Food Sciences and Consumer Sciences; Hospitality, Leisure, Sport and Tourism; Linguistics; Politics and International Relations; Social Work & Policy; Sociology Town and Country Planning on <http://www.qaa.ac.uk/academicinfrastructure/benchmark/> (Accessed 15/06/05)
   See the Harold Shipman case <http://www.the-shipman-inquiry.org.uk/home.asp> (Accessed 15/06/05), the Alder Hey Inquiry <http://www.rlcinquiry.org.uk/> (Accessed 15/06/05), the Bristol Royal Infirmary Inquiry <http://www.bristol-inquiry.org.uk/final_report/index.htm> (Accessed 15/06/05) the BSE Inquiry <http://www.bseinquiry.gov.uk/> (Accessed 15/06/05) and the Foot and Mouth Disease Inquiry <http://archive.cabinetoffice.gov.uk/fmd/> (Accessed 15/06/05).
3. Examples of proposed assessment methods within Professional Ethics:

   DIT Defining Issues Test (Rest *et al.* 1999)
   TESS Test for Ethical Sensitivity in Science (Clarkeburn, 2002)
   ERT Ethical Reasoning Tool (McAlpine, Kristianson & Poroch, 1997)
   DEST Dental Ethical Sensitivity Test (Bebeau,1994)
   Perry Questionnaire (Perry, 1999)
   SRM Sociomoral Reflection Measure (Basinger, Gibbs & Fuller, 1995)

MJI		Moral Judgement Interview (Colby *et al.*, 1987)
FCM		Four Component Model (Rest, 1983)
MES		Multidimensional ethics scale (Reidenbach & Robin, 1990)
PROI		Professional Role Orientation Inventory (Bebeau, Born & Ozar, 1993)
REST		Racial Ethical Sensitivity Test (Brabeck *et al.*, 2000).

REFERENCES

Alderson P., Farsides, B. & Williams, C. (2002) Examining ethics in practice: health service professionals' evaluations of in hospital ethics seminars, *Nursing Ethics*, vol. 9, no. 5, 508-521
Animals in Scientific Procedures: <http://www.homeoffice.gov.uk/comrace/animals/reference.html#> (Accessed 15/06/05)
Ashcrof, R. E. (2000) Teaching for Patient-Centred Ethics, *Medicine, Health Care and Philosophy*, 3, 287–295
Barnbaum, D. R. (2001) Teaching Empathy in Medical Ethics, *Teaching Philosophy*, vol. 24, no. 1, 63-75
Basinger, K. S., Gibbs, J. C. & Fuller, D. (1995) Context and the measurement of moral judgment, *International Journal of Behavioral Development*, 18, 537-556
Bebeau, M. (1994) Influencing the moral dimensions of dental practice, in Rest, J. & Narvaez, D. (eds.), *Moral development in the professions*, Hillsdale, NJ: Erlbaum, 121-146
Bebeau, M. J., Born, D. O. & Ozar, D. T. (1993) The development of a Professional Role Orientation Inventory, *Journal of the American College of Dentists*, 60, 27–33
Botes, A. (2000) A comparison between the ethics of justice and the ethics of care, *Journal of Advanced Nursing*, vol. 32, no.5, 1071-075
Boyd, K.M. ed. (1987) *The Pond Report. Report of a working party on the teaching of medical ethics*. London: IME Publication
Brabeck, M. M., Rogers, L. A., Sirin, S., Henderson, J., Benvenuto, M., Weaver, M. & Ting, K. (2000) Increasing Ethical Sensitivity to Racial and Gender Intolerance in Schools: Development of the Racial Ethical Sensitivity Test', *Ethics and Behavior*, vol. 10, no. 2, 119-137
Carnall, D. (1995) New broom at the top? An interview with Anders Milton, the chairman of the World Medical Association's Council, *British Medical Journal*, 311, 620-622
Clarkeburn, H. (2002) The Aims and Practice of Ethics Education in an Undergraduate Curriculum: reasons for choosing a skills approach, *Journal of Further and Higher Education*, vol. 26, no. 4, 307-315
Clarkeburn, H. (2002) A Test for Ethical Sensitivity in Science, *Journal of Moral Education*, 1 December 2002, vol. 31, no. 4, 439-453
Colby, A., Kohlberg, L., Speicher, B. *et al.* (1987) *The Measurement of Moral Judgement*, vol. 1-2. New York: Cambridge University Press

Cornelius, N. & Laurie, N. (2003) Capable Management: An interview with Martha Nussbaum, *Philosophy of Management*, 3: 1, 3-16

Dundee University School of Nursing & Midwifery on: <http://www.dundee.ac.uk/nursingmidwifery/index.html?org_id=1> (Accessed 15/06/05)

Edward, C. & Preece, P. E. (1999) Shared Teaching in Healthcare Ethics: A Report on the Beginning of an Idea, *Nursing Ethics*, Vol. 6 (4), 299-307

Forsburgh, R. P. (2001) Teaching virtue theory using a model from Nursing, *Teaching Philosophy*, 24:2, 155-166

Gastmans, C. (1998) Challenges to Nursing Values in a Changing Nursing Environment, *Nursing Ethics*, 5 (3), 236-245

Gilligan, C. (1982) *In a Different voice: Psychological Theory and Women's Development*, Cambridge: Harvard University Press

Gillon, R. (1999) *Philosophical Medical Ethics*, Chichester: John Wiley & Sons

Goodman, K. W. (1998) Bioethics and Health Informatics: An Introduction, in Goodman, K. W. (ed.) *Ethics, Computing and Medicine*. Cambridge: Cambridge University Press

Gould, J. B. (2002) Better Hearts: Teaching Applied Virtue Ethics, *Teaching Philosophy*, vol. 25, no. 1, 1-25

Greenhalgh, T. & Hurwitz, B., (1999) Narrative based medicine: Why study narrative? *British Medical Journal*, no. 318, 48-50

Greenpeace: <http://www.greenpeace.org.uk> (Accessed 15/06/05)

Halpern, J. (2003) What is Clinical Empathy? *Journal of General Internal Medicine*, vol. 18, no. 8, 670-674.

Henry, C. (1995) Mismatch of Policy and Practice, in Henry, C. (ed.) *Professional Ethics and Organisational Change in Education and Health*. London: Edward Arnold

Henry-Tillman, R. *et al.* (2002) The medical student as patient navigator as an approach to teaching empathy, *The American Journal of Surgery*, vol. 183, 6, 659-662

Murray, M. E. (2002) Moral Development and Moral Education: An Overview on <http://tigger.uic.edu/~lnucci/MoralEd/overview.html>(Accessed 15/06/05)

Jaeger, S. M. (2001) Teaching health care ethics: the importance of moral sensitivity for moral reasoning, *Nursing Philosophy*, vol. 2, no. 2, 131-142

Levitt, M. (1995) 'Higher Education and Values in Henry C. (ed.) *Professional Ethics and Organisational Change in Education and Health*. London: Edward Arnold

Malin, N. A, Wilmot, S. & Beswick, J. A. (2000) The use of an ethical advisory group in a learning disability service, *Journal of Learning Disabilities*, vol. 4 (2), 105-114

McAlpine H.; Kristjanson L. & Poroch D. (1997) Development and testing of the ethical reasoning tool (ERT): an instrument to measure the ethical reasoning of nurses, *Journal of Advanced Nursing*, vol. 25, no. 6,1151-1161

McNulty, M. (2002) Teaching Applied Ethics Effectively, *Teaching Philosophy*, Volume 21, Number 4, 361-372

Milgram, S. (1983) *Obedience to Authority: An Experimental View*. New York: Harper/Collins.
MRC Centre for Best Practice for Animals in Research on: <http://www.mrc.ac.uk/index/public-interest/public-ethics_and_best_practice/public-use_of_animals_in_research> (Accessed 15/06/05)
NHS Direct Online: <http://www.nhsdirect.nhs.uk/index.asp> (Accessed 15/06/05)
Nuffield Council on Bioethics: <http://www.nuffieldbioethics.org/home/> (Accessed 15/06/05)
Paley, J. (2002) Caring as a slave morality: Nietzschean themes in nursing ethics, *Journal of Advanced Nursing*, vol. 40, no. 1, 25-35
Patient UK on: <http://www.patient.co.uk/> (Accessed 15/06/05)
Peach, L. (Chair) (1999) *Fitness for Practice, Commissioned by The United Kingdom Central Council (UKCC) for Nursing, Midwifery and Health Visiting*: <http://www.nmc-uk.org/nmc/main/publications/fitnessForPractice.pdf> (Accessed 15/06/05)
Pellegrino, E. D. & Thomasma, D. C. (1993) *The Virtues in Medical Practice*, (Oxford: Oxford University Press)
Perry, W. G. J. (1999) *Forms of Ethical and Intellectual Development in the College Years: a scheme (San Francisco*, CA: Jossey-Bass
Pritchard, J. (1995) Applied Ethics and Managing Change in the Health Field, in Henry C. (ed.) *Professional Ethics and Organisational Change in Education and Health*, London: Edward Arnold, 24
QAA Benchmarks <http://www.qaa.ac.uk/academicinfrastructure/benchmark> (Accessed 15/06/05)
QAA Benchmark for Bioscience: <http://www.qaa.ac.uk/academicinfrastructure/benchmark/honours/biosciences.pdf> (Accessed 15/06/05)
QAA Benchmark for Dentisty <http://www.qaa.ac.uk/academicinfrastructure/benchmark/honours/Dentistry.pdf> (Accessed 15/06/05)
QAA Benchmark for Midwifery: <http://www.qaa.ac.uk/academicinfrastructure/benchmark/health/midwifery.pdf> (Accessed 15/06/05)
QAA Benchmark for Nursing: <http://www.qaa.ac.uk/academicinfrastructure/benchmark/health/nursing.pdf>(Accessed 15/06/05)
QAA Benchmark for Occupational Therapy <http://www.qaa.ac.uk/academicinfrastructure/benchmark/health/ot.pdf> (Accessed 15/06/05)
QAA Benchmark for Veterinary Science: <http://www.qaa.ac.uk/academicinfrastructure/benchmark/honours/vet_sci.pdf>, (Accessed 15/06/05)
QAA Benchmarks for Biosciences <http://www.qaa.ac.uk/academicinfrastructure/benchmark/honours/biosciences.pdf> (Accessed 15/06/05)
QAA Benchmarks for Health Professionals: <http://www.qaa.ac.uk/academicinfrastructure/benchmark/health>(Accessed 15/06/05)
Reidenbach, R. E. & Robin, D. P. (1990) Toward the Development of a Multidimensional Scale for Improving Evaluations in Business Ethics, *Journal of Business Ethics*, 9, 639– 653
Rest, J. R. (1983) Morality, in Mussen, P. H. (ser. ed.), Flavell, J. & Markman, E.

(vol. eds.), *Handbook of Child Psychology: Cognitive Development*, Vol. 3. Wiley: New York, 556-629

Rest, J., Narvaez, D., Bebeau, M. J. & Thoma, S. J. (1999) A neo-Kohlbergian approach: The DIT and Schema Theory, *Educational Psychology Review*, 11 (4), 291-324

Sanson-Fisher, R.W. *et al.* (2002) Trialling a new way to learn clinical skills: systematic clinical appraisal and learning, *Medical Education*, vol. 36, no. 11, 1028-1034

Scott, P. A. (1998) Professional Ethics: are we on the wrong track? *Nursing Ethics*, vol. 5, no. 6, 477-496

Seedhouse, D. (1998) *Ethics: The Heart of Health Care*. John Wiley & Sons: Chichester, 39

Sellman, D. (1997) The Virtues in the Moral Education of Nurses: Florence Nightingale Revisited, *Nursing Ethics*, vol. 4, no. 1, 3-11

Smith, K.V. & Godfrey, N. S. (2002) Being a good nurse and doing the right thing: a qualitative study, *Nursing Ethics*, vol. 9, no. 3, 301-312

Welcome Trust Biomedical Ethics Programme on: <http://www.wellcome.ac.uk/doc_WTD003247.html> (Accessed 15/06/05)

Worldwide Fund for Nature: <http://www.wwf.org.uk/core/index.asp> (Accessed 15/06/05)

11
"Wisdom cries aloud in the street"

Using service-learning to teach ethics across the curriculum

Elizabeth Weiss Ozorak

Despair over the moral condition of the rising generations is nothing new: in the early years of the 20th century, psychologist William James called "moral flabbiness... our [American] national disease."[1] Yet the present time, on our side of the Atlantic at least, seems particularly devoid of a shared moral compass. This lack is conspicuously evident among adolescents and young adults, who are far less likely to vote and join civic organizations and more likely to identify material wealth as their top priority than their older counterparts are now or were at their age. This has led American liberal arts colleges to embrace civic engagement as the new mandate for higher education. While I am skeptical of the stampede to embed civic values and ethics in the liberal arts curriculum – perhaps because I remember the stampede of the very same institutions to disengage from any hint of value bias during the 1970s, when I was an undergraduate – I believe it to be an important move. If we accept that higher education ought to be about the business of inculcating ethical awareness in young people, then we need to consider pedagogies that will allow us to do that across the curriculum, not merely in a subset of courses earmarked as courses about ethics.

Based on a growing body of research, I will argue that service-learning provides one of the best opportunities for teaching ethical aspects of all kinds of disciplines as well as one of the best preparations an undergraduate institution can offer students for the kinds of ethical dilemmas they might face in the 'real world'. Service-learning is defined as the learning that occurs when community service work that meets real community needs is integrated into an academic course, such that the academic requirements and service requirements of the course are mutually illuminating. There is evidence that service-learning has a broad impact on the attitudes and aspirations of college and university students and that this impact is significantly greater than that of community service undertaken outside of a course context, even though such service does cause some change in attitudes (Astin, Sax and Avalos, 1999; Astin, Vogelgesang, Ikeda and Yee, 2000; Moely, McFarland, Miron, Mercer & Ilustre 2002; Morgan and Streb, 2001).

Moral reasoning is one kind of thinking that seems to be enhanced – qualitatively – by service-learning (Boss, 1994; Neururer and Rhoads, 1998; Leming, 2001). In particular, the 'ethic of care' first described by Carol Gilligan (1982) seems to develop through work that invites greater identification with those who are initially construed as very different from oneself. What remains is to delineate the mechanisms and trajectories by which service-learning fosters moral development. I suggest that basic cognitive mechanisms of awareness, attention and categorization or schematization account for some of the change, but that some is also due to practice in developing ethical heuristics to address a shifting set of situations.

Morality is inescapably social, arising as it does out of a particular culture's web of beliefs and people's experiences of bumping up against one another. Although certain broad moral principles may appear to be stable across cultures and generations – for instance, the Judeo-Christian rule 'you shall not steal' has been taught and enforced in many countries for many centuries – it is also true that the definition of 'stealing' has been far from consistent across time and culture. That is to say, all cultures distinguish between moral and immoral, and most categorize stealing as immoral, but they do not necessarily include the same behaviors in the category of stealing. For example, the notion that one's ideas are personal property and should not be stolen is relatively modern: protection of written or printed ideas became part of British common law only in the 18th century, as printing presses made printed matter widely available. Today the technology of the internet makes it so much easier to copy another person's material – with or without their permission – that new areas of law have developed to address ambiguities of ownership that could not have existed prior to computers and on-line exchange of information.

There are also areas of ambiguity even within time and culture. As a teacher who favors group work on projects, I routinely struggle with the difficulty of evaluating individual performance in what is essentially a collective thinking environment, where students may honestly not know whose ideas were whose to begin with. I persist in the struggle because I believe that it is at least as useful for students to learn to work together as it is for them to get nuanced feedback on their own work. Interestingly, students attend to different ethical aspects of group work than I do: they become hugely exercised if they see the actual workload of the project being inequitably distributed, but the ownership of particular ideas in the finished paper rarely seems to concern them.

These examples make two important points about moral thinking. First, many ethical situations are messy – that is to say, they are ill-defined problems. Either the problem itself is ambiguous, or the rules for reaching an answer or evaluating its rightness are unclear, perhaps because two goods or two evils are involved and there is no established way of quantifying them for direct comparison. Ill-defined problems do not permit the use of algorithms (rules that, if followed correctly, guarantee a right answer). Heuristics, however – rules of thumb that make a right answer more likely – can be extremely valuable in solving ill-defined problems.

Second, because so many of the problems encountered in real life are ill-defined, students must learn not only to apply heuristics that someone else has found helpful but also to invent heuristics they will need in the future to solve problems that cannot be foreseen. In my own field, psychology, we teach students early and often the ethical guidelines adopted by the American Psychological Association (APA), including avoidance of harm, informed consent for participation in research and protection of privacy. However, in our mid-level and upper-level courses we go to great lengths to help them recognize that interpretation and application of the guidelines is a moving target. Privacy, like ownership of ideas, has acquired a new set of ambiguities on the internet. For example, is a chat room private or public? If I want to study conversations in a chat room, must the participants consent to be observed?

There is a third aspect to moral education, and that is the ability to recognize situations as ethical dilemmas in the first place. Again using the APA guidelines as an example, psychologists are warned against dual roles – for example, romantic relationships with clients or, perhaps less obviously, therapeutic relationships with students in our classes. Among many important reasons for this prohibition, it avoids abuse of power in pressuring a vulnerable person into a relationship. It is helpful for students to learn to avoid these overlapping relationships, but they also need to learn the underlying ethical principles about social power dynamics and be able to recognize them as they arise in other situations. Once they identify the moral issue involved, they can use the underlying principles to generate new heuristics for action. In short, education in ethics is intended to affect *how* students think as well as *what* they think about.

All experiential learning, including service-learning, has certain advantages for long-term retention and application of knowledge. Cognitive research has amply demonstrated that when students must generate material and apply it to a variety of contexts, they recall it better than when they simply read it over, months or even years after the fact (Bjork, 2003). The more inference and problem-solving are called for, the greater the difference. What is more, material applied to oneself is more memorable than the same material applied to any other context, probably because of the way human memory is structured (Matlin, 1998). And because procedural memory (how to do things) functions a little differently than declarative memory (memory for facts), personal experience is especially critical to applications of skills and knowledge. This is the rationale for internships and residencies, but is equally true at beginning levels of disciplines – hence the need for laboratory courses.

Service-learning, however, is more than experiential learning with the community as laboratory. It has some particular strengths with respect to the agenda of moral education. First, issues of social responsibility are brought to the foreground as students are placed with social service agencies or with community organizations that have articulated a need. Their assumptions about various kinds of people are tested by their interactions on site as they meet people with problems they may not have had to deal with themselves, ranging from physical ailments to emotional disorders to a history of abuse to crisis-level poverty. Class discussions, reading and writing assignments force them to examine their assumptions and initial reactions to both the people and the work. Issues as broad as social justice and as specific as whether it is all right to offer to baby-sit for agency clients are likely to arise in the course of their work. The fact that there are obvious consequences for making good or bad choices compels most students to grow into the role they have taken on, although not always immediately.

Of course, it matters greatly what the professor's approach to these experiences is. By this I mean not simply how the service itself is set up and introduced and how the assignments are integrated with the community work, but also the professor's attitudes towards the community, service work and social justice generally. By shaping the questions that are asked as well as by responding to our students' reflections, we lead them to notice and remember specific aspects of their experiences and privilege some interpretations over others. This is why course-based community service is more powerful than volunteering alone, but it also places a considerable responsibility on faculty to think through (ethically) the consequences of their pedagogical choices for the students, the community agencies and their clients.

My students typically arrive at school with two kinds of political frameworks, both of them prevalent in American culture. Political philosopher David Lisman (1998) calls them the neoconservative perspective and the consumerist perspective. Both are highly individualistic, holding the individual largely responsible for his or her problems and believing that the less government intervenes in economic matters, the better; both hold economic freedom and the pursuit of wealth to be among the greatest goods, and both presume in one way or another that people generally get what they deserve.

It is self-evident how views of this type lead to contempt for the poor at worst, condescending sympathy at best, and generate band-aids for social problems rather than addressing their roots. This is known as 'pulling people out of the river without asking why so many are falling in.' The ethical learning in service-learning commences when students go upstream to investigate the nature of that slippery slope. Partly to counteract students' initial frameworks and force them to attend to new information, I emphasize systemic causes and responses to social problems, and I encourage them to try to understand how those problems might look from a perspective different, perhaps less privileged, than their own.

In the past few years I have systematically collected observations about service-learning from the students in my own classes. Students worked between 10 and 32 hours at one of four agencies serving the poor, the mentally ill, or at-risk youth; the class with more hours had a choice of agencies, while those with the shorter commitment were assigned to one agency. The bulk of these observations were drawn from a reflective paper assigned in each class at the end of the term. Most students found their service-learning experiences so powerful that they dominated the papers, although the assignment was not presented in those terms. I have focused on issues of poverty and the wealth gap, both here and in my courses, because increasingly it is the dominant public tension in American life (Younge, 2003) and because the sheer size of the inequity in our country renders it, for me, a moral imperative for change.[2] In addition, the school where I teach is located in an especially economically depressed area, so most of the local agencies do deal with poverty in one form or another.

The pattern that emerged from the students' narratives fits a process of qualitative change in thinking that is congruent with predictions of cognitive theory. First, different aspects of experience are attended to; second, as the new information fits poorly with existing ideas or schemas, adjustments to those schemas become necessary; this in turn alters students' interpretation of information and also causes them to identify ethical elements in a much broader range of situations than previously. Ultimately, the more sophisticated students rethink their definitions of service itself and the point of their involvement in the community – which is to say, they begin to compile a rather different heuristic toolbox. Examples from students' narratives will illustrate this process of change.

Most of my students, initially at least, did not construe their community service in ethical terms, but simply as a course requirement. The pay-off for them, beyond passing the course, involved feeling good about themselves for making a difference in someone else's life. The first disequilibration came when students did not immediately feel good about what they were doing. Interacting closely with poor people was a new experience for most, and they were stunned by differences as simple as the lack of dental care.[3] They acknowledged that service-learning is an especially powerful mechanism for learning hard truths: 'It was not until I was confronted with these toothless men and women in old, ragged clothing that I realized this was *real*,' confessed a first-year student. 'Words and stories of poverty don't last, but the images instilled in my head will be with me forever... Service-learning is necessary because of its effectiveness in producing awareness.'

As students became more conversant with problems faced by the poor, they often commented sympathetically on the plight of those they met through service, and some clearly began to identify with those they helped. 'This woman looked so tired,' said one. 'She must have only been in her twenties, but her eyes looked as old as forty.' 'I see the strenuous pressures they are under and could not imagine what it would be like to have the weight of their worlds on my shoulders,' said another.

Identification often led to a self-critical stance. 'I feel so selfish!' several of the students wailed, contrasting their own creature comforts with the lack of resources endured by those they served. The number of clothes they owned, their grumpiness at having to walk to work in the cold, their stable family situations, even their pillows and blankets, all came under scrutiny as they absorbed the hard truths of life in poverty. In other words, their own level of privilege became an ethical issue where it had not been before. Even in the throes of their discomfort, students recognized the value of their newfound awareness: 'I've realized that if everyone had the same [disinterest in social issues] as me, the country would be in bad shape.' '[Service] has taught me things that I would have rather not known,' wrote another student, 'but now, I am glad that I do know them.'

If it is but a step from sympathy to identification, it is a shorter step from self-scrutiny to reinterpretation. Several of the students showed evidence of dissonance resolved through reframing: 'Prior to this, I thought [poverty] was their fault;' 'I've gotten rid of a lot of stereotypes.' This too was sometimes cast in a self-critical light: 'I can't believe I thought someone would choose to be poor!'

Students who had logged more experience in service were more likely to identify specific areas of growth in their own thinking. Though the tone was often self-critical, the focus was heuristic, pointing towards new ways of reasoning. 'I am more aware now of those barriers [in society] of who is 'capable' and 'incapable' of performing tasks,' wrote one. Another said, 'I tend to baby people with handicaps or differences... [This class] made me a little uncomfortable that I treat people this way,' adding, 'You cannot overgeneralize; it is not good for you as a volunteer or the population you are serving.'

The most experienced and sophisticated students demonstrated the reorientation of vision that results from major schematic restructuring. This often took the form of recognizing collective interdependence. 'Poverty affects the community as a whole,' wrote one such student. These students also seemed to be rethinking the social order. 'Although I have had courses related to this area, I never looked critically at the reasons behind the problems,' wrote one student. 'I was forced to get to the root of the problem and think of possible solutions,' said another. 'I found that many decisions made [in a community] have a large impact or influence on others.' A third was more confrontational: 'We need to ask questions of the system, like, "Why can't we change it?"'

These students sometimes turned their critique on their own service participation. 'Previously, I always had the mindset that doing service was making *me* a better person,' one wrote. 'I realized through experience...[that] the purpose is not to make me a better person, but to help *others* get into a better life situation.' Another cautioned, 'We sometimes use services as an excuse for not helping people.' Paraphrasing Saul Alinsky, she added, 'You cannot do things for people that they can do for themselves... I am going to stop being a service and start being a server.' A student with almost a life-long experience of service and activism due to the involvement of her family underscored this idea that service must be turned on its head: 'We must empower people to change their own situations.'

The development of cognitive complexity, ethical or otherwise, is not a simple linear process. While it may also be the case – indeed, as a professor, I hope it is the case! – that sophomores and juniors are generally better equipped for critical thinking than freshmen, these observations show that a bright first-year student with adequate service experience and reflection is quite capable of cognitive restructuring. In addition, schemas continue to change throughout the lifespan, so it is likely that students who engage in service-learning for years, as well as the faculty who teach them, go through repeated cycles of disequilibration and restructuring. By building service-learning into a variety of courses across the curriculum, we offer students to revisit ethical principles in the light of real-world community issues, refining over time a heuristic toolbox that will serve them well in the years beyond their formal education.

NOTES

1. <u>The Letters of William James</u>. From a letter to H.G. Wells, 11 September 1906.
2. In 1999, the average CEO made 458 times as much as the average production or nonsupervisory worker. See M. Lanzarotta (2001), Across the great divide: The wealth gap challenges American ideals. *Impact Press, August-September 2001.* Available: http://www.impactpress.com/articles/augsep01/divide80901.html.
3. In the U.S., routine dental care is not covered by most basic health insurance plans, and the poor are typically uninsured anyway. As a result, their dental problems must become a clear emergency to qualify for treatment, so the poor are often readily identifiable by the state of their teeth.

REFERENCES

Astin, A. W., Sax, L. J. and Avalos, J. (1999) Long-term effects of volunteerism during the undergraduate years. *The Review of Higher Education,* 22, 187-202

Astin, A. W., Vogelgesang, L. J., Ikeda, E. K. and Yee, J. A. (2000) *How service learning affects students* (executive summary). Los Angeles, CA: Higher Education Research Institute, UCLA. Available : http://www.gseis.ucla.edu/slc/rhowas.html

Bjork, R. (2003) *How students learn vs. how they think they learn.* Address at Allegheny College, Meadville PA, June 2003

Boss, J.A. (1994) The effect of community service work on the moral development of college ethics students. *Journal of Moral Education,* 23, 183-198

Gilligan, C. (1982) *In a different voice: Psychological theory and women's development.* Cambridge, MA: Harvard University Press

Leming, J. S. (2001) Integrating a structured ethical reflection curriculum into high school community service experiences: Impact on students' sociomoral development. *Adolescence,* 36, 33-45

Lisman, C. D. (1998) *Toward a civil society: Civic literacy and service learning.* Westport, CT: Bergin & Garvey

Matlin, M. W. (1998) *Cognition* (4th ed). Fort Worth, TX: Harcourt Brace

Moely, B. E., McFarland, M., Miron, D., Mercer, S. and Ilustre, V. (2002) Changes in college students' attitudes and intentions for civic involvement as a function of service-learning experiences, *Michigan Journal of Community Service Learning,* 9, 18-26

Morgan, W. and Streb, M. (2001) Building citizenship: How student voice in service-learning develops civic values, *Social Science Quarterly,* 82, 154-169

Neururer, J. and Rhoads, R.A. (1998) Community service: Panacea, paradox, or potentiation? *Journal of College Student Development,* 39, 321-330

Younge, G. (2003) American dream tarnished by widening wealth gap. *The Guardian Unlimited,* 24 January 2003. Available: http://www.guardian.co.uk/usa/story/0%2C12271%2C881137%2C00.html

12
The challenge of raising ethical awareness*
A case-based aiding system for use by computing and ICT students

Don Sherratt, Simon Rogerson
and N. Ben Fairweather

INTRODUCTION AND AIMS OF THE RESEARCH

Information and Communication Technology (ICT) is a comparatively new profession. The unique features of ICT, such as its speed of transmission, globalisation, anonymity, and ability to manipulate information, can create many problems for those who develop and use the technology. The pace of technological development has been so rapid that the new technologies have been implemented before a full consideration of the ethical issues raised by their use can be made (Bynum, 1998).

All professional activity has social consequences (Campo *et al.*, 201, 215). Professionals should be aware of the consequences of their actions and be prepared to accept responsibility for them. However, Bynum and Moor (2000, 5) suggest that little progress has been made in addressing the ethical issues associated with ICT because of a lack of a clear understanding of computer ethics. Students, the future ICT professionals, are often perceived to have little understanding of the ethical issues associated with the use of ICT (Fleischman, 2001, 173). Some governments, particularly in the

---

*This paper first appeared in *Science and Engineering Ethics*, Volume 11, No. 2 (April), 2005, pp. 299-315. © Opragen Publications; www.opragen.co.uk. Reproduced by permission.

Western world, and most professional computing bodies, have turned their attention to the problem[5,6] and instigated measures to include consideration of social, legal and ethical issues in undergraduate and postgraduate computer-related courses (see ACM, 2001; Thompson, 2001).

The research outlined in this chapter is part of a wider project to establish a theoretical basis for, and the development of, an educational courseware tool that will assist students to recognise, understand and consider more deeply the ethical issues that may arise from the use of ICTs. Rahanu's (1999) case-based reasoner was an initial output of this wider project. This particular tool builds upon that experience. It will retrieve a nearest matching case(s) to a given scenario from a library of ethically analysed real-life cases chosen to reflect the range of conflicts arising from unethical computer use.

THE CHALLENGE OF RAISING ETHICAL AWARENESS

There is considerable debate concerning the most effective way of raising students' awareness of the ethical issues that they will possibly encounter in their future careers. Munro and Munro (2002, 643) have identified that, especially in the medical, engineering and computing disciplines, it is essential that students be taught to recognise ethical issues, and encouraged to consider the social and legal consequences of their actions. Woodcock and Armstrong (2001) suggest that exposing students to a variety of relevant ethical experiences can produce significant changes in students' ethical awareness. Other authors consider that the most effective approach to raising awareness is to target an individual's personal ethical code by the use of pertinent case studies (Fleischman, 2001, 173; Liffick, 1995; Spinello, 1997, xii; Pena et al., 1999).

Stanoevska et al. (1998, 23-1) consider that classification and retrieval procedures, transforming simple data into knowledge, are required before knowledge can be reused with efficiency. They identify two categories of knowledge: tacit and explicit. Tacit knowledge is internal, personal intuition and insight. Explicit knowledge is external, codified, and available with some form of transmission medium. The two form a cyclical knowledge creation process (Figure 1) which can be mapped to the development of personal ethical values. How, then, can codified knowledge and a transmission medium be developed and deployed to target students' personal ethical codes?

Much experience, particularly in the engineering and science disciplines, has developed through the inspection and analysis of former events. This information can be incorporated into case studies. These can be used to transfer to students the experiences gleaned from detailed inspection,

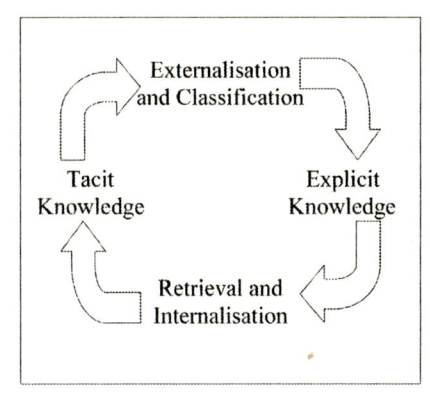

Figure 1. The Tacit-Explicit Knowledge Cycle (Adapted from Stanoevska et al. 1998)

speeding up recognition of the issues raised. The use of case studies for examination and discussion by students is the preferred method of instruction suggested by the ImpactCS committee (ACM, 2001; Martin et al., 1995). However, the use of case studies can bring disadvantages. Complex cases are often summarised for the sake of readability or to emphasise a particular issue required by the curriculum, thus losing some of the factual richness that would be of benefit to students. Students may see the précised studies as phoney, and lose interest in the analysis and discussion of the very points that the cases were designed to illustrate. Clearly any approach using case studies needs to recognise these pitfalls.

The recent recognition by governments and the courts that unlawful use of ICT must be addressed is now beginning to produce an interesting, accessible and relevant source of teaching material. The publication of legal case transcripts on the Internet has provided ready access to those areas that were formerly the privileged domain of lawyers (Widdison 2001). Court transcripts, legal commentaries, and articles from reliable trade and national press sources provide case details that can be used as a library of reference material.

Student awareness of ethical issues can be improved by providing examples of matching, ethically interesting episodes from the library, so forming an 'aide-memoire' for comparison with the students' assignment scenario. The use of current, relevant material is a stimulant to students, who are able to identify and empathise with the participants in the action, and to develop their own personal intuitions and insights.

The ubiquity of ICTs, and their use by those who are not ICT professionals (in the sense of belonging to an ICT professional organisation), raises the possibility that anyone employing the technologies has the ability to use ICT intentionally or unintentionally in unethical actions. This would suggest that all who use ICTs should be aware of, and observe, some key ethical principles.

PREVIOUS WORK

A number of authors have developed instruments that are designed to assist in raising awareness of the ethical issues posed by the use of ICTs. Kallman and Grillo (1996) devised a system for ethical analysis and decision making. Maner (1998) developed a web-based interactive survey tool using scenarios to compare one's own ethical views with those of a world-wide audience. Rahanu's (1999) tool uses artificial intelligence (AI) techniques to retrieve cases from a library of ethically analysed case studies addressing the issue of professional malpractice in failed information systems.

While in some ways useful, the retrieval vectors for Rahanu's system are not applicable to a range of ethical issues wider than those involved in failed information systems. Rahanu's case library, however, provided a useful resource. Analysis of the Rahanu cases suggests that most involve failure to keep promises. Rahanu's term 'failed information systems' does not immediately convey any suggestion of unethical or unlawful behaviour. For our wider purposes, the classification might therefore more helpfully be described as 'contractual issues' rather than 'failed information systems'.

ICT has also permeated most other professions, allowing traditional wrongdoings to be perpetrated more rapidly, widely and effectively than ever before. Most enterprises become involved in contractual issues. ICT faces the same dilemmas as many other professions. Rahanu's system therefore addresses ethical, social and legal issues common to the contractual problems faced by many organisations.

Rahanu's concept has the potential for development for use within any discipline where ethical issues need to be considered, not just those arising from failed information systems. It should be possible to develop a set of vectors for use in a retrieval process that will address a range of ethical issues common to most professions. Examination of the codes of conduct and practice for other professions reveal that they follow closely the principles adopted by ICT professional bodies. The case library developed as part of this research draws heavily on ICT case law. Other professions also generate their own volume of case law that may be used to assemble similar libraries for use by students in those areas. The concept therefore has the potential to be transferred to other professions.

The following sections suggest how the Rahanu concept may be generalised to address unethical actions within any sector of ICT.

THE BASIS FOR A RETRIEVAL ENGINE

The selection of a 'similar' matching case from a library of pre-analysed cases can be difficult. Some retrieval systems adopt a semantic approach, attempting to match cases through the identification of word associations. Others attempt to apply rule-based algorithms, and follow the propositional calculus format used in relational database management systems. In so doing, they attempt to apply AI techniques to mimic human intelligence.

Zeleznikow and Hunter (1994) discuss at length the application of AI principles to the domain of legal case retrieval, and find that the appropriateness, acceptability and usefulness of AI systems are a question of degree. The greater the need for human reflection, intuition and judgement then the less appropriate is an AI system that is closed, self-sustaining and incapable of human intervention. For this reason, the type of AI techniques used and the manner in which they are used are most important. Systems that replace human activity are likely to be closed and use rigorous techniques to emulate the human performance. Systems acting as support or guidance for human activity are more likely to have multiple intervention points and simpler techniques.

Moor (2000, 221) notes that it is of concern to many critics of artificial intelligence that the activities of computers are matters of calculation, and not judgement. Computers process information dispassionately. Dreyfus (2000, 199) states that a computer has no built-in pre-understanding of how our world is organised. Before a computer can undertake AI actions, it needs to be primed with human knowledge and judgement (Moor, 2000, 217). Ethical concepts do not lend themselves to semantic or logic-based retrieval as the many important nuances present in ethical scenarios are ignored. Slight changes of context or date can mean that, for a similar set of case conditions, very different courses of action may be ethical. No two ethical dilemmas are ever likely to be set in exactly the same context. Consequently, the reduction of the potential range of actions available to the human operators to a simple rule-based algorithm is impossible to achieve.

While rule-based systems may be confounded if they attempt to obtain a precise match on all fields, other systems may use AI techniques that are closed, self sustaining and incapable of human intervention. Neither technique is what is required for the stimulation of students' deeper thinking processes. An exact match will not encourage discussion and reflection of ethical issues. Wiener (1988, 21) suggests that the more probable the message, the less information it conveys. Similarly, the more exact the match, the less the student will need to think about the relationships between the scenario and the matching case presented by the retrieval tool. Students' imaginations must be stimulated to recognise and explore the nuances and differences between cases, and to 'bridge' between their given scenario and the retrieved case presented by the tool. However, a case that appears to the student to bear no, or minimal, relevance may not provide stimulation either. There needs to be a gap to bridge, but to be useful it cannot be wider than the student's ability to build the 'bridge'.

The Development of a Retrieval Algorithm

The retrieval of ethical analyses from the case library presents many challenges if suitable similar cases are to be identified and presented to students. Kolodner (1993, 31) suggests that cases are contextualised pieces of knowledge representing an experience. These do not lend themselves to the application of rule-based systems for several reasons (Kolodner, 1993, 93-94):

- Rules in a rule-based system look for patterns. Cases in a case library are constants that may not contain any definable or repeatable patterns but will contain certain vectors that can be discretely identified;
- Rule-based systems require an exact match for retrieval. Cases are retrieved usually on partial matching;
- Rules are applied iteratively on a cycle of microevents. Cases are retrieved first in their entirety, presenting an entire solution immediately, which may then be refined and adapted to provide a final answer;
- Rules are small, usually independent, pieces of domain information. Cases are large chunks of domain knowledge, much of which may be redundant;
- Rules are based on a mechanism rather than addressing content;
- Rule-based systems are more applicable when the domain is well understood. Case-based systems are more applicable to domains where the underlying model is not clearly understood.

Kolodner (1993, 540) discusses the opportunities presented for the retrieval of cases using casebased reasoning techniques. She notes that these can range from a fully repairing, predictive system to a simple retrieval system that transfers reasoning from the computer to the user. The proposed retrieval tool does not require a fully-fledged case-based reasoner. The predictive and repairing facilities are inappropriate when dealing with ethical issues, a domain often not fully understood by the students. Students need to retain ownership of the reasoning (thinking) process. There should be no student passivity with the retrieval or interpretation of the case. The input of data for use in the retrieval paradigm is part of the reasoning process. If the tool is allowed to usurp the human elements of the reasoning process, it will block student thinking.

Thagard (2000, 49) believes that much in artificial intelligence research is not concerned with modelling human thought processes. It is focused towards the construction of algorithms designed to perform well on complex tasks, regardless of whether the algorithms correspond to human thinking. The proposed retrieval tool is required to act simply as a 'reminding' system, guiding and supporting the human-centred thinking process to reach a suitably similar case. Kolodner (ibid., 60-71) describes such retrieval-only and advisory systems. Furthermore, the systems described are not required to include any complex computer code. Any system that guides a user through a retrieval process may be included under the generic heading of case-based reasoning. The degree of interactivity and artificial intelligence is entirely within the control of the designer (Thagard, 2000, 540-543). It is therefore acceptable for a system to be developed that merely assists the user to navigate successfully through a series of questions. Such systems are classified by Kolodner as case-based aiding systems.

Case-Based Aiding

From the above it can be seen that it should be possible to develop a case-based aiding system that:

- Follows many of the principles of case-based reasoning systems, but does not involve the mechanistic application of rule-based algorithms for retrieval;
- Describes cases in terms of neutral, dispassionate vectors;
- Allows students to retain control of the reasoning process;
- Presents suitable similar cases, but allows the user mentally to adapt and merge information from several cases where appropriate in order to arrive at a suitable evaluation of an ethical action;
- Does not attempt to process input data to give a computationally interpreted or adapted result;
- Guides students' navigation through the system, suggesting relevant questions that will lead to a suitably similar case(s) within the case library.

This suggests the use of a 'conversational' interface, interacting with the students in a natural, sensible manner (Kolodner, 1993, 556-561) Such systems are particularly useful for inexperienced students, and adopt the metaphor of a novice in conversation with an expert. The system guides the novice through a sequence of questions based upon the experience of the designer concerning what the novice might reasonably be expected to ask next. This raises the question of how the conversational elements of the interaction may be modelled.

The Retrieval Tool Paradigm

Moor (2000, 226) suggests that the conversational responses can be modelled as nodes of a decision tree. He recognises that, during a normal conversation, the possible choice of sensible response strings that might be used in a conversation is huge. However, if the conversation is contextualised, the number of choices can be reduced so that the number of nodes is restricted to a manageable level.

Moor also believes that following a conversational tree is not AI. So long as the computer follows a path of sensible responses supplied by the designer, selected in sequence by the user, the machine will have the appearance of a Turing machine, but will simply be an inert tool. No inherent reasoning, adaptation or merging need take place. The navigational direction is entirely under the control of the user.

Schweighofer (1999) suggests that hypertext links can form the basis for the representation of a structure allowing the indexation and classification of a document collection. The nodes of the hypertext system form the basis for the navigational structure that permit navigation through the document collection to a relevant case or cases. The system thus 'walks the user through' the retrieval process.

These concepts appear to match exactly the requirements for the retrieval of ethical analyses. It therefore seems possible that a tree structure, constructed using hypertext links and posing navigational queries based on contextualised ethical principles to the user, is a fruitful area for research.

The Selection of Retrieval Vectors

There now comes the issue of what substantive queries should be asked of the user to enable them to use the case-based aiding system. Kallman and Grillo (1996, 9) suggest that anyone using computers should consider the following issues when contemplating the effects of the use of the computer and making a defensible decision for their actions:

- Legal issues and limitations;

- Availability of Guidelines;
- Consequentialism;
- Rights and Duties, involving
  - Personal duties;
  - The rights to know, to privacy and to property;
  - Professional responsibilities;
- Kant's Categorical Imperative.

These criteria may provide a basis for the classification and retrieval of ethically analysed cases, and be adapted to fit the requirements of a retrieval, in a way that facilitates the use of those cases in a case-based aiding system as described above.

Pattern-matching retrieval seems to offer a possible case identification system. This uses Boolean logic, asking simply whether a particular factor is present in the case, regardless of its influence upon the outcome. The responses are limited to 'Yes' or 'No', giving a simple algorithm. Cases may be 'described' by the presence or absence of the factors. Smyth and McKenna (1999, 343) suggest that the method is most effective using a restricted range of cases. If a large case library can be partitioned using recognised classifications, the final retrieval can be successfully achieved using the Boolean responses as retrieval vectors.

Difficulty in retrieval of 'matching' cases is not unique to ethics. A similar problem exists in law, where semantic or logic-based models give difficulty with legal document retrieval systems (Schweighofer, 1999). It is therefore possible that progress made in research upon the retrieval of legal cases can offer potential solutions for the retrieval of ethical cases also.

Curran and Higgins (2000) have investigated this system for retrieval of legal documents. The pattern of the Boolean responses may be matched to similar patterns for other cases contained within the case library as in Figure 2. Curran and Higgins examined the area of company directors' duties towards small shareholders, and found it possible to develop rudimentary retrieval vectors for this legal domain that would lend themselves to Boolean

Stored Case	Problem Situation
Factor 1	
Factor 2	Factor 2
Factor 3	
Factor 4	Factor 4
Factor 5	Factor 5
Factor N	

Figure 2. Factor Matching (adapted from Curran and Higgins (2000))

responses. The system operated successfully if an area of law could be discretely identified. This suggests that if instances of ICT ethical malpractice could be broadly contextualised into areas such as contractual issues or property ownership, following the concept of keywords, it should be possible to apply suitable ethically based questions as vectors to identify specific areas of ethical malpractice.

THE DEVELOPMENT OF THE RETRIEVAL SYSTEM

The retrieval tool model is that of a decision tree. Each node in the tree addresses an ethical issue. For a decision tree to work effectively, it is necessary to split the analysis process quickly into discrete paths. This concept mirrors the contextualisation needed for the retrieval of the ethical analyses. The tool first contextualises the case, bursting the retrieval process into a number of discrete ethical domains. It then applies Boolean logic to determine the occurrence of specific ethical principles within a case. Finally, fine-tuning is carried out by applying professional and personal moral duties to the retrieval process, allowing navigation to a suitable matching case or cases.

Contextualisation

A series of real-world ethical scenarios was researched and examined. The ethical, social and legal issues raised by the cases were identified. It became evident that the contextualisation of unethical acts requires consideration of environment, culture and jurisprudence, all related to the country in which the act arises. This vector is one of the most important for the successful retrieval of relevant cases, and is a convenient start point for the tool.

The cases were then used to test whether sub-division might be achieved within each country domain. Two areas were of interest: the main issue raised by the unethical act, and the violation of personal rights. Examination of the test cases suggested that the main issues highlighted fell within the broad categories listed in Figure 3. These are not mutually exclusive, but usually one will be more dominant. The tool requests that the students select the issue they perceive to be the most important.

It was also found that most scenarios examined contained violations of one or more of the rights to privacy, to property and to know, recognised by Kallman and Grillo (1996, 13) as being of significance to ICT ethical analysis. Identification of the violations of the different rights provided a further sub-division of the case library.

The combination available from the country, main issue addressed and

No.	Class
1.	Promises/contracts
2.	Personal rights/freedoms
3.	Harm
4.	Computer misuse
5.	Information use
6.	Property ownership

Figure 3. Main Issue Raised by the Case.

rights violation classifiers provides a very powerful partitioning mechanism for the case library. They provide 480 discrete areas within which Boolean responses to the presence of ethical and professional principles may be identified.

Applying Ethical and Professional Normative Principles

The test cases were checked against the criteria of Kallman and Grillo (1996, 9) to determine if it was possible to use these issues as retrieval tool vectors. Most issues lent themselves well to Boolean responses, and these were incorporated into the retrieval tool interface.

However, it is not necessary to apply all potential questions in the tool interface in order to retrieve a case. Some questions are irrelevant to retrieval in some contextual areas. A database was set up containing a full set of data from the responses to all questions relating to each of the library cases, including the categorisation data and null responses where the question was irrelevant to retrieval. The cases were sorted into their appropriate categories. Each group of cases was used to run a series of experiments to determine which questions were relevant for retrieval within that context. It was found that many of the decision paths within the contextual areas required submission of the questions in different sequences if a good separation of the cases was to be achieved.

Those questions in each contextual area that did not contribute to the retrieval process were removed. It was possible, using the shortened decision paths, to separate the cases into discrete cases, or alternatively into small clusters of cases addressing similar ethical principles.

Cases frequently involve more than one ethical issue. Case clusters may have some cases with common ethical issues, and others with issues making a particular case unique. Cases can be separated or subclustered using the combinations of the professional principles shown in Figure 4. In particular clusters of cases grouped by the Boolean questions, this provides the ability to match cases into smaller groups of two or three cases according to the

No.	Duty
1.	Trust
2.	Integrity
3.	Truthfulness
4.	Justice
5.	Beneficence/Nonmaleficence
6.	Self-Improvement
7.	Gratitude/ Reparation

Figure 4. Professional Duties.

No.	Duty
1.	Maintain Confidentiality
2.	Maintain Impartiality
3.	Maintain Professional Relationships
4.	Maintain Efficacy
5.	Duty of Care to Others
6.	Competence
7.	Avoid Inducements and Bribes

Figure 5. Personal Moral Duties

professional criteria identified. It presents a choice of cases for consideration and encourages exploration and evaluation of the issues raised from several viewpoints.

Finally, further sub-division may be required within the small clusters of cases provided by the 'professional duty' classifier. Kallman and Grillo (1996, 14) suggest that all people have personal moral duties, shown in Figure 5. Although available for inclusion in the retrieval tool, this sort mechanism has not yet been needed, but has been included in one decision path to test its effectiveness.

Once the retrieval process has been completed, the tool presents the user with a brief description of the case or cases. Hypertext links then lead the user to the full ethical analysis of each case.

THE EXPANSION OF THE CASE LIBRARY

At present, the environment addressed by the tool is limited to that of British or North American culture and jurisprudence examining the area of unethical computer use. However, the tool is capable of including cases from other cultures and problem domains as suitable cases arise.

The principle of a decision tree is that it functions best when a large number of cases are included. A reduced case base restricts the scope and efficiency of retrieval. Before the full efficacy of the tool can be realised, it will be necessary to populate further US and UK areas of the case library. Furthermore, students may have differing perceptions of the main issue addressed by a case. Cases are often not clear-cut, and may fall equally justifiably into more than one of the 'main issue' categories. Students must be able to navigate to an appropriate case regardless of which start-point is used. The construction of the tool allows this multi-standpoint approach, but will require the inclusion of a substantial number of additional cases for a fully effective retrieval operation.

The case library for this tool includes ten cases developed by Rahanu, but needed more cases for effective operation. The library was therefore expanded to contain twenty-two contractual cases from the UK. It was also necessary to include additional cases to populate a further area of the case library. The area of US privacy was selected, and thirty-three cases from this area have been included.

EMPIRICAL TESTING

Initial testing of the tool has begun. Two areas are being investigated: the usability of the tool, and the effect of the tool upon a student's ethical awareness.

The tool has undergone a pilot assessment for usability by students within the United Kingdom. Students who have used the Rahanu tool have commented favourably upon their first impressions of the new tool. Several useful suggestions upon usability issues have been received, and modifications included in the interface.

Some informal experimentation by students who used the tool to match a case against their assignment case has demonstrated its ability to retrieve relevant cases. It has also raised the point that the retrieved cases do not always immediately appear to address the areas anticipated by the student, a point addressed earlier in this chapter. Some thought and evaluation is required on the part of the student to interpret the issues raised, a strong point in favour of the tool. Initial informal testing therefore seems to suggest that the tool is able to achieve one of its major objectives: that of stimulating deeper thought upon ethical issues raised by new scenarios.

There is an element of subjectivity in a student's performance when undertaking an ethical analysis of a given scenario which prohibits the assignment of absolute scores. It is therefore not feasible to reduce the assessment of change in ethical awareness to a comprehensive statistical analysis. The testing seeks only to identify trends in the change of students' ethical awareness using a simple two-stage survey technique.

Students are given a simple case study to analyse, and asked to complete a brief questionnaire seeking responses to ethical issues identified within the case study. Students are then encouraged to use the case retrieval tool to retrieve a suitable matching case and to undertake a more detailed analysis. The survey is then repeated. The comparison of the students' 'before' and 'after' responses will give an indication of the effect that the use of the tool has produced upon the students' ethical awareness of the issues raised by the case study.

The students may use the tool within a group or individual environment. However, it is important that students complete the surveys individually, without contemporaneous input from their colleagues, to determine whether their own ethical understanding has changed.

THE HUMAN RESEARCH PROTOCOL

The research protocol used for the testing of the tool was that required by the Human Research Ethics Committee of De Montfort University, Leicester, UK. The principal points of the protocol are:

- The rights of students will be respected.
- Students are not obliged to participate in the research. Students may withdraw from the research at any time without providing any reason for doing so.
- No personal, private identifiable data is to be collected. The data collected will identify only a student's perception of their ethical understanding concerning the issues raised by the case study or the usability issues of the retrieval tool.
- Student responses to the questionnaires will be kept strictly confidential. All responses will be anonymised during processing.
- Students will be required to choose a personal identifier known only to them for entry on the 'before' and 'after' response questionnaires for the ethical awareness evaluation so that the researcher can match 'before' and 'after' responses.
- No attempt will be made by the researcher to identify individuals taking part in the survey from their chosen identifier.
- The data obtained from the responses will be used only for the evaluation and development of the retrieval tool.
- Students have a right to place their responses in an envelope for return to the researcher without the tutor seeing their responses to the questionnaire, and to see that the envelope is sealed.
- Once received by the researcher, the questionnaire sheets will be kept within secure facilities at the home of the researcher.
- Once the paper questionnaires have been processed, they will be destroyed. No personal or private information will be disseminated to others.

PILOT TESTING

Pilot testing of the tool was carried out in Malaysia in July 2003 using a UK contractual case, that of SAM v Hedley, for the assessment. More stringent testing of the tool will be carried out in the UK during the 2003/4 and 2004/5 academic years.

Additionally, it is intended that in future semesters the tool will again be used by students in Malaysia, and in the United States. This will provide an assessment of its acceptability in different ethnic and cultural environments.

ANALYSIS OF ETHICAL AWARENESS PILOT TEST QUESTIONNAIRES

Forty-one Malaysian and Taiwanese students at university in Kuala Lumpur agreed to take part in the research. From these, twenty-five pairs of responses were found to be valid. A number of students either completed only one questionnaire, or had failed to use the same personal identifier on the 'before' and 'after' questionnaires, thus preventing the matching of the individual student's responses. Students' responses were examined from three viewpoints:

1. the number of students who changed their responses to any of the questions after using the retrieval tool,
2. which issues were the subject to the greatest reconsideration,
3. the perceived ease of answering the questionnaire after using the retrieval tool.

THE NUMBER OF STUDENTS CHANGING THEIR RESPONSES AFTER USING THE TOOL

Figure 6 shows a graphical representation of the responses of students who altered their response to the questionnaire after using the tool. The pilot indicates that twenty-two of the twenty-five students (88%) changed their perception of at least one issue raised by the questionnaire. Fifty-two percent changed their perception on 25% or more of the issues raised. Twenty percent of students changed 50% or more of their perceptions of the ethical issues.

Three students did not change their responses to any of the questions. The reason for this is not known. It suggests that these students held very firm ethical beliefs and that the tool did not prompt reconsideration of the

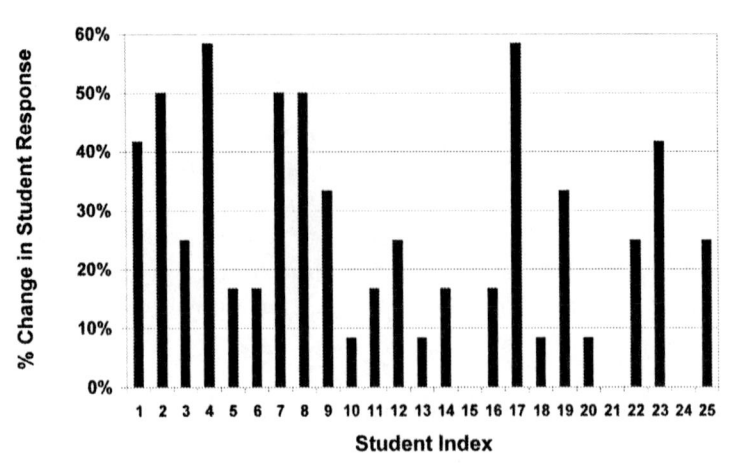

Figure 6. Percentage Change of Awareness by Student

issues raised by the test scenario. Alternatively, students may not have entered into the spirit of the research and simply repeated from memory the responses to the questions. However, the latter explanation is less likely as the students were not told that the test for ethical awareness was to be repeated, and had no need to memorise their 'before' responses.

ISSUES SUBJECT TO THE GREATEST RECONSIDERATION

Figure 7 indicates the number of students altering their perception of each ethical issue. Two of the issues addressed by the questionnaire, broken promises and truthfulness, are qualities that are personal and internalised. The others are qualities that require the student to consider the issues from the perspective of another. It would be expected that, following theories of moral development, individuals who have developed a high degree of moral maturity would be able to 'inhabit' the personae of others, and to recognise the ethical dilemmas that a case study presents. The high number of changes indicated suggests that the students taking part in the research have yet to reach this degree of maturity.

Furthermore, those issues that have attracted a change in response of more than 25%, (broken promises, abuse of power, unfair action, caused harm, and the Golden Rule), are all issues associated with contracts and the conduct of business. The case study addresses the issues of contract limitation and exclusion clauses. The responses suggest that students were not familiar with the implicit promises and conditions contained within the area of contract law. However, the level of change indicated suggests that students

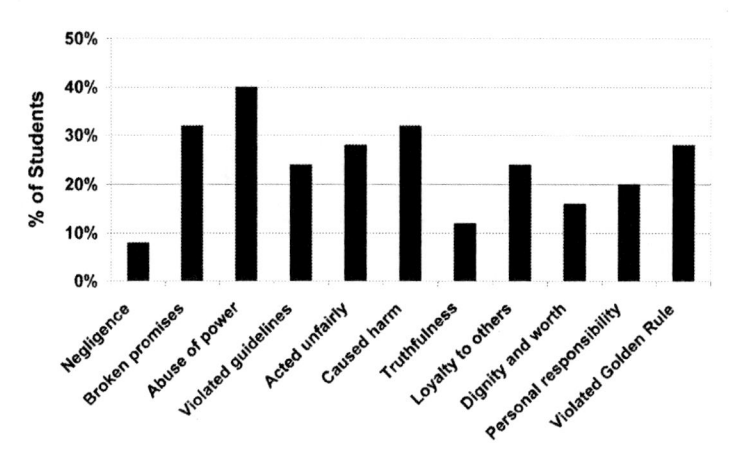

Figure 7. Change in Awareness by Issue.

have an inherent attitude towards contract and promissory commitments that follows their cultural background. Hofstede (1994, 26) finds that many south-east Asian cultures have a power distance index (PDI) of 60-100. This suggests a culture where high value is placed by society on obedience and conformity, acceptance of the status quo where individuals tend not to trust one another or to disagree with one another. Business practices thus tend to be very different from those of western cultures where PDI scores are typically 35-40, suggesting a much more open, competitive society.

EASE OF ANSWERING QUESTIONS AFTER USING THE RETRIEVAL TOOL

Figure 8 indicates the change in perception of the difficulty in answering the ethical awareness questionnaire. Forty percent of students changed their responses following use of the tool. Of these, 24% found the questions easier to answer and 16% found them more difficult.

Of those who made the same response to the difficulty of answering the questions after using the tool, 44% found the questions difficult and 16% found them easy. One interpretation of these results would be that the tool facilitates the analysis of the given scenario by some students, but prompts others to recognise that the scenario may not be so simple and clear-cut as it first appears. Unfortunately, the results could also be interpreted as consistent with the tool enabling some students to short-cut ethical analysis, while confusing others. The results obtained to date can now be used as a baseline for a further series of more stringent tests to be carried out on a

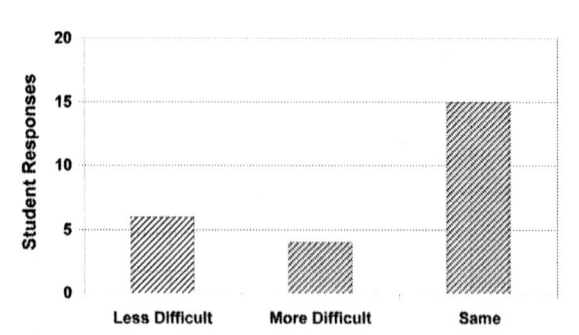

Figure 8. Ease of Answering Questions After Using Tool

wider selection of students. These will help to resolve whether the changes brought about by using the tool are helpful.

CONCLUSION

The literature provides evidence of the need for the development of a tool to raise students' ethical awareness and understanding of the ethical issues inherent in the use of ICTs. Furthermore, there is a coherent ethical basis for the technological development of the tool. The use of a hypertext decision tree linked via Boolean retrieval techniques to a library of pre-analysed ethical scenarios offers a promising way forward. This would suggest that it is possible for the tool to be developed to meet its stated objectives.

The pilot studies and informal feedback suggest that the students like using the tool, finding it easy and intuitive to use. The studies also suggest that the tool achieves its aim of promoting students' deeper thinking upon ethical issues.

The questions posed by the tool during the retrieval process seem applicable to a wide range of business and social scenarios, suggesting that the tool is transferable to other professions. However, some additions to the choices offered by the tool interface may need to be made and suitable case libraries would need to be developed.

REFERENCES

ACM (2001) *Computing Curricula 2001, Computer Science Volume, Chapter 10 - Professional Practice.* <http://www.acm.org/sigcse/cc2001/cs-professional-practice.html>. (Date Accessed: 10/07/2003)

Bynum, T. W. (1998) *Ethics in the Information Age.* <http://www.southernct.edu/

organizations/rccs/resources/research/global_info/bynum_info_age .html>. (Date Accessed: 10/07/2003)
Bynum, T. W. and Moor, J. H. (2000) How Computers are Changing Philosophy, in: Bynum, T. W. and Moor, J. H. eds. *The Digital Phoenix: How Computers are Changing Philosophy.* Revised Edition, Oxford: Blackwell, 1-14
Campo, J. D., Barroso, P. and Weckert, J. (2001) Teaching Computer Ethics: A Comparative Study. *Proceedings of the Fifth International Conference on The Social Impacts of Information and Communication Technologies, ETHICOMP 2001,* Gdansk, Poland, 18–20 June, 2001, Volume 1, 215–222
Curran, K. and Higgins, L. (2000) A Legal Information Retrieval System. *Journal of Information, Law and Technology, 2000, Vol. 3.* <http://elj.warwick.ac.uk/jilt/00- 3/curran.html> (Date Accessed: 10/07/2003)
Dreyfus, H. L. (2000) Response to My Critics, in: Bynum, T.W. and Moor, J.H. eds. *The Digital Phoenix: How Computers are Changing Philosophy,* Revised Edition. Oxford: Blackwell, 193- 212
Fleischman, W. M. (2001) The Role of Imagination in a Course on Ethical Issues in Computer Science. *Proceedings of the Fifth International Conference on The Social Impacts of Information and Communication Technologies, ETHICOMP 2001,* Gdansk, Poland, 18–20 June, 2001, Volume 1, 171–183
Hofstede, G. (1994) *Cultures and Organisations: Software of the Mind.* London: HarperCollinsBusiness.
Kallman, E. A. and Grillo, J. P. (1996) *Ethical Decision Making and Information Technology: An Introduction with Cases.* New York: McGraw-Hill
Kolodner, J. (1993) *Case Based Reasoning.* Morgan Kaufmann, San Mateo, CA
Liffick, B.W. (1995) Analysing Ethical Scenarios. *Proceedings of an International Conference on the Ethical Issues of Using Information Technology, ETHICOMP95,* De Montfort University, Leicester, UK, 28-30 March, 1995
Maner, W. (1998) ICEE: Online Ethical Scenarios with Interactive Surveys and Real-time Demographics. *Proceedings of an International Conference on the Ethical Issues of Using Information Technology,* Erasmus University, Rotterdam, 25-27 March, 1998, 462-470
Martin, D., Huff, C., Gotterbarn, D. and Miller, K. (1995) Curriculum Guidelines for Teaching the Consequences of Computing. *Proceedings of the ACM/SIGCAS Symposium on Computers and the Quality of Life (CQL '96),* Philadelphia, PA, USA, 14 February, 1996, 73-85
Moor, J.H. (2000) Assessing Artificial Intelligence and Its Critics, in: Bynum, T.W. and Moor, J.H. eds. *The Digital Phoenix: How Computers are Changing Philosophy,* Revised Edition. Blackwell, Oxford: 213-230
Munro, K., and Munro, K. (2002) The Challenge of Teaching Ethics in a Multi-Cultural University Setting: A South African Perspective. *Proceedings of ETHICOMP 2002,* 13-15 November, 2002, Universidade Lusiada, Lisbon, Portugal, 643-660
Pena, R., Botía, J. and Extremera, J. (1999) Teaching Ethics Embedded in Technical Subjects. *Proceedings of the Fourth International Conference on the Social and Ethical Impacts of Information and Communication Technologies,*

ETHICOMP'99, Libera Universita Internatzionale degli Studi Sociali, Rome, 5–8 October, 1999

Rahanu, H. (1999) *Development of a Case-based Reasoner as a Tool to Facilitate Understanding of the Ethical and Professional Issues Invoked by Failed Information Systems Projects.* Ph.D. Thesis, University of Wolverhampton, Wolverhampton, UK

Schweighofer, E. (1999) The Revolution in Legal Information Retrieval or: The Empire Strikes Back. *Journal of Information, Law and Technology, 1999, Vol. 1.* http://elj.warwick.ac.uk/jilt/99-1/schweigh.html (Accessed: 10/07/2003)

Smyth, B. and McKennac, E. (1999) Footprint-Based Retrieval. *Proceedings of the Third International Conference on Case-Based Reasoning, ICCBR-99, Seeon Monastery, Munich, Germany. 27-30 July, 1999, 343-357.* <http://www.cs.ucd.ie/staff/bsmyth/home/crc/iccbr99c.ps> (Accessed: 10/07/2003)

Spinello, R. A. (1997) *Case Studies in Information and Computer Ethics.* Prentice-Hall, Upper Saddle River, New Jersey. *Raising Ethical Awareness: A Case-Based Aiding System for Computing Students Science and Engineering Ethics, Volume 11,* Issue 2, 2005 315

Stanoevska-Slabeva, K., Handschuh, S., Hombrecher, A. and Schmid, B. F. (1998) Efficient Information Retrieval: Tools for Knowledge Management. *Proceedings of the Second International Conference on Practical Aspects of Knowledge Management (PAKM98)*, Basel, Switzerland, 29-30 October, 1998, 23-1 to 23-6. http://sunsite.informatik.rwth.aachen.de/Publications/CEURWS/Vol13/paper23.ps (Accessed: 10/07/2003)

Thagard, P. (2000) Computation and the Philosophy of Science, in: Bynum, T.W. and Moor, J. H. eds. *The Digital Phoenix: How Computers are Changing Philosophy.* Revised Edition, Blackwell, Oxford: 48-61

Thompson, J. B. (2001) Slowly Reaching Towards Software Engineering Professionalism: A Report on Recent Activities Across the World. *Proceedings of the Fifth International Conference on The Social Impacts of Information and Communication Technologies, ETHICOMP 2001,* Gdansk, Poland, 18–20 June, 2001, Volume 1, 14–21

Widdison, R. (2001) Some Current Legal Issues in Legal Information Retrieval. *Proceedings of the 16th BILETA Annual Conference, 9-10 April, 2001, University of Edinburgh, Scotland.* http://www.bileta.ac.uk/01papers/widdison.html (Accessed: 02/01/02)

Wiener, N. (1988) *The Human Use of Human Beings: Cybernetics and Society.* Boston: Houghton Mifflin

Woodcock, L. and Armstrong, B. (2001) Legal Awareness: Issues in Computing Ethics. *Proceedings of the Twelfth Australasian Conference on Information Systems,* 4-7 December 2001, Southern Cross University, New South Wales, Australia

Zeleznikow, J. and Hunter, D. (1994) *Building Intelligent Legal Information Systems.* Deventer, The Netherlands: Kluwer Law and Taxation Publishers

13
An approach to developing ethical sensitivity in student nurses

Patricia Perry and Janis Moody

There are many ethical challenges facing tomorrow's graduates and the response of providers of higher education preparing students to meet these challenges, is of vital importance. In the healthcare context this relates to teaching ethics to students to prepare them for the 'real world' and the ethical decision-making inherent in any realm of practice. In nursing programmes, the balance of learning is fifty percent clinical practice and fifty percent theory (Nursing and Midwifery Council, 2004a). The focus of this chapter, however, relates to theoretical ethical content and its application to practice in the form of a module entitled 'Ethics in Healthcare'. One of the main aims of this module is to prepare our students in a way that helps them make sense of ethics in clinical practice and to develop their ethical sensitivity. Our understanding of this term is that students should be able to 'recognise values and value conflicts' (Fry and Johnstone, 2002, p.182) as this is essential to identification of situations which involve moral distress or dilemma.

Teaching ethics in nursing will be considered in general terms and then more specifically in relation to an ethics module and the methods used to facilitate learning in this module. In order to establish the historical context a brief overview will be provided of how ethics teaching in nurse education has developed. Consideration will be given to the current situation taking into account the various external and internal influences and drivers.

There has been increasing emphasis placed on ethics in the nursing curriculum and the reasons for this are multi-faceted. From a review of relevant literature it is apparent that nursing has always incorporated some form of ethical preparation for students (Fry, 1989; Allmark, 1995; Sellman, 1997). The current momentum to include formal ethics education in nursing courses at both pre- and post-registration levels has, however, taken place within the last two decades or so and is the result of a number of recent developments. There is now a general agreement that ethical decision making is an essential component of professional nursing practice, as evidenced by the burgeoning literature on ethics in nursing and the current emphasis on ethics in the nursing curriculum. There are a number of reasons for this. Societal issues such as rapidly developing technology, an ageing population, distribution of scarce resources, and the changing role of the nurse have resulted in an escalation in the number of ethical issues faced by nurses in their day-to-day work. This has led to an increasing realization of the underlying moral dimension of healthcare practice in general and nursing practice in particular (Scott, 1998). Further, the professional nurse of today is expected to be accountable for all aspects of professional and ethical decision making. Thus, it is essential that modern nurses acquire and practice the skills of ethical reasoning in order that they are able to understand, participate in and influence a complex health care system. As well as societal influences there may be another reason for the current emphasis on ethics in the nursing curriculum. It could be viewed as part of the professionalising process with the related emphasis placed on codes of professional conduct and accountability (Scott, 1998).

All nursing courses in the United Kingdom (UK) are now required to include ethics in the curriculum, although there is considerable variation in the content of ethics courses and the teaching methods used to assist in the acquisition of ethical reasoning (Parsons *et al.*, 2001; Nolan and Markert, 2002; Woods, 2005). The reform of nurse education which occurred as a result of the Project 2000 curriculum (UKCC, 1986) represented a major change in nurse education and professional nursing structures. In the Project 2000 curricula ethics was recognised as being a central component of nurse preparation and the need for a comprehensive ethics input into basic nurse education was clearly articulated in this document. The next major re-organisation of nurse education in 2001 was based on the document entitled 'Partnerships in development and delivery: Fitness for Practice – Implementation in Scotland, Curriculum Guidelines for Pre-registration Nursing Programmes', known as 'Fitness for Practice' (National Board for Nursing, Midwifery and Health Visiting for Scotland [NBS], 2000), which served to further emphasise the importance of ethical and legal content for nursing programmes. Undoubtedly, this was the result of some of the issues previously mentioned as well as an increasingly knowledgeable and litigious society.

The challenge to nurse educators has been and continues to be how to integrate the required professional, ethical and legal content into an already overcrowded curriculum and to make it meaningful to practice. The approach we have taken is an integrated curriculum approach which entails weaving an identifiable strand of content throughout the programme (Ryden et al., 1989). Thus, the ethical and legal content is identifiable at various stages of the programme. A two-pronged approach is taken, in that, ethical content is included in a variety of modules and there is also a specific module, which focuses solely on ethics and law. This module takes place in the second year of the Diploma of Higher Education in Nursing and Bachelor of Nursing Degree (Adult) programmes. Prior to undertaking the module, Ethics in Healthcare, students will have achieved competencies in professional and ethical issues in theory and practice modules in Year 1.

As a result of the far-reaching nature of ethical and legal issues in healthcare provision, the aims of the module are multi-factorial. Our stated aim is to allow students to examine ethical, professional and legal aspects of healthcare provision. To achieve this students are required to develop an understanding of relevant theories and principles and relate these to a variety of pertinent issues derived from practice. Further, it is expected that during the course of lectures, discussions and seminars students will become more aware of their own moral values and will be encouraged to examine and question the justificatory basis of these values. In addition to raising awareness, it is expected that on completion of the module students will have the ability to recognise ethical situations in practice at micro and macro levels and to contribute to ethical decision-making within a healthcare setting with the support of clinical staff. There is an expectation that these skills will continue to develop over the course of the programme.

The theoretical approaches to teaching ethics and ethical decision-making which are utilised in Ethics in Healthcare will now be considered. The principle-based theoretical perspective is the dominant approach used in this module and other ethics content throughout the curriculum and the reasons for this will be explored. Consideration will also be given to the relevance of other theoretical approaches and the need to more fully integrate these into our teaching, as this is one of the main challenges we face in developing this module.

Ultimately, there is no definitive theory for ethical decision-making in nursing. There are a range of approaches taken which include treating it variously as a branch of philosophy, bio-ethics, medical ethics, professional conduct or moral education. This uncertainty has its origins in the fact that there is not a theoretical approach to ethical deliberation which is wholly relevant to nursing (Allmark, 1995).

Ethics and ethics education in nursing has traditionally been dominated by ethical theories and principles which have evolved in biomedicine (Fry, 1989; Doane, 2002). Ethical principles are guides to moral decision-making and moral action, and focus on the formation of moral judgements in practice (Beauchamp and Childress, 2001). Ethical situations can be analysed in terms of these principles and guidance for behaviour can be obtained from them (Allmark, 1995). The moral agent is someone who objectively analyses ethical dilemmas and utilises principles and rules to help them make and justify their decisions.

There has been criticism of this approach and its relevance to nursing has been questioned, as it does not take account of the importance of relationships between the individuals involved, but requires application of ethical principles in an objective and impartial manner (Fry and Johnstone, 2002). This has led to an increased awareness that nursing ethics must be considered as more than a branch of medical ethics and adherence to a set of principles. In light of this, it is evident that other relevant ethical theories need to be taken into account such as the 'ethic of care' which emphasizes human relationships, interconnectedness and caring. Noddings (1984), has built on Gilligan's (1977), theory of moral development in women, and this has led to an ethic of care theory which encompasses concepts relating to the importance of human relationships, moral obligation, moral good and moral justification (Fry and Johnstone, 2002) which has clear applicability in the nursing context.

Virtue theory is another important approach to ethics which has an almost hidden influence on the formation of ethical values in relation to professional behaviour in nursing. As with an ethic of care, virtue ethics does not include a framework of principles into which ethical issues or dilemmas are required to fit. Instead it relates to 'what sort of person one ought to be and what sort of life one ought to live' (Tschudin, 2003, p.65).

The cultivation of virtues, or dispositions, does not normally fall under the umbrella of any discrete part of the modern nursing curriculum, but instead forms part of the hidden curriculum and relates to professional behaviour as demanded by nursing's code of professional conduct (Sellman, 1997). Nursing continues to insist upon professional behaviour both in the work and personal sphere as evidenced by the demands of the NMC code of professional conduct: standards for conduct, performance and ethics (Nursing and Midwifery Council, 2004b) and on the basis of this it would seem that nurses are required to aspire to exemplary moral standards (Sellman, 1997). Articulation of these virtues or moral standards could be considered as part of the role of the nurse educator when attempting to develop ethical sensitivity in students.

The principle-based approach, the ethics of care and virtue ethics do not, however, need to be viewed as separate realities. Nurses should have knowledge of different perspectives and should be able to use them appropriately depending on the situation. The different approaches should be considered as complementary rather than in opposition.

The principle based approach to ethical decision making provides a framework on which to base decisions but on its own is a rather sterile approach. It needs to be supplemented by an overarching caring approach with some attempt to articulate this effectively for practicing nurses. Taking this type of pluralistic approach requires a broad knowledge base and the confidence to incorporate differing perspectives and make them meaningful to practice. If this is to become a reality student nurses need to be conversant with a variety of ethical approaches and this is no easy task given the lack of specialised nurse teachers with the ability to integrate and make meaningful the varied approaches to ethics which are relevant to nursing. Although the principle-based approach is currently predominant in Ethics in Healthcare and other ethics input throughout the curriculum, reference is made to other theoretical approaches, how they relate to each other and to practice. Our aim is to move towards a more integrated approach and to more effectively articulate this for students in order to enhance their ethical sensitivity.

In the module the nursing process is the framework which has been adapted as a model for ethical decision-making (Thompson *et al.*, 2000). This allows students to apply the different theoretical approaches in the context of an already familiar decision-making model. Students are introduced to the nursing process in Year I as a framework for planning nursing care and thus its relevance to nursing is appreciated. The nursing process entails assessment, planning, implementation and evaluation and it has been adapted to take into account the relevant ethical theories and principles which students are introduced to in the module.

Thus far, discussion has focused on why nurses are required to study ethics and the challenges that are of current and future concern for those teaching, as well as those undertaking nursing programmes and registering as nurses. Consideration is now given to the preparation of our students for the challenges of clinical practice and how we attempt to keep this grounded in the real world. What follows is an outline of the key learning, teaching and assessment strategies used in the module with particular reference to the use of seminars and seminar presentation as assessment. This includes explanation of how we encourage students to engage in learning and endeavour to provide an environment that is conducive to the development of ethical sensitivity.

As ethics has become a necessary part of the nursing curriculum, it could be assumed that there is consensus within nurse education regarding the content and method for teaching student nurses this subject. Unfortunately this is not so. While professional bodies promote consideration of the subject (Nolan and Markert, 2002), and the module content is guided by the recommendations indicated in the Fitness for Practice document (NBS, 2000), there is little evidence on which to base module design. As with medical education, which underwent a formal enquiry into ethics education for doctors (the Pond Report, 1987), investigation into the teaching of ethics in nursing, midwifery and health visiting throughout the United Kingdom was undertaken. The Institute of Medical Ethics in collaboration with the Royal College of Nursing conducted this work and their findings and recommendations were published in 1991 (Gallagher and Boyd, 1991). Some of their recommendations have been adopted by individual institutions, but no consensus statement, such as the document issued by the teachers of medical ethics and law (Consensus Statement, 1998), is apparent.

Undoubtedly, professional guidelines, curricular documents and research-based recommendations are important to the development of ethics modules, as they reflect the concerns and requirements of regulating bodies, educational institutions and professional organisations. However, of fundamental importance is the Fitness for Practice document (NBS, 2000). This brings together the statutory and professional requirements relevant to pre-registration nurse education and provides a framework for all pre-registration nursing programmes. It consists of four domains, one of which is the Professional and Ethical Domain, and it indicates the outcomes and competencies relating to professional, ethical and legal issues, nurses must achieve in order to progress on the programme and register as a nurse. A proportion of the outcomes are addressed within the Ethics in Healthcare module.

However, in addition to this requirement, the process of module content selection should be dynamic rather than static as there is a need to respond to what might be called 'bottom up' as well as 'top down' considerations. This requires lecturers to identify ethics topics emerging from the care setting and to maintain module content that is relevant for changing clinical practice and thus relevant to the challenges facing our students. Therefore, the module content reflects the regulatory body's guidance, concerns identified by clinical staff and the education, nursing and ethics literature. At present this includes topics such as responsibility and accountability and use and abuse of power.

The learning, teaching and assessment strategies adopted by the module team are master lecturers followed by associated seminars. Master lectures are used to introduce new theoretical concepts and ethical topics to the student cohort and the seminars enable further exploration and discussion within a seminar group (25–30 students). The assessment is a seminar presentation undertaken in a small seminar presentation group (three students) which is lecturer and peer assessed. The lecturer assessment considers achievement of the module learning outcomes and the specific learning outcomes students prepare for their seminar presentation. Peer assessment is completed prior to presentation by those in the seminar presentation group and is their assessment of their peers' participation in the process of developing the seminar presentation.

One of the aims of small group learning, in the form of seminar groups, is to advance the topic that has been introduced in the lecture. Although seminars traditionally involve reading a paper, which is then presented by one member of a group and followed by group discussion (Quinn, 2000, p.371), the module uses a topic-centred approach. This requires students to review and reflect on the topic area using guided reading and take an active part in seminar discussion. The role of the lecturer, initially, is to lead the seminar group discussion and serve as a role model concerning this activity. However, over the course of the module, as students become familiar with the seminar activities and module content and develop confidence, the lecturer moves to a facilitative role and eventually students lead their own seminar which is their module assessment.

The seminar groups provide a suitable forum for discussion. This is an important method for the module as it gives students the opportunity to express themselves in terms of the concepts under study, allows for closer contact between teacher and student and it can enable development of a variety of communication skills (Jacques, 2003). While discussion is important, providing a challenging focus for consideration is equally so. Examination of the ethical component of current professional guidelines, codes of practice, clinical scenarios, case studies or a particular law, for example the Adults with Incapacity (Scotland) Act 2000, can promote active learning and enhance ethical sensitivity.

An example of this is the introduction of a brief scenario, related to a topic area such as truth-telling, by the lecturer. Students can then be organised into smaller groups and asked to identify any ethical issues which arise in the scenario, with different groups considering it from the perspective of a patient, a nurse and a relative. Once sufficient time has been given for this, feedback and discussion can be undertaken as a class or by another approach such as buzz groups. During the activity students may at first consider the scenario a practical concern but through discussion different moral values often become apparent, some of which may conflict and are worthy of further consideration. This can be extended to discussion of what the nurse should do in the situation and on what moral basis this action could be justified.

Such methods can enable the lecturer to clarify the lecture content and link important concepts to clinical issues. For students, it provides variety in learning and makes the relevance and applicability of the module content explicit. Further to this, the discussion in small groups can promote student learning by raising student interest (Race, 2001) and stimulating individuals to share their views, reconsider their attitudes and explore a range of issues (Reece and Walker, 2000). While these are important activities, it is also essential that such exploration challenges students to consider not only their personal values and views but to consider those of the patient, their families and other members of the care team.

There are a number of influences on the effective use of the seminars. A particular concern is the grouping of students, as the nature of the seminar group will have an effect on the learning that takes place and is significant for student engagement. The student group size varies but a cohort is approximately 200 students and there are two cohorts a year. Our approach is to use established reflective groups consisting of students who share their experiences of clinical practice on a regular basis within the university environment. For our purposes reflective groups are combined, with approximately 25–30 students forming a seminar group. This number of participants is over the limit of recommended small group size (Reece and Walker, 2000) and could consequently affect the process of discussion and quality of interaction between participants (Quinn, 2000). However, the mix of students provides an element of familiarity with others, from reflective sessions, that can enhance discussion while still offering opportunities for new relationships to develop.

The variety of previous experience (life and work) and academic backgrounds of students are also influential concerning seminar group functioning. Often student groups are diverse and it is possible to have an ex-telecommunications engineer sitting next to someone who has worked as a health care assistant for many years and a recent school leaver. It is therefore essential to develop knowledge of the group to be able to draw on the wealth of experience students possess and to meet the particular educational needs of the student group

A further influence on student learning will be the lecturers. The module team are registered nurses of varying clinical backgrounds, such as care of the older person or accident and emergency care, and most of the team have undertaken further study in the field of ethics, philosophy or ethics and law in addition to nurse teaching. We have continued links with clinical settings which help to maintain an awareness of issues concerning patients and clinical staff. Each member of staff also has responsibility for a reflective group as described and is experienced in small group learning and teaching.

As previously mentioned the assessment of the module is a seminar presentation. This maintains the continuity of the module and requires students, within a presentation group of three, to select a topic for development and presentation. Our expectations of students are that they access and retrieve relevant literature, prepare, organise, and present the key issues concerning their topic to other members of the seminar group. Time is also set aside for those presenting to answer questions from the class and it is expected that a larger group discussion will ensue.

In providing a degree of educational choice regarding their chosen topic we hope to encourage students to engage with the ethics content. However, some limitations on topic selection are inevitable to ensure students can achieve the stated module learning outcomes (Crooks et al., 2001). Nevertheless students can focus on a topic of interest linked to the module themes and present it in their own style via their preferred medium. This has sometimes resulted in students choosing to role play a scenario and discuss this with the class or has involved thoughtful use of video clips to illustrate key ethical issues. Overall providing some aspects of choice can imbue a sense of ownership of the topic and is meaningful for students.

Another factor concerning choice of topic is that students may have a desire to focus on a topic but do not see the connection between it and the module content. Exploring this carefully with the seminar presentation group can usually resolve this situation. It can help students to fulfil their needs and if effectively facilitated, contributes to the learning process. Of course, we often learn something during this process as students regularly suggest excellent topics for presentation that we have not considered.

In addition to the presentation students also provide a summary paper and a reference list. This requirement has a number of aims, which are made explicit to students at the beginning and throughout the module, but in particular undertaking these activities aims to consolidate both the seminar presentation group cohesiveness and strengthen the seminar presentation. Overall the process of preparation necessary for seminar presentation makes it less likely that students will take a superficial approach to learning, as success necessitates a level of engagement with the content which can result in deep learning (Cole and Chan, 1994).

Throughout the module the lecturer acts as a lecturer/facilitator. This will involve acting as a resource person to provide information concerning the general running of the module, the organisation of seminars, seminar presentations and audio-visual resources and guides to enable students to 'focus in' on their chosen topic for assessment. However, we consider facilitation (and the associated skills) to be of crucial importance to managing the learning experience. Creating an atmosphere to enable students to learn, giving them the opportunity to learn by doing, where they can gain feedback from their peers and lecturer in a 'safe and supportive environment' (Race, 2001, 149) are our main objectives.

In conclusion, there are many challenges for tomorrow's graduates such as meeting the needs of a changing society, increased accountability in practice and an expanding and sometimes diverse role. It is essential that the students of today are prepared appropriately to respond to such challenges, particularly those concerning ethics and decision-making. As already suggested one of the main challenges for nurse teachers is to make ethics meaningful for student nurses and to develop an eclectic approach which incorporates a variety of theoretical approaches that are relevant to nursing. Further to this the development of ethical sensitivity can be seen as an important precursor to moral development. This is something, which we are currently attempting to develop within our ethics teaching across the nursing curriculum. Further, by adopting the approach to teaching, learning and assessment as outlined, and being flexible in our role as teacher/facilitator, we hope to adequately prepare students for the demands of future practice.

Currently, the authors are engaged in review of this module as part of the wider evaluation of the pre-registration nursing curriculum. Influences on this activity are the student module evaluations, external examiner review, the Scottish subject benchmark statement for Nursing (Quality Assurance Agency for Higher Education, NHS Scotland and the Scottish Executive, 2002) and the Standards of proficiency for pre-registration nursing education (Nursing and Midwifery Council, 2004a).

REFERENCES

Allmark, P. (1995) Uncertainties in the teaching of ethics to students of nursing, *Journal of Advanced Nursing*, 22, 374-378

Beauchamp, T. L. and Childress, J. F. (1994) *Principles of Biomedical Ethics* (4th edition). Oxford: Oxford University Press

Cole, P. G. and Chan, L. K. S. (1994) *Teaching principles and practice* (2nd edition). New York: Prentice Hall

Consensus Statement by teachers of medical ethics and law in UK medical schools (1998) Teaching medical ethics and law within medical education: a model for the UK core curriculum, *Journal of Medical Ethics*, 24, 188-192

Crooks, D., Lunyk-Child, O., Patterson, C. and LeGris, J. (2001) Facilitating Self-Directed Learning; in Rideout E. (ed.), *Transforming nursing education through problem-based learning*. London: Jones and Bartlett Publishers

Doane, G. H. (2002) In the spirit of creativity: the learning and teaching of ethics in nursing, *Journal of Advanced Nursing*, 39 (6), 521-528

Fry, S. (1989) Teaching ethics in nursing curricula, *Nursing Clinics of North America*, 24 (2), 485-497

Fry, S. and Johnstone, M. J. (2002) *Ethics in Nursing Practice, A Guide to Ethical Decision Making* (2nd edition). Oxford: Blackwell Publishing

Gallagher, U. and Boyd, K. M. (eds.) (1991) *Teaching and Learning in Nursing*

Ethics. Harrow: Scutari Press

Gilligan, C. (1977) In a different voice: women's conceptions of self and morality, *Harvard Educational Review*, 74 (4), 481-517

Institute of Medical Ethics, Working Party on the Teaching of Medical Ethics (1987) *Report of a Working Party on the Teaching of Medical Ethics* - chairman, Sir Desmond Pond - The Pond Report, edited by Kenneth M. Boyd, London, IME Publications

Jacques, D. (2003) Teaching small groups, *British Medical Journal*, 326, 492-494

National Board for Nursing, Midwifery and Health Visiting for Scotland (2000) *Partnerships in development and delivery: Fitness for Practice – Implementation in Scotland, Curriculum Guidelines for Pre-registration Nursing Programmes*. Edinburgh: NBS

Noddings, N. (1984) *Caring: A Feminine Approach to Ethics and Moral Education*. Berkeley: University of California Press

Nolan, P. W. and Markert, D. (2002) Ethical Reasoning Observed: A longitudinal study of nursing students, *Nursing Ethics*, 9(3), 243-258

Nursing and Midwifery Council (2004a) *Standards of proficiency for pre-registration nursing education*. London: NMC

Nursing and Midwifery Council (2004b) *The NMC code of professional conduct: standards for conduct, performance and ethics*. London: NMC

Parsons, S., Barker, P. J. and Armstrong, A. E. (2001) The Teaching of Healthcare Ethics to Students of Nursing in the UK: A Pilot Study, *Nursing Ethics*, 8 (1), 45-56

Quality Assurance Agency for Higher Education, NHS Scotland and the Scottish Executive (2002) *Scottish subject benchmark statement – Nursing*, Gloucester, QAA

Quinn, F. M. (2000) *Principles and Practice of Nurse Education* (4th edition). London: Stanley Thornes

Race, P. (2001) *The Lecturer's Toolkit, A Practical Guide to Learning, Teaching and Assessment* (2nd edition). London: Routledge Falmer

Reece, I. and Walker, S. (2000) *Teaching, Training and Learning, A Practical Guide* (4th edition). Sunderland: Business Education Publishers Ltd

Ryden, M. B., Duckett, L., Crisham, P., Caplan, A. and Schmitz, K. (1989) Multi-Course Sequential learning as a model for content for content integration: Ethics as a prototype, *Journal of Nursing Education*, 28 (3), 102-106

Scott, P. A. (1998) Professional Ethics: Are we on the wrong track? *Nursing Ethics*, 5 (6), 477-485

Sellman, D. (1997) The Virtues in the Moral Education of Nurses: Florence Nightingale Revisited, *Nursing Ethics*, 4 (1), 3-11

Thompson, I. E., Melia, K. M. and Boyd, K. M. (2000) *Nursing Ethics* (4th edition). Edinburgh: Churchill Livingstone

Tschudin, V. (2003) *Ethics in Nursing, The Caring Relationship* (3rd edition), Edinburgh, Butterworth-Heinemann

United Kingdom Central Council for Nursing, Midwifery and Health Visiting (1986) *Project 2000: a new preparation for nurses, midwifery and health visiting*. London: UKCC

Woods, M. (2005) Nursing Ethics Education: Are We Really Delivering the Good(s)? *Nursing Ethics*, 12 (1), 5-18

WEB SITE

Adults with Incapacity (Scotland) Act 2000 home (accessed 25.05.05): (http://www.scotland.gov.uk/about/JD/CL/00016360/home.aspx

14
Teaching ethics in higher education

Thomas Borchmann and Poul Bonde Jensen

INTRODUCTION

The growing number of ethics courses and ethics programmes within higher education in the Western World can probably be seen as a result of a variety of different factors, including among other things a felt need for a better preparation of students for the ethical challenges within their future professions and the often claimed complexity of modern life in general. Whether this need is seen as stemming from changes within society, changes within the professions, or changes within the student population, it is often fulfilled through the design and implementation of supplementary curricular modules introducing either professional codes of conduct or ethical reasoning. This leaves a critical examination of the form and content of the curriculum as such and its potential contributions to the experienced problem not covered.

In this chapter we will argue that the task of preparing students for the ethical challenges within their future professions ought not to be considered without prior reference to the more general task of supporting future practitioners in their acquisition of critical agency. The major reason for this claim is the belief that a new practitioner without a perception and overall understanding of him/her self as an equal, responsible and critically committed agent could easily fall prey to authoritarianism or opportunism and engage in the instrumental reasoning reigning in a lot of professional practices. In the first part of the chapter, support for this belief is offered by drawing on lessons derived from the works of William Perry (Perry, 1970) and Paulo Freire (Perry, 1970). In the second part of the chapter, a variety of curriculum activities, which supposedly can support the student's acquisition of critical agency within a future professional practice, is outlined and discussed.

LESSONS FROM PERRY AND FREIRE

At a first glance, it might seem odd to try to bring together Perry's study of forms of ethical and intellectual development among Harvard college students and Freire's thoughts on critical education, stemming from adult literacy training in the 'Third World' in order to draw some common lessons; odd because Freire's view of educational activities as emancipating processes and his practical engagement with a formulation and realization of a pedagogy of the oppressed in more than one sense could be conceived to be worlds apart from Perry's interest in mapping the intellectual 'metamorphoses' of privileged freshmen. On the other hand, these oddities need not necessarily be stressed; ignoring their different focuses and risking a lot of gross oversimplifications, we will try to show that they both offer important lessons of the necessity of supporting students/practitioners in their quest for the acquisition of critical agency, as well as a broad variety of equally important lessons on the possible threats and obstacles to this acquisition. Lessons, which also leave us sceptical about the value and sufficiency of attempts to prepare students for the ethical challenges within their professions, which just take the form of rehearsals of codes of conduct or supplementary courses in ethical reasoning, but otherwise leave the curriculum unchanged.

Perry's scheme of intellectual and ethical development

In our view, the scheme developed by Perry and his colleagues convincingly maps a series of progressive stages of cognitive and ethical development, which can be used to characterize the actual and possible development of students in their overall journey from adolescence into adulthood or to characterize changes in the relations between a subject and the world, which have to be lived through almost every-time he/she enters a new context or domain (Knefelkamp, 1999; Borchmann, 2003). The four major stages - which all display possible ways of perceiving the world, the self, and the relation between the two by focussing on different ways of perceiving the character and origin of knowledge, value, and responsibility, are:

1. *Dualism* in which students/new practitioners see the world/a particular

practice through a conviction that right and wrong answers exist for everything and look to authorities for these – be it in the personalized form of other living beings or just 'theories' – as they – and not themselves – are regarded as 'holders of truth'.
2. *Complex dualism/ multiplicity*, in which students/new practitioners acknowledge the existence of uncertainty and the existence of oppositional views, but either regards these as mere opinions or assumes the perspective of the most persuading authority, still not trusting themselves.
3. *Relativism*, in which students/new practitioners acknowledge conflicting or contradictory viewpoints and change their perceptions of authorities as the only available source of answers, but have not yet developed – and to some extend are actively resisting – personal stances which are both committed, responsible and tolerant.
4. *Commitment in relativism*, in which students have developed personal stances, are able to make commitments, but also understand the need of examining and supporting these (Perry, 1970). The four stages include nine detailed positions or sub-stages, that vary in complex ways which will not be explained in detail here. Instead we will focus shortly on the major transitions from dualism to relativism, and from relativism to commitment in relativism.

The transition from dualism to relativism mainly involves the recognition of uncertainty. However, this transition is always threatened by a regress into an even more intolerant dualism or an entrenching in proprietary absolutism as the initial embrace of relativism involves a loss of a previously felt security; a felt security, which can both stem from having a fixed and comforting worldview and from a more fluid submission to the authority of others. A successful transition from dualism to relativism, that is an acceptance of uncertainty and the embracing of relativism, provides, however, no safe haven in the long run and can lead to opportunism, dissociation or despair if not succeeded by a further transition from relativism to commitment in relativism. This transition requires among other things the student/practitioner to act on his/her own beliefs and experiences, but also an acceptance of the contextual qualities of knowledge and an acceptance of the existence of criteria for evaluating competing views.

Freire on consciousness and emancipation

For Freire servile submission, opportunism and despair are also in focus along with other manifestations of self-destructive tendencies: Fatalism, horizontal violence, love of oppressors, self-depreciation, lack of confidence and emotional dependence. These manifestations are however not viewed as a result of youth or an unsuccessful entrance into a new practice, but instead as general outcomes of a historical conditioning imposed by social relations of domination. Developing his own vocabulary to describe the different stages of human development, Freire distinguishes between *semi-intransitive consciousness, naive transitive consciousness and critical consciousness*, which all convey different types of relations between the subject and the world. The *semi-intransitive* stage marks a consciousness that lives passively within a given reality, where interest centres almost totally on matters of daily survival. It is marked by fatalism and an authoritarian acceptance of the given social order. The *naive transitive* stage is characterized by a greater capacity to actively engage others and the world through inquiry and action – or in the existential vocabulary of Freire, by an initial 'Being *with* the World' rather than just 'Being *in* the World' – but also by a tendency to hold focalized views of problems and a vulnerability to sectarian irrationality, that is the entertainment of dualism or an unreflective absolutism. Finally, the *critical-transitive* stage is characterized by an open embrace of others and the world, a depth in perspective and a non-focalized, structure-oriented interpretation of problems as well as openness to revision and reconstruction of views held.

For Freire the movement towards a critical consciousness also requires changes in the way the individual perceives the world, him or her self, as well as knowledge. In order to be with the world rather than just in it, one has to change one's view of the world and the given social order as something that is static or inevitable and instead regard it as a historical reality susceptible of transformation. This changed perception is among other things linked to an understanding and 'profanization' of knowledge and theoretical perspectives as 'the creatures of hitherto men', that is historical deposits, which can serve as means to maintain, rather than means to neutrally describe or challenge the present social order.

By locating the origins of the passive and fragmented consciousness both in existing social relations of dominance and in the more abstract colonization of the life world by administrative logics (see Allman, 1999; Morrow and Torres, 2002), Freire can be said to point to a growth potential – or reservoir of potential insight – residing in an examination of why we think, what we think, that does not only direct itself towards the possible reasons for a belief, but also towards its possible causes. In other words: you must take to heart the dialectical lesson – that man is both a product and a producer of social life – and critically examine knowledge and perceptions held as they may be systematically permeated by oppressive ideology or simply "locked" or fragmented due to their dependencies on existing vocabularies or views. The process of developing critical consciousness, which for Freire also includes transformative action, is named 'Conscientization', a term, which has been popularized and widely used leading sometimes to a dilution of its action component and sometimes to a dilution of its origin in a critique of a class-divided and dependent society.

Of the importance of keeping a focus on critical agency, when considering the task of preparing students for ethical challenges within their future professions

In the introduction to this chapter we stated a scepticism about the value and sufficiency of attempts to prepare students for the ethical challenges within their professions, which just took the form of rehearsals of codes of conduct or supplementary courses in ethical reasoning, but otherwise left curriculum both unexamined and unchanged, and claimed that the task of preparing students for the ethical challenges within their future professions had to be seen as a task, that ought not to be considered without prior reference to the more general task of supporting future practitioners in their acquisition of critical agency. The main reason for this claim was the belief that a new practitioner without a perception and overall understanding of him/her self as an equal, responsible and critically committed agent could easily fall prey to authoritarianism or opportunism. Whereas the everyday experiences of working life alone might confirm the reality of these threats, both Freire and Perry offer us frameworks that enable us to understand some of the causes of these mishaps. Leaving their differences aside, they both remind us that active and critical agency cannot be taken for granted, but have to be conceived as something which has to be acquired by a series of troublesome transitions; transitions in which students/ practitioners ideally move from a passive, submissive and non-reflexive consciousness to a more active, engaged and critical consciousness, but also risk a regress into a holding of intolerant dualisms, a stranding in opportunism, an equally irresponsible dissociation or a frustrated despair.

Having argued for the importance of keeping the notion of critical agency in focus, when theorizing about the preparation of students for ethical challenges within their future professions, we will next turn our attention towards the question of how the acquisition of critical agency can be supported within the curriculum. Here, we are neither going to spend time on criticisms of curriculum activities, which in our view (at best) do nothing to support this acquisition, nor on commenting on the recent pressures on schools and universities to become producers of technically trained workers for whom the demands of responsible citizenship are subordinated to the vicissitudes of the marketplace. Rather, we will focus on a variety of activities used in curricula, that we have been responsible for, or participated in.

SOME SUGGESTIONS FOR CURRICULUM ACTIVITIES

A rich literature exists, which either seeks to derive curriculum prescriptions from the Perry Scheme (e.g. Capossela, 1993; Thoma, 1993; Kloss, 1994; Grossmann, 1994 among others) or discusses different ways of materializing Freire's prescriptions of dialogical peer circles as well as the possible roles and role-imperatives for the non-oppressive, but also "non-assistencialistic" learning-facilitator (e.g. Carr and Kemmis, 1985; Gadotti, 1996, among others). However, here we will limit ourselves to the suggestion and discussion of a range of activities, which have been used – and are being used – in curricula that we ourselves have been responsible for developing, just as we will avoid a specific focusing on principles for teacher-student – or rather; learner-learner interaction. The activities we will focus on are 1) *the confrontation and analysis of opposing views and perspectives*, 2) *the exploration of multi-voiced real-life cases*, 3) *mini research projects, and 4) the critical-reflexive practicum.*

The confrontation and analysis of opposing views and perspectives

The first activity we will suggest, we have labelled 'the confrontation and analysis of opposing views and perspectives'. One might argue that this is in fact something we have always done within curriculum as such, but here we will focus on the confrontation and analysis of opposing views and perspectives as an activity in itself. Regarded as a separate curriculum activity, the confrontation and analysis of opposing views and perspectives can, of course, unfold in a variety of different set-ups; oral exercises, written assignments, etc., just as it can also serve as a principle for the composition of one or more lectures. With regard to exercises and assignments we will, however, argue for the value of not making these activities of a kind which has to be engaged in individually. The reason for this is that a group- or pair-organization in our view also carries important potential within it with regard to a de-centring of authority as well as the offering of mutual peer support.

Viewed in the light of the Perry scheme, the rationale for making the confrontation and analysis of opposing views and perspectives a core activity in the curriculum is, of course, to invite (or challenge) dualistic thinkers to change their perception of knowledge, as well as allowing "multiplists" and (early) relativists to observe that diversity in perspectives is more than a diversity in mere opinion. Whereas oppositional views and perspectives in the Perry approach might here be seen as being related to differences in e.g. the anthropologies underlying the perspectives, the lessons derived from Freire do, however, also point to selections of other kinds of oppositions. One example is a presentation of a perspective or piece of knowledge claimed as value-free over against a claimed value-laden-ness of the same perspective/knowledge. Such oppositions are not hard to find within our own discipline of 'organisational theory and management theory', where the introductions to the merits and insights of the different schools of thought and the description of their progressive historical development, which can be found in main stream textbooks, can be confronted by labour-process theory (e.g. Braverman, 1974) or other critical and de-constructivist readings; readings in which ideas are not treated independently of their material context and where the claims to progress and knowledge advancement are also related to broader discourses of ethics and politics in order to display other patterns of continuity and progression (e.g. Hollway, 2000: Warring, 1992 among others). Such oppositions cannot only be said to stimulate changes in the student's perceptions of knowledge but also to permit a certain 'de-sacralization' of theories and authorities as 'holders of truth'.

The exploration of multi-voiced real-life cases

The second activity we will suggest is the exploration of multi-voiced real-life cases. By a multi voiced real-life case is meant a presentation of a real-life event in which everyone involved or concerned are given a voice. Whereas the benefits of the use of cases are praised from many directions - be they real-life cases, purely fictive ones or worst case- and many restrictions are put on the organization of case material (see Erskine *et al.*, 1998), an emphasis on the benefits of a multi-voiced case is rarely found. Hence, we will try to formulate a rationale (or 'ethionale') for multi-voiced cases here. However, we would claim that a real-life case holds a potential for a de-sacralization of authorities, which a purely fictive one does not.

A multi-voiced real-life case can, of course, be seen as yet another way of confronting students with the reality of diversity and pluralism. It can, however, also be seen as an opportunity to confront and juxtapose the dominant voice of the powerful with the normally silent voice of the powerless. Given the emphasis on the confrontation of dominant and dominated voices, it might be somewhat tempting to conceive the activity of exploring multi-voiced real-life cases as a variant of 'testimonials' in which privileged groups (or potential oppressors) are confronted with less privileged groups (or victims of oppression) in order to establish sympathy with the otherwise 'distant other' (or believed to find again the 'humanity' lost through their shared comparisons of the 'equally' dehumanizing effects of having power in excess – or a total lack of it). However, such a classification would ignore other and more straight-forward learning potentials residing in such a juxtaposition; learning potentials, which stem from the fact that also the road towards becoming an oppressor is layered with experiences of strategic action – be it both in the form of acts of dominance and in the form of acts of submission. To give a short example, when we introduce students to cases which deal with the classical theme of 'organizational participation', we aim to stimulate the students and ourselves to explore, among other things, the question of possible obstacles to a successful unification of the quest for effectiveness with the quest for power sharing, but also the 'strange' fact that this question historically has come to supersede interests in the conditions for a realization of work-place democracy. We often find that students are not only willing to use the popular phrase 'resistance to change' to label or designate a dominant human obstacle to the successful realization of this unification, but also to credit it with the status of a clear and adequate account. This willingness is however somewhat changed, if we ask students before-hand to list their own reasons for sometimes resisting offers to participate and discuss whether the diagnosis 'resistance to change' would be a clear and adequate description or a good and just starting point for the identification of possible explanations and/or a formulation of possible action-strategies to overcome this resistance. Here, we find that they are both very able to contest the clarity of the diagnosis and to suspect a series of inferior motives of strategic defocusing and responsibility placement underlying its use, just as they are able to offer a variety of rational reasons for rejecting offers to participation and a listing of warranties and/or requirements, which have to be given or fulfilled in order to overcome their resistance. Afterwards, when we introduced a practitioner, in this case an ordinary post-worker, to present his experiences with, and ambivalence towards, what at first glance, appears as unproblematic offers to increased participation within his workplace, we also find that the students are able to 'mirror' their own worries. This mirroring also allows the student to realize the rationality in the ambivalence of the post-worker, rather than just to see him as a sentimental or over-worried individual, who might or might not be an object for their sympathy.

Most of the cases we use stem from action research projects, which we have participated in within different organisations. This allows us to present 'data' – and sometimes also living co-researchers – as sources and resources for the students' explorations. Some of these cases are sketched in Borchmann and Jensen (2002) and Borchmann (2003). As an inspiration for the build-up of cases from a variety of sources, see also Boje (1998), who among other things presents an exemplary juxtaposing of Nike's official claims on ethical conduct with the voices of workers at Nike's over-sea factories, as these are present in a variety of reports on abusive labour practices. A good collection of small cases is also to be found in Corbett's *Critical Cases in Organizational Behaviour* (1994).

Mini research projects

The third activity we will focus on is mini research projects. As the name suggests, mini research projects are activities where students themselves conduct research; that is they try to answer, explore, solve or shed light on one or more problems or questions, which supposedly carry a potential for exemplary learning and therefore are allowed to serve as a reference point for the students' choice of theories to be studied and methods to be applied. The overall idea or rationale behind the use of mini research projects is of course to change the students' view of knowledge as something that is given – or a commodity, which can be acquired from others – into a view of knowledge as something which anyone can attempt to construe. Other important gains can, however, also be hoped for. Among these are the practical experiences of influence, self-authority and responsibility. Scope and length of the project-activities can differ. At Aalborg University half the students' time is spend on this kind of project-work from the first semester onwards. In each semester the students organize themselves in project groups and have to complete a project under the guidance of a supervisor. The projects are guided by an overall and fairly wide semester theme, which, along with the courses and supervision offered, should support exemplary learning. In our present practice the concept of exemplary learning can be said to be credited with conflicting meanings coming originally from the different definitions given by Wagenschein (1968) and Negt (1981). In the first definition the idea of exemplary learning simply means exemplary for a specific field or discipline. In the second the learner acquires an exemplary transition in consciousness with regard to his or her perception of the problem addressed. For a short introduction to the two concepts of exemplary learning and some reflections on their diverse implications for the perceptions of problems, as well as the scope of possible action strategies for problem-solving within curriculum development – see Borchmann and Lindhardt (2004).

The critical-reflective practicum

The final activity we would like to suggest here is the critical-reflexive practicum. By a critical–reflexive practicum we mean a practicum that not only aims at giving the student an introduction to a future professional practice, but also supports the student in directing both a critical and reflexive attention to the first meeting with professional practice. Different ways of supporting and stimulating these reflections are well known, including self-monitoring and/or feedback from both internal and external supervisors, although the critical reflections often have a tendency to be directed solely towards the student and not the practice or student-practice relation. Whereas a practicum is still not part of a lot of curricula in higher education, the present tendencies to just add this activity to the curricula need not necessarily be praised. Least of all if this only has the form of an unsupported, unsolicited 'legitimate peripheral participation'. An alternative way of designing an entrance into practice, which we experimented with at the Aarhus School of Business, could perhaps be labelled the transformative practicum. Here we coupled pairs of students with a practitioner and had these 'trios' conduct a practice-development project within the practitioner's organisation. During the six-month period in which the projects ran, both students and practitioners participated in a series of workshops, which all introduced to their critical action-research, while at the same time working with their projects within the organisations of the practitioners. For the organisations involved, the outcome of these projects can best be described as a series of collaboratively achieved deconstructions and reconstructions of understandings and local practices. For the students, one outcome among a lot of others was a changed view of their future practices as arenas for further inquiries and objects of possible change.

SUMMARY AND CONCLUSION

In this chapter we have argued for the importance of keeping the notion of critical agency in focus when theorizing about the preparation of students for the ethical challenges within their future professions. Our reason for doing so was to question the present tendency to just add supplementary ethics modules to the curriculum, leaving a questioning and examination of the content and form of existing curricula to itself. Our reason for the choice of focus on critical agency was the belief that a new practitioner without a perception and overall understanding of him/her self as an equal, responsible and critically committed agent could fall prey to authoritarianism or opportunism and engage in instrumental reasoning present in a lot of professional practices. This belief can of course be criticized for being overly negative in its view of both potential practitioners and practices, but even so, it might still serve to remind us of a series of important considerations, which otherwise could be forgotten or lost.

In the second part of the chapter we have suggested a variety of curriculum activities, which supposedly can support the student's acquisition of critical agency. All of these can be looked upon as activities, which allow for rich variations as well as further development within the different curricula of the professions. We hope that our suggestions might serve as sources of inspiration. Alternatively they can also serve as reminders of what used to be considered virtues in higher education and perhaps also of what used to be considered well-known vices.

REFERENCES

Allmann, P. (1999) *Revolutionary Social Transformation – Democratic Hopes, Political Possibilities and Critical Education*. London: Bergin & Garvey

Boje, D. (1998) How Critical Theory and Critical Pedagogy can unmask Nike's Labour Practices. *August Meeting of the Academy of Management Meetings*, San Diego

Borchmann, T. (2003) *Om kompetenceudvikling og aktionsforskning og kompetenceudvikling gennem aktionsforskning*. Department of Organization and Management. The Aarhus School of Business. DK

Borchmann, T. and Jensen, P. D. (2002) Aktionforskning som medium for praksisudvikling. *Conference "Aktionsforskning"*, Aalborg Universitet

Borchmann, T. and Lindhardt, S. (2004) Doing almost the same thing for somewhat different reasons - A note on variations within the Aalborg Model. In Kolmos, Fink and Krogh, eds. *The Aalborg PBL Model – Progress, Diversity and Challenges*. Aalborg University Press

Braverman, H. (1974) *Labor and Monoploy Capital: The Degradation of Work in the Twentieth Century*. New York: Monthly Review Press

Carr, W. and Kemmis S. (1985) *Becoming Critical*. London: Falmer Press

Capossela, T. (1993) Using William Perry's Scheme to Encourage Critical Writing. In Capossela, T. (ed.), *The Critical Writing Workshop: Designing Writing Assignments to Foster Critical Thinking*. Portsmouth: Boynton/Cook

Corbett, M. (1994) *Critical Cases in Organisational Behaviour*. London: MacMillan

Erskine, J. A. et al. (1998) *Teaching with Cases*. Richard Ivey School of Business. The University of Western Ontario; Ivey

Freire, P. (1970) *The Pedagogy of The Oppressed*. New York: Seabury

Freire, P. (1973) *Education for Critical Consciousness*. New York: Seabury

Gadotti, M. (1996) *The Pedagogy of Praxis – A Dialectical Philosophy of Education*. Albany: State University of New York Press

Hollway, W. (2000) *Work Psychology and Organizational Behaviour – Managing the Individual at Work*. London: Sage

Knefelkamp, L. (1999) "Introduction". In Perry, W.G. (ed.), *Forms of Ethical and Intellectual Development in the College Years – A scheme*. San Francisco: Jossey-Bass

Kloss, R. J. (1994) A Nudge is Best Helping Students Through the Perry Scheme of Intellectual Development, *College Teaching*. Vol. 42, no. 4

Grossman, R. W. (1994) Encouraging Critical Thinking Using The Case Study Method and Cooperative Learning Techniques, *Journal on Excellence in College Teaching*, 5 (1)

Morrow, R. and Torres, C. A. (2002) *Reading Freire and Habermas – Critical Pedagogy and Transformative Social Change*. New York: Teachers College Press

Negt, O. (1981) *Sociologisk fantasi og eksemplarisk indlæring*. København: Kurasje

Perry, W. (1970) *Forms of Ethical and Intellectual Development in the College Years – A scheme*. Holt, Rinehart and Winston

Thoma, G. A. (1993) The Perry Framework and Tactics for Teaching Critical Thinking in Economics, *Journal of Economic Education*, vol. 24: 2

Wagenschein, M. (1968) *Zum begriff des Exemplarischen Lehrens in "Verstehen Lehren"*. Basel: Beltz Verlag

Warring, S. (1992) *Taylorism Transformed – Scientific Management Theory since 1945*. Chapel Hill: University of North Carolina Press

15
Enabling professions

Simon Robinson

Much of the work in the book to this point has been focusing on particular professions. In this chapter I want to look at one approach to the concept of professions as a whole. I will focus first on the view that professions tend to fulfil a disabling role in society. I will then argue that a core role of the professions is actually to enable and empower, principally the client but also possibly other stakeholders. Whilst this is not an exhaustive view of what a profession is, it is a plausible view of at least important aspects of the work of the professions. I will then examine the relationship of empowerment to client autonomy. Finally, I will look at how pre-professional education might develop the professional as enabler.

DISABLING PROFESSIONS

Ivan Illich's critique of the professions is radical (1977). He suggests that the professions rose from the Middle Ages as soon as the definition of pastoral human need began to emerge. In this light the priesthood became the key 'arbiter' of the right way to live, taking away the responsibility from the individual. With the rise of the modern professions, far from this providing a disinterested service, power was simply transferred from the church to them.

Illich has several arguments. Firstly, professional expertise is anti-democratic, taking away responsibility and power from the individual, but also in many cases from governments, who will base decisions on expert judgement. Secondly, dependence upon the professions is further reinforced by the development of the consumer services model. In medicine, for instance, this leads to the view that health is connected to the consumption of health services.

This means that the success of the government and the health professions is measured by how well the service is supplied, and thus to an increase in the expectation of the potential client. All this leads to the generation of further demand and to the need for more professionals to fulfil that demand.

Thirdly, the professions in all this exceed their limits. They move from competent practitioners to 'ideologues', who claim the power to state what is in the client's interest and prescribe what should be done. No profession is immune from this use of power and Parker even suggests that the profession of philosophy as practised in the public sphere, might do this (Parker, 1994). Illich contrasts such an approach with the pattern of the professional giving his judgement and then allowing the client to decide what should be done about this

There can be no question that there is some truth in this model of the view of professions as disabling. As Campbell (1985) notes, the medical profession have often been seen as 'gods', who knew the best interest of the patient. Moreover, as Bauman argues, the example of the Holocaust shows how the division of labour and the growth of the expert could assist government in disabling society as a whole (Bauman, 1989).

However, there are problems with Illich's argument. Despite the evidence of the professional as disabling, it is equally true that professional bodies have increasingly been reflecting on how the professional can enable the client. The nursing profession has focussed on the empowering of the patient, and often too upon advocacy (O'Connor, 1987). The medical profession has begun to revolutionise the education of doctors through the development of interpersonal skills and a concern for the autonomy of the patient (exemplified in the debate about advance directives, see Kendrick and Robinson, 2002, 70 ff.).

Secondly, Illich's view of the proper professional-client relationship is simplistic. It assumes an individualistic liberal understanding of the whole process, such that the professional will simply communicate the data, and the client will make the appropriate decision. The autonomy of the client is seen simply as a right to be respected. However, the client for many reasons may not be in a position to make a decision, and may need to be enabled both to understand the significance of the data and how best to respond. Autonomy in this sense is something which is more relational, involving learning and possibly development. I will return to this in more detail shortly.

THE PROFESSIONS AS ENABLING

In different ways May (1985) and Koehn (1994) suggest that the role of the professional is precisely to enable the development of autonomy. May contrasts the image of the professional as adversary, fighting disease or fighting against the opposition in the courtroom, with the professional as teacher. This, he argues, involves a transformative process, with the client developing the capacity to make decisions, or the ability to make them in different contexts. May is careful to stress that such teaching would not be paternalistic but would involve a collaboration between one or more professionals and the client around the project, be that health, legal challenges, or an engineering project.

Koehn takes this further, arguing that the professional does not simply seek to avoid harm but to develop the best for the client. Developing the best can only be discovered in dialogue with the client. In this light Koehn stresses the importance of the professional enabling the client to articulate his need through developing his particular narrative. The starting point for the professional is listening to the client (Koehn, 2004, 175 ff.).

Close to these is the view of Schoen (1983). Schoen argues for reflective practice as being central to professional development. This includes an understanding of the professional's own role in any context, noting both limitations and opportunities. Schoen suggests also that a key part of the professional response is to treat the client as a reflective practitioner. As a reflective practitioner the client would be empowered, learning, as well as using, knowledge, insight and abilities in working out the particular problem.

AUTONOMY

At the heart of much of this is the role of the professional in enabling the client to make an autonomous decision. At the outset, however, this view of the professional as enabler or teacher might seem to be problematic. The liberal view, as noted above, is that it is simply for the professional to communicate the truth of his judgement, in the best way possible, and for the client to work this through in his context. This asserts a form of negative autonomy, parallel to Berlin's negative freedom (1969), in which the client's right to self governance is respected. The substance of that respect is that the professional does not try to influence or coerce the client.

However, whilst such respect is necessary it is not sufficient for the practice of autonomy. Autonomy, which involves the client taking responsibility for working through a decision, may need more positive assistance. This is parallel to Berlin's view of positive freedom, the freedom to achieve something, often requiring support of some kind, not simply the freedom from coercion.

This points to a more complex definition of autonomy. Clement (1996) suggests that autonomy is not a state to be respected but is rather a capacity to make and carry out our own decisions. Any capacity has to be learned and will involve dealing with many possible constraints. It is thus, often, a function of a relationship or relationships that enable the person to take responsiblity for his own decision making. Part of this involves the development of critical thinking, part an internal awareness of what ideas and feelings are driving the person, and part an awareness of the wider social and physical environment and the issues involved. In the light of that, autonomy is not simply a given but rather something that is continuously developing.

The question of autonomy in the professional/client relationship is also affected by the issues of responsibility and the wider relationships involved in any situation. Whilst the client relationship is central to the professional it is not the only one of importance. The professional engineer, for instance, has responsibilities to the client but wider responsibilities to the future generations and to the environment. Any building, if badly constructed or constructed in such as way as to ultimately adversely affect the environment, will affect not simply the client, but the many possible victims. This is the principle responsibility of non-maleficence, above all do no harm. In addition the professional, following Beauchamp and Childress (1989), will look for the best outcome for the client (beneficence). For professions such as medicine this involves seeing the patient's illness in a broader horizon than dealing with the immediate problem, enabling him to develop the best possible management of the condition, including possible lifestyle changes. Such changes may not be initially desired by the client or patient. For professionals such as engineering the best outcome for the community or the environment may go against the interest of the client. In that case the responsibility of the professional to the other stakeholders minimally means that he has to challenge the view of the client. This does not necessarily mean an adversarial challenge. There may be other ways of working through the issues. However, minimally, the professional cannot simply leave the client to make their own autonomous decision. The wider responsibility dictates some form of challenge.

In addition the professional has responsibility to the profession as such and to the maintenance of standards and relationships that will ensure continued trust. It could be argued that the independence of the professional, such that he does challenge the client, is ultimately for the client's good. The case of Enron, where the accountants' challenge was insufficient to counter the bullying response of the client business, is a good illustration (Sims and Brinkmann, 2003). Furthermore, not only did this lead ultimately to the downfall of Enron, it also involved, in one sense, a lack of autonomy on the part of Enron management. Their focus on the narrow outcomes of profit and success had blinkered them to the wider issues, and made them incapable of wise decision making. The concern with responsibility takes the debate on autonomy beyond the negative or positive views, to one that sees autonomy tied to identity and thus to working through personal and professional meaning in relation to one's culture and context (see Riceour 1977). This involves the individual taking responsibility for making meaning, as a 'part of ongoing communities defined by reciprocal bonds of obligation, common traditions and institutions.' (Ikonomidis and Singer, 1999, 523).

Clearly the range of what any of this might involve in terms of responding to autonomy in a professional context will vary. It can be illustrated with four different cases.

A civil engineering firm was asked to develop a runway in the Falkland Islands after the war with Argentina (Armstrong et al., 1999). The client, the UK Government, was clear about the need for this. In order to make a final decision the engineering firm had to bring together all the necessary data, about the different stakeholders, including the environment. The unusual features of the project included the remoteness of the site, and the need to make a minimal impact on a fragile local ecosystem – where penguins far outnumbered human beings. All of this was taken care of in the development of the project, which included an ethical and environmental audit. The findings were given to the client who then, in discussion with the engineers, was able to make its final decision about where the runway should go. The client was capable of making a decision, and therefore had the capacity for autonomy but could not make that decision without significant discussion with the engineers. They needed information and dialogue for the autonomous capacity to be exercised. Such a model is straightforward and could be played out in many different areas, such as medicine and the law. It would easily fit into the more liberal view of the professional role as well as the enabling view.

There are also far more complex cases which move more towards the enabling view. The Challenger space shuttle 51-L disaster is a good example. I have looked at this in more detail elsewhere, both the case as a whole and how it affects the autonomy of the professional (Robinson, 2002, 2005). Here then I will only mention the autonomy of the client. First, the immediate client was the American Government, acting through NASA. The engineers involved worked for Morton-Thiokol Industries (MTI), who were responsible for building the solid fuel rocket boosters. Also involved were the Marshall Space Flight Centre (responsible for the propulsion system). The autonomy of the client in this situation is not straightforward. NASA had immense political and financial pressures on them to launch, connected to the maintenance of the shuttle programme. There were further pressures to time the launch with the U.S. president's State of the Union speech. There were then a number of different values and perceived priorities which radically affected the capacity of the client to make a reasoned judgement. The situation was further exacerbated by financial pressures on MTI, who depended on the government contract for survival. This presents a classic case of the profession as part of an industry under pressure trying to relate to a client who wanted a professional judgement that supported their pressing objectives. Autonomy in this situation required an articulation and critical examination both of the values underlying the rush to launch, and of the criteria for launching. At no point was this done. In fact the pressure was rather to affect the engineers of MTI who initially could not accept the rush to launch. Enabling the client to take an autonomous decision in this situation would demand that the professional, the engineer, maintain his professional judgment and ask the client to provide clear scientific ground for not accepting that judgement. The very act of having to articulate such grounds would have helped the client to clarify its own values in the situation and so achieve a more autonomous decision. Perhaps the most disturbing aspects of the Challenger case, which demonstrates a lack of autonomy on the part of the client, i.e. showed them incapable of making a rational and well thought out decision, was the fact that their view of the health and safety standards was so radically different from the professional's. One observer noted that the NASA estimates of safety were 'to the point of fantasy' (Robinson, 2001, 118). This led to the development of a criterion of safety away from 'unsafe until proven otherwise' to 'safe unless proven otherwise'. Given that the conditions prior to launch involved a temperature of 29°F, never before experienced in the shuttle programme, and the high risk nature of the enterprise in any case, the failure of the launch was inevitable. Whilst the engineers stood out for some time they eventually accepted this change of criteria, and were later puzzled as to when the change occurred. The liberal argument might say that the task of the professional in all this could not have been to convince the client not to launch. This was someone else's responsibility, so the argument goes. The argument against this in this case is twofold. Firstly, this was part of an ongoing relationship which was precisely a learning one. Secondly, the trust of the professional depends upon the truth being fully argued for, not simply communicated. This includes ensuring that the client understands the consequences of any action. In a similar case an engineer took to his client a written statement which clarified that the client understood what the consequences of the action would be in the judgment of the professional, and asked the client to sign this, before the professional 'signed off' on the project. The effect of this was a speedy acceptance of the engineer's judgement, because it enabled transparency, and thus enabled the client to see that responsibility in this situation had to be clarified. Where this is not articulated then it is easy to avoid issues of responsibility. Hence, alongside any clarification of values runs the clarification and negotiation of responsibility. The professional can either take responsibility for that, or ensure that this is done by someone else. He can't avoid addressing this issue and in addressing it the client's autonomy is developed.

A third case highlights a more complex view of autonomy. A retired professor had experienced a major disabling stroke and subsequently pneumonia. The family, his wife and two middle-aged sons, were faced with the question of whether they should accede to his advance directive living will, which asked that he should not receive any treatment in this situation (see Kendrick and Robinson, 2002). The professionals worked through the issues with family, finally leading to the father's wishes being accepted. The question of client autonomy was very complex. It involved not only a patient who was not competent but also a family who had to make a decision. In working through the issues it was clear that all needed to clarify and work with both their own and other values before they could come to a decision. The decision was not simply a rational one but one involving many different feelings, which resonated with the very different relationships that each person had with the patient. To come to an autonomous decision, not being pressured by the professionals or by any members of the family, required real learning in that context. The enabling role in this situation need not have been the doctor, indeed it was shared by doctors and nurses. The important thing at this point is that the professional ensures that someone is fulfilling that role. In this case then, autonomy was essentially relational, in that it required key relationships, and the values embodied in them, to be acknowledged and worked through.

Finally, there are professions, such as counselling, psychotherapy, social work, teaching and nursing where an essential part of the professional aim is precisely to enable the development of autonomy (Robinson, 2001; Rogers, 1983). In psychological therapy, for instance, the point of therapy is precisely to enable the client to work through factors which disable autonomy. In one respect this may be working at affective blocks, often involving negative shame or guilt, which prevents the client from fully reflecting on data, values and responsibility (Robinson, 2001). The core values for the professional in enabling this are unconditional positive regard, empathy and congruence (such that the professional is able to maintain a rational, consistent and holistic stance). However, the point of the exercise is to enable the client to develop her own empathy, positive regard and congruence. In this area of professional enabling it is possible to see the client as being enabled to develop not simply core skills, such as communication, but central abilities and virtues. Swift *et al.* (2002) note the development of such virtues in patients with chronic illness. Robinson (2001) notes in psychological therapy the way in which the development of such virtues in the patient arises from the practice and development of moral meaning embodied in the relationship.

I have suggested then a broad range of areas in which the professional affects the autonomy of the client. At one end of the range the professional is simply giving the client data, enabling a better understanding of the situation. At the other end of the range the professional is actually building up the autonomy of the client through the relationship, enabling a greater awareness of different values in the situation and the articulation and practice of responsibility. It is thus plausible to argue that at least part of the role of the professional, in certain contexts, involves not simply respecting autonomy but actually enabling or developing it. Such an autonomy, moreover, may involve helping the client, and those related to the client, to reflect on and articulate their core values and the values which underlie the situation. This suggests a view of autonomy which goes beyond the negative or positive idea, to one of moral autonomy- the capacity to work through the ethical implications of a situation.

PRE-PROFESSIONAL LEARNING

If the professional is to develop this role of the enabler then professional and pre-professional development needs to take account of it. Restricting myself in this chapter to pre-professional learning, I would argue that this requires two important elements: the development of a decision making framework, and the development of moral virtues or capacities alongside professional skills.

A framework is critical for several reasons. It:

- provides a basis for systematic moral reflection;
- ensures that moral reflection is part of the core professional decision making method;
- provides a vehicle for examining underlying values and purpose. Aristotle notes the importance in any ethical decision making of reflecting on the telos, or purpose (Megone, 2002);
- provides a means of reflecting on the integrity of the person and of the organisation;
- provides the same framework for professional ethical development and for enabling the client and others to reflect on practice.

Such a framework can be developed through initial student reflection on scenarios, case studies or role play (Robinson and Dixon, 1997), and typically involves:

- *Data gathering.* Recording and analysing the major stakeholders, the issues involved, possibilities and constraints. Stakeholders here means all those with an interest in the situation. This can also involve an analysis of the power distribution amongst stakeholders, something relevant both to the calculation of resources and the negotiation of responsibility.

- *Value clarification and analysis.* This part of the framework picks up the Koehn point about developing the capacity of the professional to listen to the story of the client. For all people or organisations there are values which are implicit in their narrative and practice. What is lacking for most is the chance to articulate those values and begin to develop a positive critical stance towards them. This is not about breaking down values but rather the stating of and relating to values. Values emerge most effectively through the development of the person's or group's narrative. This acts as the vehicle for reflection and actually owning and testing those values and purposes (Freeman, 1992). Such reflectivity is sharpened when the values of different stakeholders are reflected on. This leads to intertextual dialogue, in which those involved listen to each others' narratives, and are further challenged, to recognize value congruence and explain value conflicts and what they involve. Van der Ven (1998) notes the importance of this for moral development. This further leads to re-examination of the person's own values and the ground for them. In all of this the student is able to articulate personal, professional and public values, to see where very different values need to be held in tension and to see other values might have to be maintained or stood for against others. Much of this is learning through engaging difference, both affectively and cognitively. It is most effective through ethics team teaching which brings together representatives from different perspectives, such as management, professional, and academic, and through case studies and simulations (Robinson and Dixon, 1997).

- *Outlining and negotiating responsibility.* Recent research involving families has stressed that this is the most common way of developing and testing ethical identity (Williams, 2004; Finch and Mason, 1993). This research found that few families refer to principles or a religious framework but rather negotiate how each member of the family will take responsibility for issues such as the care of an elderly relative. This is a particularly important skill for the professional for several reasons which impact on client autonomy. Firstly, some clients in the caring professions, as Illich noted, collude with the paternalistic approach of some professionals, looking to the professionals to take responsibility for the success of therapy and refusing to be engaged in the process. It is therefore important that professional can help the client to develop responsibility. The development or acceptance of responsibility may be a key part of a successful outcome, and the negotiation of responsibility enables this to happen. Secondly, as noted above, the areas of professional responsibility can often be unclear. This can be clarified and generated through the effective use of contracts, written and unwritten, in areas such teaching or counselling. The very act of working through contract and expectations is, in effect, negotiating responsibilities in the relationship, reflecting on and developing the purpose of that relationship. Thirdly, negotiation of responsibility is connected to accepting the limits of competence in the professional, often leading to referral to another professional, or agent involved in the situation. Once again, team teaching and student centred methods, such as simulation, can be used to help students identify and develop negotiation skills.

The final stage of the framework involves examining the different options in the light of the constraints and possibilities and values and responsibilities, deciding which to implement, and plan for it. This is the actual embodiment of the values and responsibilities.

Such a framework is looking not to develop normative or prescriptive ethics. It is rather aiming to develop professional agency and moral autonomy in relation to the several social structures that may be part of any situation, and as such it is not value free. The framework will enable the pre-professional to begin developing his autonomy. The development of this recognises that the debate about values in any profession is a matter of continued debate and dialogue. It is not simply prescribed. The development of the framework also provides the professional with a tool for enabling the capacity for self governance in the client. Seedhouse (1998) writes of creating and maintaining autonomy in the client. The danger in using the concept of creation is that it ignores the client's role in that creation. The role of the enabling professional is to let go of the power, so often associated with the professions, and to enable the client to take and share power. The articulation of values, and the negotiating of responsibility all are part of that learning to use and share power.

Core to such a process of reflection and learning are capacities or virtues which relate to the skills of the professional. I suggest that three central ones are empathy, integrity and respect.

Empathy, involves an awareness of the other. It is not a total identification but rather involves epistemic distance, enabling better perception of the other and ensuring that the person does not over identify with the needs of the other (Robinson and Dixon, 1997, 341). This is crucial for the operation of professional competence and independence. The communication of empathy is also important in enabling the client or other stakeholders to articulate their story. Empathy in the learning context can be developed both through the student practicing critical reflection, and through intertextual dialogue.

Solomon (1992) suggests that integrity is not a single virtue but a collection of virtues. However, it can be seen as a more dynamic basis to character itself, involving:

- Integration of the different parts of the person, cognitive, affective and somatic. This leads to holistic thinking.
- Consistency of character between values and practice; between past, present and the future; and in different contexts.
- Taking responsibility for the articulation of value and embodiment of value in practice. This is very close to what Aristotle refers to as phronesis, or practical wisdom (Megone, 2002). It involves the capacity to reflect on the telos (purpose) of the person or group and ensure its embodiment in practice. This is an intellectual virtue that supports the moral virtues.

It is impossible for complete integrity to be attained. Hence, integrity has to involve the capacity to reflect and learn. Whilst integrity is best learned through practice, and therefore is best learned and developed in professional practice itself, it can be focussed on and developed through reflective techniques (not least in progress files) and through intertextual dialogue.

Empathy, integrity and phronesis are important bridges between technical skills and the ultimate, irreducible ethical attitude of respect (Robinson, 2005). Respect can be seen in terms of unconditional positive regard (Rogers 1983). This adds appreciation and valuing to awareness of the other, and provides the basis of an inclusive and unconditional covenant or pledge between the professional and client (Koehn 1994). Just as the medical profession is there for the patient regardless of ability pay or any other condition, the civil engineering or architect is there for future generations who will use their buildings. Any specific contract works out how that covenant is fulfilled. Appreciation and valuing of the other again can develop through intertextual dialogue and practice reflection.

CONCLUSION

I have argued in this chapter that at least part of the professional's task is to enable the articulation and development of autonomy in the client, and sometimes in other stakeholders. Part of that autonomy involves articulating moral meaning and responsibility, and underlying this is an implicit view that responsibility cannot be predetermined but only be negotiated in practice.

It is perhaps not very far from that to imagine that the professional might have a responsibility to society, which involves contributing to the meaning of civic responsibility, and so contributing to a much wider enabling. Hence Reeck (1982) argues for the professions as guardians of civic values. Tawney (Terrill 1973, 168) before him suggested that the professions might contribute to social values, embodying and enabling the values of service and democracy. For Tawney democracy was precisely about the development of reflectivity and taking responsibility for decisions, hence his concern for instigating 'experiments in democracy', literally enabling communities themselves to develop self governance.

REFERENCES

Armstrong, J. Dixon, J. R. and Robinson, S. (1999) *The Decision Makers: Ethics in Engineering.* London: Thomas Telford
Bauman, Z. (1989) *Modernity and the Holocaust.* London: Polity Press
Beauchamp, T. and Childress, J. (1989) *Principles of Biomedical Ethics,* 3rd ed. Oxford: Oxford University Press
Berlin, I. (1969) Two Concepts of Liberty. In Quinton, A. (ed.), *Political Philosophy.* Oxford: Oxford University Press, 141-154
Campbell, A. (1985) *Paid to Care.* London: SPCK
Clement, G. (2001) *Care, Autonomy, and Justice.* Boulder: Westview Press
Kendrick, K. and Robinson, S. (2002) *Their Rights: Advance directives and living wills explored.* London: Age Concern
Koehn, D. (1994) *The Ground of Professional Ethics.* London: Routledge
Ikonomidis, S. and Singer, P. (1999) Autonomy, liberalism and advance care planning, *Journal of Medical Ethics,* 25: 522-527
Illich, I. (1977) *Disabling Professions.* London: Marion Boyars
Finch, J. and Mason, J. (1993) *Negotiating Family Responsibilities.* London: Routledge

Freeman, M. (1993) *Rewriting the Self*. London: Routledge
May, W. (1985) Adversarialism in America and in the professions. In: McLean, U. (ed.), *The End of Professionalism?* Edinburgh: The Centre for Theology and Public Issues, Edinburgh University, Occasional Paper no. 6, 5-19
Megone, C. (2002) Two Aristotelian approaches to business ethics. In: Megone C. and Robinson, S. J. (eds.), *Case Histories in Business Ethics*. London: Routledge
O'Conner, M. A. (1987) Health/illness and healing /caring- a feminist perspective. In: Orr, J. (ed.), *Women's Health in the Community*. Chichester: Wiley
Parker, J. (1994) Moral Philosophy – another 'disabling profession'? In: Chadwick, R. (ed.), *Ethics and the Professions*. Aldershot: Avebury
Reeck, D. (1982) *Ethics for the Professions: A Christian Perspective*. Minneapolis: Augsburg
Riceour, P. (1977) *The Rule of Metaphor: Multi-disciplinary studies of the creation of meaning in language*, trans. Czerney, R. Toronto: Toronto University Press
Robinson, S. and Dixon, J. R. (1997), The Professional Engineer: Virtues and Learning, *Science and Engineering Ethics*, Vol.3, Issue 3
Robinson, S. J. (2001) *Agape Moral Meaning and Pastoral Counselling*. Cardiff: Aureus
Robinson, S. (2002) Challenger Flight 51- L. In: Megone, C. and Robinson, S. (eds.), *Case Studies in Business Ethics*. London: Routledge, 108-122
Robinson, S. (2005) *Ethics and Employability*. York: Learning and Teaching Support Network
Rogers, C. (1983) *Freedom to Learn*. Columbus: Merrill
Schoen, D. (1983) *The Reflective Practitioner*. New York: Basic Books
Seedhouse, D. (1998) *Ethics: The Heart of Health Care*. Chichester: Wiley
Sims, R.R. and Brinkmann, J. (2003) Enron Ethics (Or: Culture Matters More Than Codes). *Journal of Business Ethics*, July, vol. 45, no. 3, 243-256
Solomon, R. (1992) *Ethics and Excellence: Cooperation and Integrity in Business*. Oxford: Oxford University Press
Swift, T. L., Ashcroft, R., Tadd, W., Campbell, A. and Dieppe, P. (2002) Living Well Through Chronic Illness: The Relevance of Virtue Theory to Patients With Chronic Osteoarthritis. *Arthritis and Rheumatism (Arthritis Care and Research)*, Vol. 47, No. 5, 2002, 474-478
Terrill, R. (1973) *R.H.Tawney and his times*. London: Andre Deutsch
van der Ven, J. (1998) *Formation of the Moral Self*. Grand Rapids: Eerdmans
Williams, F. (2004) *Rethinking Families*. London: Calouste Gulbenkian Foundation

Printed in the United Kingdom
by Lightning Source UK Ltd.
105897UKS00001B/154-390